Marie
Nightingale's
favourite
recipes

...

Over
350 'keepers'
from
Nova Scotia's
favourite
food editor

...

NIMBUS
PUBLISHING

Nimbus Publishing Limited
P.O. Box 9301, Station A
Halifax, N.S. B3K 5N5
(902)-455-4286

Design/Illustration: Kathy Kaulbach, Halifax

Printed and bound in Canada

Canadian Cataloguing in Publication Data

Nightingale, Marie.
Marie Nightingale's favourite recipes
Includes index.
ISBN 1-55109-022-8

1. Cookery, Canadian—Nova Scotia style.
2. Cookery—Nova Scotia. I. Title.
TX715.6.N54 1993   641.59716   C93-098664-4

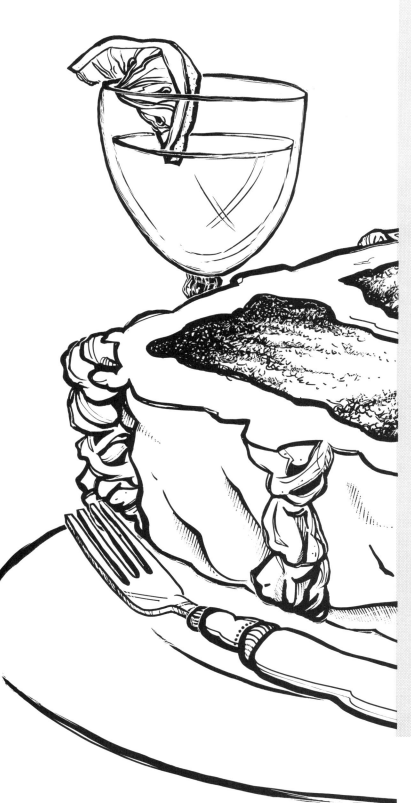

CONTENTS

...

...

To Frank, Gary, and Bobby,

who created the memories.

And to Craig, Candice,

Ashley, Christa, and Corey,

who love to hear Nana

snitch on their daddies and uncles.

PREFACE

E ver since my first cookbook, *Out of Old Nova Scotia Kitchens* proved to be such a success, I have been asked many times when I was going to write another.

I wasn't ready. Was I afraid that a second book would fall far short of the mark? My brother Ray thought so. I don't think he was right. In fact, I think I was happy doing the things I was busy doing—organizing a festival for four years, and then working as the food writer for *The Chronicle-Herald* and *The Mail-Star*. This kept me in touch with food. And for 13 years with these newspapers, I have never been at a loss for a subject.

Then, three years ago, Dorothy Blythe, of Nimbus Publishing asked me if I would consider writing *Out of New Nova Scotia Kitchens*. I knew the time was right.

While she had the nutritional 90s in mind, I felt there was another period that should be documented first. The comfort foods of the 50s and 60s should be recorded before they became lost to us. These are the foods I cooked in my first kitchens. The foods my sons grew up on.

I didn't do any cooking before I was married. First, because I was too busy having fun. And second, because my grandmother, who raised me from the age of ten, couldn't abide waste. Any time I asked if I could do some cooking, she would actually put aside whatever she was doing and come to the kitchen with me. She was one of those wonderful cooks who used instinct and "feel" instead of a measuring cup. And as she added a little of this and a little more of that, I found I was doing nothing but the stirring. (There was no electric mixer to lighten my task.) My creative juices went sour. I became bored.

It wasn't until Laurie and I were married, in 1951, that I was able to lay claim to a kitchen of my own. I began to experiment. And to learn.

First, it was in a little rented bungalow on Retreat Avenue, off Dutch Village Road, in Halifax. Five years later, we moved to Greenwood Avenue in the city's south end. This is where my sons, Frank, Gary and Bobby grew up. After 25 years in this neighbourhood, we still consider it home.

When I set up my first kitchen, changes were happening in the culinary world. I found myself caught in the metamorphosis that stretched between my grandmother's time and my own. The wonderful sameness of my grandmother's meals—roast chicken on Sundays, shepherds' pie on Mondays, fish on Fridays, baked beans on Saturdays—was a reflection of her era.

While my mother may have started out with much the same routine, the Great Depression quickly changed the menu. I remember being happy to have the hash, bannock and molasses Mother prepared for us kids, as she reserved the small piece of beefsteak or pork chop for my father.

Gradually, during the years leading up to World War II, meals were pretty much returning to the basics—meat loaf, liver and onions, fish, rabbit stew, baked beans—the whole wonderful works. Then the war, with its dreaded ration book, turned things around again.

It was after V-E Day that the major changes began. Now, we had casseroles. And Spam! Makers of this canned meat product switched their focus from supplying the army, navy and air force (the services had their own identities in those days) to wooing the consumer.

Food companies began hiring home economists to develop recipes that would create a demand for the company's products. The time of the food fads had begun.While people with longer memories tried to dig in their heels, it was useless. Change would have its way.

A young hostess would be mortified if she mistakenly served the same dish twice to the same guests, and so she kept records of what was served to whom. Even family meals must have constant variety.

Food was a favourite topic of conversation at the koffee klatches where we young mothers tried to find reasons and solutions for all the changes that were, bit by bit, turning our lives around.

And if one of those women even hinted at the idea of going out and getting a job, the rest of us probably reserved our shock and disapproval until after she had left.

This book was written in an effort to recapture the comfort foods of the time. It's also a collection of memories.

APPETIZERS

B ack in the days when small envelopes were permitted to go through the mail, we got our share of the "Come for cocktails" invitations. This was the way to entertain before dinner parties took hold.

The invitation list usually depended on the size of the home. Some could cope with only about ten people, while others could handle 100 or more. To make room, furniture was often taken to the basement or the attic—nobody sat down anyway. Sometimes two couples jointly engaged the facilities of a private club for their parties, and all they had to do was choose the appetizers to be served—and be there before the guests started arriving.

Although we preferred to host smaller parties of up to 20 in our home on Greenwood Avenue, on occasion we joined with another couple for a larger party at Ashburn Golf Club. One time we "borrowed" Laurie's mother's home which easily accommodated 100 people.

Since I was doing the catering on that occasion, I didn't change into my party dress until after I had everything arranged. Minutes before the guests were to arrive, I slipped upstairs and changed into a beautiful white shantung silk sheath with a lace bodice. How I loved that dress! But when I came downstairs and asked Laurie's mother how she liked it, she thought it was a slip and told me I didn't have time for any tomfoolery. "Go upstairs and put your dress on," she admonished. All I could think of was the price tag of that "slip."

Meatballs and bacon-wrapped scallops probably topped the popularity list of appetizers served at these parties, but pickled shrimp and lobster rolls weren't far behind. I liked to have at least three kinds of hot appetizers, and lots of cold ones to keep people eating while they sipped. Although we always tried to insist on making coffee the "one for the road," there wasn't the general awareness of drinking and driving back then, and "designated drivers" hadn't been invented.

Although I still make some of these appetizers today, they are usually served to six or eight guests prior to dinner. The Nuts and Bolts are still part of our Christmas tradition. Like turkey, they're an essential.

Appetizer Meatballs

1 pound (500 g) lean ground beef
1/2 teaspoon salt
1/4 teaspoon pepper
1/4 cup ketchup or chili sauce
1 tablespoon Worcestershire sauce
1/4 cup finely chopped onion
1/2 cup crushed corn flakes
1/2 cup evaporated milk (do not substitute regular milk)

I always say that when you find something easy, stay with it. I've been making these easiest of meatballs for more than 30 years. I mold them, put them in the oven and forget about them until the timer signals they're done. And, because these meatballs freeze well before or after cooking, it's possible to make them days or weeks before entertaining.

• Combine beef, salt, pepper, ketchup, Worcestershire sauce, onion, corn flake crumbs and evaporated milk in large mixing bowl. Shape into tiny meatballs.

• Place in 9 x 13-inch pan and bake at 400°F (no need to turn) for 12 to 15 minutes or until browned.

• Insert a toothpick into each meatball and serve with hot barbecue sauce. Makes 3 dozen meatballs.

Chafing Dish Meatballs and Wieners

2 pounds (1 kg) lean ground beef
1 egg
1 onion, finely chopped
pinch each of salt and pepper
1 ½ cups grape jelly
1 12-oz. bottle chili sauce
juice of a lemon
2 pounds (1 kg) wieners

When I first tried these meatballs and wieners, I found the younger crowd loved them. The adults didn't turn up their noses either.

• Combine beef with egg, onion, salt and pepper in large bowl. Mix thoroughly. Shape into about 50 small meatballs.

• In saucepan, combine jelly, chili sauce and lemon juice. Stir to blend well over medium heat until jelly melts.

• Add meatballs and simmer for an hour.

• Cut wieners on the diagonal into 1/2-inch slices and add to saucepan. Continue simmering until wieners are cooked.

• Transfer to chafing dish and serve hot.

Chinese Garlic Ribs

During my family's early years, we usually went out for Chinese food or brought it home. But, occasionally, I prepared these ribs for appetizers. No matter how many I made, it was never enough.

I used to get the butcher to crack the ribs into 1 ½-inch long pieces so they would be easy to cut apart at home.

1 ½ pounds (750 g) back
    spareribs, cracked into
    1 ½-inch lengths
1/3 cup cornstarch
1 teaspoon garlic salt
1/4 cup vegetable oil

Sauce:
1 garlic clove, crushed
1/4 cup chopped onion
1/4 cup chopped celery
2 tablespoons vegetable oil
1 cup pineapple juice
1 chicken bouillon cube
1/2 cup chili sauce
2 teaspoons cornstarch
1 tablespoon sherry
1 teaspoon each of soy sauce
    and lemon juice
1 tablespoon brown sugar

• Cut sparerib pieces into separate ribs, break into 1-inch lengths. Place in plastic bag with cornstarch and garlic salt and shake to coat.

• Heat 1/4 cup oil in 9 x 13-inch pan. Place ribs in pan and turn to coat with oil.

• Bake at 375°F for 35 to 40 minutes, stirring once or twice.

• Drain and let cool. If preparing early, store in casserole dish in refrigerator until ready to use.

• In saucepan, sauté garlic, onion and celery in 2 tablespoons oil.

• Add pineapple juice, bouillon cube and chili sauce and simmer for 5 minutes.

• Combine cornstarch and sherry in small bowl and stir until smooth. Add to mixture in saucepan, stirring until slightly thickened.

• Flavour with soy sauce, lemon juice and brown sugar to taste.

• Pour sauce over ribs, cover and bake at 350°F for 30 minutes. Turn into chafing dish, if desired, to keep hot.

Onion Appetizer

If you like onions, you'll like this simple appetizer.

• Lightly toast several slices of bread on one side only. Cut four small circles from each slice. • On untoasted side of each round, place a thin slice of white onion. Top with a teaspoon of mayonnaise. Sprinkle with grated parmesan cheese. • Place rounds on a cookie sheet and bake at 400°F until mayonnaise puffs up and cheese is golden. Serve hot.

Teriyaki Steak Appetizers

1 ½ pounds (750 g) sirloin
   steak, 3/4-inch thick,
   slightly frozen
1/4 cup vegetable oil
1/4 cup soy sauce
1/4 cup honey
1/2 cup finely chopped onion
1 garlic clove, crushed
1/2 teaspoon ground ginger

I don't remember which came first, the hibachi or the teriyaki steak appetizers. It doesn't matter, since these little strips of beef grilled on bamboo skewers proved to be one of the most popular appetizers that my husband ever prepared. Laurie has always been in charge of the barbecue and, though not as adventuresome as some male cooks, he knew when he had struck gold. The steak slices more easily if it is slightly frozen.

• Cut steak across the grain into long strips that are 1/16-inch wide, or as thin as you can slice them (no more than 1/8-inch or they won't thread nicely).

• In plastic bag, combine oil, soy sauce, honey, onion, garlic and ginger. Add steak strips and tie. Marinate in refrigerator for at least 4 hours.

• Lift strips from marinade, shaking to remove excess liquid. Thread strips onto small bamboo skewers which have been soaked in water.

• Place on hibachi or barbecue grill and broil over medium heat, turning and brushing with marinade, just until well browned. Serve hot.

Lobster Cheese Rolls

1/2 cup butter
8 ounces (250 g) processed
   cheese
1 pound (500 g) lobster meat,
   cut finely
2 loaves very fresh, sliced
   white bread
melted butter for brushing

I make these delicious little lobster rolls to keep in the freezer until an appetizer is needed. Since our family is more careful about salt intake these days, I look for a salt-reduced processed cheese.

• Cut butter and cheese into small pieces. Melt in top of double boiler over simmering water.

• Add lobster and stir to combine.

• Remove crusts from bread. Roll each slice with rolling pin to prevent cracking.

• Spread thin layer of lobster mixture almost to edges of bread. Roll and place, in single layers, in containers and freeze until ready to use.

• Before serving, cut each roll in half and brush with melted butter.

• Defrost and bake at 450°F for 10 to 15 minutes. Makes 60 to 70 rolls.

When Ashburn Golf Club opened for the sesaon, among the hot appetizers served were these bacon-wrapped scallops, which were all the rage. The free parties have come to an end but it's still possible to make these appetizers at home with excellent results. Choose good quality scallops that are as close in size as possible.

- Rinse scallops well. Remove all grit and bits of shell. Dry thoroughly with paper towels.

- Fry bacon until partially cooked but still pliable. Drain on paper towels.

- Cut in half and wrap around scallops, overlapping ends slightly. Secure with toothpicks. If preparing early, cover and store in refrigerator until ready to use.

- If baking, place on rack in a pan. Bake at 475°F until bacon is crisp, turning once. If broiling, place on rack in a broiler pan and place about 4 inches from heat. Broil for about 5 minutes, turning once. Watch closely to prevent burning. Serve hot.

Note: Cooked chicken livers, cooked cocktail sausages, smoked oysters or stuffed olives may also be wrapped in bacon and baked or broiled as above.

Bacon-Wrapped Scallops

small to medium-sized scallops
bacon
toothpicks

My first fondue pot didn't have a heat control so I made these delicious cheese fingers in a deep fryer.

- Cut cheese into 40 strips, 1/2-inch thick and 1 ½ inches long. Coat each piece with flour. Dip in egg and roll in bread crumbs. Dip again in the egg and the crumbs.

- Heat oil in fondue pot or deep fryer to 375°F. (Maintain heat throughout cooking, to prevent soggy or overcooked food.) Fry each cheese stick for 25 to 35 seconds. Do not overcook.

- If desired, serve with a sauce made by combining 1 cup sour cream and 1 teaspoon curry powder.

Fondue Cheese Fingers

1 (8-ounce/250g) package
    unsliced mozzarella cheese
1/3 cup flour
2 eggs, beaten
1 ¼ cups dry bread crumbs

Toasted Mushroom Rolls

1 pound (500 g) fresh
   mushrooms
1/2 cup butter or margarine
6 tablespoons all-purpose flour
1 teaspoon salt
2 cups blend (light cream)
1 tablespoon minced chives
2 teaspoons lemon juice
2 sandwich loaves white bread
melted butter

These delicious mushroom rolls have long since replaced my earliest efforts, which was opening a can of cream of mushroom soup, spooning it on thinly rolled bread slices, rolling up, brushing with butter, and placing them on the broiler pan to lightly brown under a hot broiler. Good, indeed — but these are better.

• Wipe mushrooms with damp paper towels. Dice. Sauté in butter for 5 minutes.

• Blend in flour and salt. Stir in blend and simmer until thickened.

• Add chives and lemon juice.

• Remove crusts from bread. Roll each slice with rolling pin to prevent cracking. Spread thin layer of mushroom mixture almost to edges of bread. Roll up.

• Place, in single layers, in containers and freeze until ready to use.

• Before serving, cut each roll in half and brush with melted butter. Defrost and bake at 450°F for 10 to 15 minutes. Makes 70 to 80 rolls.

Toasted Cheese Squares

1 loaf unsliced, day-old bread
1/2 cup melted butter or
   margarine
8 ounces (250 g) cheddar
   cheese, grated

Another memory from my earliest cooking days is of these toasted cheese squares. They take a little time, but isn't that the case with most good things?

• Remove crusts from bread. Cut into 1-inch slices, then into approximately 2 dozen 1-inch cubes.

• Brush on 5 of the 6 sides with melted butter.

• Roll in grated cheese.

• Place cubes, unbuttered side down, on wire rack. Cover cookie sheet with foil and place rack on cookie sheet.

• Broil for about 2 minutes or until cheese has melted and is nicely browned. Serve hot.

This has always been a favourite appetizer in our house. It's great for a party as the shrimp must be prepared at least 24 hours in advance and will keep a week or more in the refrigerator.

- In large saucepan, cover shrimp with boiling water.

- Add celery tops, pickling spices and 1 tablespoon salt. Cover and simmer for 5 minutes.

- Drain and cool with cold water.

- Peel shrimp and remove veins under cold water.

- In shallow dish, alternately layer shrimp and onion. Lay bay leaves on top.

- Combine oil, vinegar, capers with juice, celery seed, Tabasco and 1 teaspoon salt in small bowl. Mix well and pour over shrimp.

- Cover shrimp and chill at least 24 hours, basting occasionally with marinade. Keeps at least a week in refrigerator.

Pickled Shrimp

2 ½ pounds (1.25 kg) fresh or
    frozen shrimp
1/2 cup celery tops
1/4 cup mixed pickling spices
1 tablespoon salt
2 cups sliced onion
6 bay leaves
1 ¼ cups vegetable oil
3/4 cup white vinegar
3 tablespoons capers and juice
2 teaspoons celery seed
dash of Tabasco
1 teaspoon salt

My family loved all of the appetizers I made with cheese. This simple spread, however, was reserved for adults only.

- Blend cheese, butter, rum, lemon rind and olives.

- Spoon into small dish and serve with an assortment of crackers. Makes about 1 ¼ cups.

Rum Cheese Spread

1/2 pound (250 g) sharp
    cheddar cheese, grated
1/4 cup butter or margarine,
    softened
1 tablespoon rum
grated rind of a lemon
1/4 cup finely chopped ripe or
    green olives

Nut-Crusted Cheese Ball

1/4 cup soft margarine or butter
2 tablespoons brandy or white
    wine
1 package (4 ounces/125 g)
    cream cheese, softened
8 ounces (250 g) cheddar
    cheese, grated
2 or 3 dashes of Tabasco
dash of black pepper
1/2 cup chopped nuts

In the 50s and 60s, a cheese ball was always the centre of attraction on a table of appetizers. I like both the flavour and appearance of this one. I often decorate the top with something to represent the occasion.

• Cream margarine with brandy or wine.

• Add cheeses; blend well.

• Season to taste with Tabasco and pepper.

• Form mixture into a ball, then roll in nuts.

• Wrap and chill. Bring to room temperature to serve.

Cheese Olives

1 jar (about 45) pimiento-
    stuffed olives
1/2 cup shredded, sharp
    cheddar cheese (at room
    temperature)
1/2 cup butter, softened
dash of Worcestershire sauce
1 cup all-purpose flour
1/4 teaspoon salt

I'm not sure when or how these appetizers came about but I do remember that my husband's sister Melda introduced them to me. I rarely look at a cookbook published in the 60s or 70s that doesn't include cheese olives.

• Drain olives and place on paper towels to dry.

• In large bowl, combine cheese, butter and Worcestershire sauce. Beat until smooth.

• Sift flour with salt. Add to cheese dough, mixing well.

• Mold approximately 1 teaspoon dough around each olive to make small balls.

• Arrange balls 2 inches apart on ungreased baking sheets. Chill in freezer until hard.

• Bake at 425°F for 12 minutes or until lightly browned. Serve hot. Makes about 45 appetizers.

These crispy wafers are very handy to keep in the freezer for unexpected guests. But be forewarned—they are as addictive as potato chips or peanuts. If you don't want them to bite back, be careful with the cayenne pepper.

Crispy Cheese Wafers

2 cups all-purpose flour
1/4 teaspoon salt
2 or 3 generous shakes of
    cayenne pepper
8 ounces (250 g) sharp cheddar
    cheese, shredded (at room
    temperature)
1 cup margarine or butter,
    softened
2 cups crisp rice cereal

• Sift flour, salt and cayenne into large bowl.

• Cut in cheese and margarine with pastry blender or 2 knives until mixture resembles coarse meal.

• Add rice cereal and mix well.

• Shape dough into 1-inch balls and place on greased baking sheets. Flatten with fork.

• Bake at 350°F for 12 to 15 minutes or until lightly browned. Cool and store in tightly covered container. Makes 5 to 6 dozen wafers.

These impressive little puffs or bouchées are so easy to make. For added convenience, they can be baked ahead and frozen up to a month. Thaw at room temperature for about two hours before filling.

Bouchées

1/2 cup water
1/4 cup butter or margarine
1/8 teaspoon salt
1/2 cup all-purpose flour
2 eggs

• Heat water in a medium-size saucepan set over high heat. Add butter and salt and bring to a boil. Remove from heat.

• Add flour and stir vigorously with a wooden spoon until mixture leaves side of pan and forms a ball.

• Add eggs, one at a time, beating until each egg is thoroughly blended. Continue beating until mixture is glossy.

• Drop by teaspoonfuls onto greased cookie sheets, about 2 inches apart. Mound paste and swirl tops.

• Bake at 400°F for 15 to 18 minutes or until very lightly browned. Turn off oven.

• Remove from oven and cut two slits on sides of each puff. Return to oven for 10 minutes to dry. Remove from oven and cool.

• Fill with chicken, ham, lobster or other seafood filling. Refrigerate until serving time. Makes approximately 40 small bouchées.

Sardine Dip

1 package (8 ounces/250 g)
   cream cheese, softened
1/2 cup sour cream
1 can (4 ounces/113 g) sardines
   in oil, drained
1 tablespoon minced green
   onion
1 tablespoon lemon juice
pinch of salt
dash of paprika

There were many dips making the rounds in the 60s, when packages of cream cheese were being softened and blended with anything that suited the cook's tastebuds. I have chosen this one as representative, since sardines happen to suit mine.

• In medium-sized bowl, combine cheese, sour cream and sardines. Beat until smooth.

• Add onion, lemon juice and salt, mixing well.

• Spoon into serving dish and sprinkle with paprika.

• Serve with crackers or potato chips. Makes about 2 cups.

Nuts and Bolts

1 pound (500 g) butter
1 tablespoon Worcestershire
   sauce
2 ½ teaspoons seasoned salt
1 teaspoon garlic salt
1 box Cheerios (425 g)
1 box Shreddies (675 g)
1 box pretzel sticks (225 g)
2 cups salted peanuts

At Christmas, we always have nuts and bolts made ahead and stored in the freezer for the friends and relatives who call in to share a little seasonal cheer. We were in a panic a few years ago, when a fire at the Cheerios plant almost knocked out the supply. Fortunately, the problem was solved in time for the season—no nuts and bolts would have been almost as serious as no Santa Claus.

• Place butter in large roasting pan and melt in oven at 250°F.

• Add seasonings and stir well.

• Add cereals, pretzels and nuts and return to oven for 1 hour. Stir every 15 minutes, lifting cereal from bottom and turning top cereal under.

• Leave in pan to cool.

• Seal in plastic bags. Store in freezer to keep very fresh.

BEVERAGES

When my paternal grandparents, Nettie and Charlie Johnston, entertained their bridge buddies, as they so often did, they served mixed drinks: one part grape juice to two parts ginger ale. The refreshing drink carried over into my early kitchens, but there were more takers from the younger set than adults.

On a hot summer's day there was nothing like homemade lemonade or limeade to quench the thirst, and for this reason there was always a bottle of sugar syrup made up and waiting in the refrigerator.

But let's face it, sugar syrup played another role. In Barbados, where Laurie and I vacationed a number of times, the simple syrup formed the base of rum punch, considered, at least by the tourists, to be the island's national drink (Bajans preferred their Mauby, made from some kind of root, but we never developed a taste for it.)

The first thing that our cook, Maureen, would do when she arrived in the morning, was to check the supply of punch. If it was low, she made up a new pitcherful, and only then would she turn to her other chores.

Although we didn't have a godfather to give us a blender for a wedding gift, it wasn't long before I brought one of those handy little appliances home. At first, I used it only for milkshakes, which kept the boys happy. They didn't even know I was bolstering those drinks with all sorts of "healthy" additions.

About three weeks before Frank was to have a couple of wisdom teeth removed, I started preparing him for the surgery and for the healing to follow. Morning, noon and night, he was given one of my special milkshakes. Unfortunately, I've lost the formula, but I do know it called for a carrot, a banana, orange juice, wheat germ and, of course, milk. I also doled out vitamins for him to take—C, B and E, as well as fish liver oil to supply A and D.

Frank might have been a little groggy when I brought him home after the extractions, but he never missed a meal and never had to take a pain killer. A week later, when he returned for a check-up, his gums had healed so well that the oral surgeon wouldn't believe it had only been a week since the teeth were pulled. Nothing will convince me that those milkshakes didn't help the healing.

Sugar Syrup

2 cups water
2 cups granulated sugar

I always used to keep sugar syrup in a jar in the refrigerator. It's a better beverage sweetener than sugar, which usually sinks, undissolved, to the bottom of the glass.

- In saucepan, stir water and sugar over moderately high heat until sugar dissolves.

- Bring to boil and continue boiling for 5 minutes.

- Cool and store in covered jar in refrigerator. Makes approximately 3 cups thin syrup.

Limeade

1 cup sugar syrup (see above)
3 cups water
rind of a lime (thin shavings with no white)
juice of 6 limes
crushed ice or ice cubes

There's nothing quite as thirst quenching as limeade served in a frosted glass. To frost glasses, simply set them on a tray in the freezer until they are covered with frost. I sometimes dip the rims in sugar and then return them to the freezer, if necessary, to refrost.

- Combine sugar syrup, water, rind and lime juice, mixing well. Pour into pitcher and refrigerate until needed.

- Serve in frosted glasses half filled with crushed ice or ice cubes. Makes 6 servings.

Lemonade

2 tablespoons lemon juice
1/4 cup sugar syrup (see above)
1 cup cold water
ice cubes
maraschino cherry or fresh mint for garnish

Lemonade was a favourite summertime refresher when my boys were young. Of course, in those days soft drinks weren't sold in two-litre bottles.

- In glass, combine lemon juice, syrup and water.

- Add ice cubes and garnish with maraschino cherry or sprig of fresh mint, if desired. Makes 1 serving.

Grape Juice Fizz

This was the drink my grandmother always served during an evening of bridge. It is just as refreshing on a hot summer's day.

1 quart (1 L) gingerale
1 pint (500 mL) grape juice, bottled or frozen
crushed ice or ice cubes

• Combine gingerale and grape juice and pour into glasses half filled with crushed ice or ice cubes. Makes 8 servings.

Cocoa Stock Syrup

Since a hot cup of cocoa is a welcome treat for all ages after winter outings, I used to find it convenient to keep this cocoa syrup on hand. It's good for cold drinks as well.

1 cup cocoa powder
1 ¼ cups granulated sugar
1/2 cup corn syrup
1 ½ cups water
1/4 teaspoon salt
1 teaspoon vinegar
1 teaspoon vanilla

• In saucepan, combine cocoa powder, sugar, corn syrup, water, salt and vinegar and mix thoroughly.

• Bring to boil, reduce heat and simmer for 5 minutes, stirring occasionally.

• Remove from heat and stir in vanilla.

• Cool and store in covered jar in refrigerator.

• To make cocoa, stir 1 or 2 tablespoons into 1 cup hot milk. For cold drink, stir same amount into glass of cold milk. Makes 2 ½ cups syrup.

Chocolate Milk Shake

Although the ice cream parlours of my youth had all but disappeared by the time I was married with children, the blender brought those old-fashioned milk shakes into the kitchen.

1/2 cup cold milk
2 tablespoons cocoa stock syrup (see above)
1 or 2 scoops vanilla ice cream

• Blend milk, syrup and ice cream in blender just until mixed.

• Pour into glass. Makes 1 serving.

Tropical Fruit Shake

1 cup orange juice
1 banana, cut in chunks
1 cup vanilla ice cream

With the potassium in bananas and the vitamin C in orange juice, I always felt good about serving this shake.

- Blend orange juice, banana and ice cream in blender until smooth.

- Pour into glass. Makes 2 cups.

Strawberry Soda

2 cups strawberries, washed and hulled
1/4 cup granulated sugar
1 pint (500 mL) vanilla ice cream
2 cans (12 ounces/355 mL each) soda water

Line up tall glasses and prepare these sodas just as they did at the drug store soda fountain. The kids will love it.

- Crush strawberries and put through sieve into small bowl.

- Stir in sugar, mixing thoroughly. Divide mixture into 4 or 5 tall glasses.

- Add scoop of ice cream and a little soda water to each glass and stir well. Add remaining soda water and top with another scoop of ice cream. Garnish with whole strawberries.

- Serve with long spoons and straws. Makes 4 to 5 servings.

Ginger Tea

1 tea bag
4 thin slices ginger root
1 cup boiling water

We discovered ginger tea in Barbados, where it was served hot to relieve indigestion. It is also soothing for a sore throat. With fresh ginger root so readily available these days, it's worth making this tea, if not to cure a cold, at least to provide some comfort.

- Add tea bag, 2 slices ginger and boiling water to heated teapot. Steep 5 minutes.

- Strain into teacup and add remaining ginger.

- Serve with honey, if desired. Makes 1 serving.

My husband Laurie always did the honours following a dinner party, preparing Irish coffee for those who wanted it.

Irish Coffee

whipping cream
3 tablespoons (1 ½ ounces) Irish whiskey
1 teaspoon sugar or sugar syrup (recipe page 12)
strong, hot coffee

- Whip cream.

- Pour whiskey into tall glass or Irish coffee glass. Add sugar and fill with coffee. Stir well and top with spoonful of whipped cream.

- Serve wrapped in linen napkin. Makes 1 serving.

Start preparing this eggnog half an hour before the guests arrive. It's important to have all the ingredients and bowls as cold as possible. I like to serve the eggnog in punch cups or old-fashioned glasses and sprinkle freshly grated nutmeg on each serving.

Rum Eggnog

12 eggs, separated
1 cup granulated sugar
1/2 cup brandy
2 cups rum
4 cups whipping cream
pinch of salt
2 cups milk
nutmeg

- Beat egg yolks until thick and light in large bowl.

- Add sugar and beat well.

- Add brandy and rum, a little at a time, stirring constantly.

- In separate bowl, whip cream. Fold into yolk mixture.

- In another bowl using clean beaters, rapidly beat egg whites and salt until fluffy. Fold whites into yolk mixture.

- Add milk.

- Pour into punch bowl and sprinkle generously with nutmeg. Serve immediately. Makes at least 50 servings.

Artillery Punch

1 quart (1 L) strong, clear tea
1 quart (1 L) rye whiskey
1 bottle red wine
1 pint (500 mL) Jamaican rum
1/2 pint (250 mL) dry gin
1/2 pint (250 mL) brandy
3 tablespoons (1 ½ ounces)
    Benedictine
1 pint (500 mL) orange juice
1/2 pint (250 mL) lemon juice
sugar syrup (recipe page 12)
Ice Ring:
5 pineapple rings
5 maraschino cherries
water

Artillery punch used to be a favourite alcoholic drink at hotel receptions in Halifax. This one was served at the old Nova Scotian Hotel, where many local receptions were held.

• In punch bowl, mix tea, rye, wine, rum, gin, brandy, Benedictine, orange juice and lemon juice. If too dry, add a little sugar syrup.

• To make ice ring, arrange pineapple rings in ring jelly mold. Place cherries in centres of pineapple rings. Add water to cover partially and place in freezer (freezing in 2 steps is necessary to keep fruit from floating). When frozen, remove and fill mold to top with water. Return to freezer.

• To remove from mold, quickly dip in hot water. Add ice ring to punch. Makes approximately 25 cups.

Tia "Marie"

2 cups water
1-inch length of vanilla bean,
    cut into 3 pieces
3 ¾ cups granulated sugar
4 ½ tablespoons instant coffee
1/2 cup warm water
1 quart (1 L) vodka
1 teaspoon glycerine

I adopted this liqueur recipe as my own after it was given to me by a friend. After saving up liqueur and liquor bottles, I began giving Tia "Marie" as gifts. It's so good that it's difficult to distinguish from the real thing.

• In large saucepan, combine 2 cups water, vanilla bean and sugar. Stir over moderate heat until sugar dissolves.

• Bring to boil and continue boiling gently for 30 minutes. Set aside to cool.

• Dissolve coffee granules in 1/2 cup warm water. Add to cooled sugar syrup.

• Strain 3 times through cheese cloth into large bowl.

• Pour in vodka and glycerine and stir well.

• Pour through funnel into 2 liqueur or liquor bottles. Cap well. Shake and allow to stand 2 weeks before using.

"One of sour, two of sweet, three of strong and four of weak." So goes the jingle by which Bajans prepared the rum punch which was the official alcoholic drink of Barbados when we visited.

- Combine lime juice, sugar syrup, rum and water and stir well.

- Pour into large bottle or pitcher and put in refrigerator to chill.

- To serve, pour into tall glasses half filled with ice. Garnish with grated nutmeg and sprigs of mint or maraschino cherries. Makes 10 8-ounce servings.

Rum Punch

1 cup lime juice
2 cups sugar syrup (recipe page 12)
3 cups rum
4 cups water
ice
grated nutmeg for garnish
sprigs of mint or maraschino cherries for garnish

What does one choose beyond an occasional rum and coke? At that time in my life it came to be an occasional Planter's Punch.

- Combine rum, sugar syrup, lime and orange juices in a blender. Pulse on and off until well mixed.

- Pour over ice cubes in a chilled 12-ounce glass.

- Fill glass with club soda. Garnish with a thin slice of lime, maraschino cherry, or both. Makes 1 drink.

Planter's Punch

1/3 cup dark rum, or less
2 tablespoons sugar syrup (recipe page 12)
2 tablespoons lime juice
2 tablespoons orange juice
club soda
slice of lime and maraschino cherry for garnish

Laurie's mother used to enjoy an occasional banana daiquiri when dining out in Florida. However, the first time Laurie attempted to make one for her at home, it was so thick she had to eat it with a spoon. He had used a whole banana.

- Blend lime juice, sugar, banana, liqueur, rum and ice in blender.

- Serve in champagne glass with short straw. Makes 1 daiquiri.

Banana Frozen Daiquiri

1 tablespoon fresh lime juice
1 teaspoon granulated sugar
1/3 of a banana
dash of orange liqueur (optional)
3 tablespoons (1 ½ ounces) rum
2/3 cup crushed ice

Strawberry Daiquiri

1 can (6 ounces/178 mL) frozen
    lemonade concentrate,
    undiluted
3/4 cup rum
3 tablespoons icing sugar
1 ¼ cups frozen strawberries,
    unsweetened
ice cubes

When we're sipping daiquiris in the hot sun, we cut back on the rum.

- Put lemonade concentrate, rum, icing sugar and strawberries in blender, then fill with ice cubes. Blend until ice is crushed and completely mixed. Makes 4 to 6 servings.

Bloody Mary

2 cups tomato juice
1/8 teaspoon Tabasco sauce
2 teaspoons freshly squeezed
    lime juice
1 ½ teaspoons Worcestershire
    sauce
1/2 cup vodka
ice cubes
fresh lime wedges for garnish

This drink was around long before Caesars became the rage.

- Combine tomato juice, Tabasco sauce, lime juice, Worcestershire sauce and vodka in pitcher and stir well.

- Pour into glasses half filled with ice cubes. Garnish with lime wedges. Makes 3 to 4 servings.

Hot Buttered Rum

1/3 cup rum, or less
1 strip of lemon peel
1 whole clove
1 cup apple cider
small pat of butter
1 long cinnamon stick

If ever there was a better cure for a cold than hot buttered rum, it had to be a raw onion sandwich washed down with hot buttered rum.

- Pour rum into a heavy mug or tankard. Add lemon peel and clove.

- Bring cider to a boil and pour in enough to fill mug.

- Top with butter and use cinnamon stick as a stirrer. Makes 1 serving.

My first step beyond opening a can of soup for lunch was to open two cans and combine them for what I then considered an "original" flavour. It might have been celery and chicken soup, tomato and pea or mushroom and asparagus. Somewhere along the way I got really fancy and opened three cans, perhaps celery soup, consommé and a can of sliced beets. I put them in the blender with a little garlic and horseradish and served up my first bowl of borscht.

It wasn't long before my interest in soup extended beyond opening cans. I started making stock and a whole new world opened up for me, the beautiful world of soup. It may have been a turkey frame that got me started or an accumulation of chicken bones. Soon I was saving all kinds of bones—from roasts, chops, steaks and chicken parts—and storing them in plastic bags in the freezer until I had enough to make a good supply of stock.

Other plastic bags started to pile up in the freezer, bags containing celery tops, broccoli stems, outer leaves of cabbage and lettuce and other washed vegetable peelings. Of course, they had to be fairly fresh, not limp and lacking in nutrients. I even started saving vegetable water to add to soups or to serve as stock for cream soups when my supplies of poultry stock ran low.

Soup making is a two-step process. First is the stock, which is chilled overnight after cooking so the fat will rise to the top and solidify, making it easy to remove with a spoon or spatula. I sometimes let the pot sit in ice water in the sink to cool before putting it in the refrigerator overnight. Then comes the soup.

I reheat the stock to boiling and then add whatever vegetables I want or have on hand—diced carrots, onions, turnips or potatoes, peas, beans, broccoli or cauliflower—as well as some seasoning and rice or pasta. If there is leftover turkey or chicken, I add it during the last few minutes of cooking time. My method for making stock follows.

SOUPS AND CHOWDERS

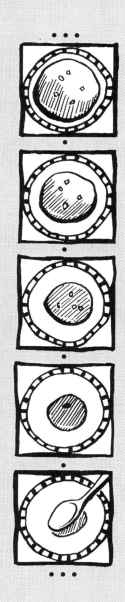

Stock for Soups

Enough bones to half fill a
    large soup kettle
cold water to cover
A handful of celery leaves
1 large onion, diced
2 carrots, chopped
2 bay leaves
6-8 peppercorns
4-5 parsley sprigs
1/4 cup vinegar
1 teaspoon salt

Stock is highly perishable and should be used within two or three days if it's kept in the refrigerator. It may also be stored in the freezer for as long as four months. When freezing stock, leave at least an inch of space at the top of the container to allow for expansion. I usually freeze it in two or four-cup lots, so I'll have the correct amount for soup making.

• Toss the bones into a large soup kettle, cover them with cold water and then cover the pot and bring it to a boil. Skim off any scum as it rises.

• Add celery leaves, onion, bay leaves, carrots, parsley, peppercorns, vinegar and salt.*

• Once the stock returns to a boil, reduce the heat and let it simmer (boiling may make it cloudy) for a couple of hours.

• Remove it from the heat, strain the liquid into another large pot or bowl and cool it as quickly as possible. When it has congealed, remove the fat from the top and spoon the stock into containers for storage or use it to make soup.

*Vinegar softens the bones so the nutrients can be withdrawn; salt tends to toughen the meat during cooking but helps extract the goodness from the bones.

Chicken and Rice Soup

4 cups defatted chicken stock
1/3 cup uncooked rice
1 cup diced, cooked chicken
salt and pepper, to taste
2 teaspoons minced parsley

Does chicken soup cure a cold? Well, my "men" were given chicken soup whenever they were sick. And I drew comfort from knowing that they breathed better, slept better, felt better, and eventually got better.

• In a large saucepan, bring stock to a boil. Add rice. Reduce heat, cover and simmer for 15 minutes.

• Add chicken, salt and pepper, if required. Simmer, uncovered, for 5 minutes longer, or until rice is tender and chicken is heated through.

• Stir in parsley and serve. Makes 4 servings.

When Sondra Gotlieb was planning a trip to Nova Scotia several years ago to research one of her cookbooks, she called to ask if I would prepare a typical Nova Scotian meal for her. As I was very busy at the time, I asked Jean Boyd to do the honours. Jean, who is an excellent cook and knowledgeable about local cuisine, agreed and received the highest accolades from Sondra in a subsequent article in Chatelaine magazine. Sondra said she never tasted better chowder.

- In large pot, render salt pork and drain off most of fat.

- Add onions and sauté until transparent.

- Add water, then potatoes. Simmer until potatoes absorb water and are cooked.

- Add seafood and cream. Simmer just until fish is cooked, 7 to 10 minutes. Do *not* allow to boil!

- Season with salt and pepper to taste. Makes 5 servings.

Jean's Rich Seafood Chowder

1/4 pound (125 g) salt pork, cut
   very finely
2 medium onions, diced
1 cup water
3 medium potatoes, diced
1 cup shrimp, diced
1 cup scallops, cut in quarters
   with scissors
1 cup chopped lobster meat
1 cup chopped haddock fillets
2 cups blend (light cream)
1 can (385 mL) evaporated milk
salt and pepper to taste

For us, a trip to the Annapolis Valley during strawberry season always means lunch at the Evangeline Tea Room in Grand-Pré. Time stands still at this little restaurant and the fish chowder, homemade scones and strawberry pie never change. Thank goodness!

- Cut haddock into bite-sized pieces.

- In large saucepan, cook onions, celery and potatoes in small amount of water for 10 minutes.

- Add fish and simmer 5 to 8 minutes or until fish is cooked.

- Slowly add blend and milk. Reheat, but do not boil.

- Season with salt and pepper. Add butter and garnish with grated carrot. Makes 4 servings.

Note: This chowder is even more flavourful when prepared ahead, chilled in the refrigerator and then reheated.

Doreen Kelly's Fish Chowder

1 pound (500 g) haddock fillets
1/2 cup chopped onion
1/2 cup chopped celery
2 cups diced potatoes
water for cooking
2 cups blend (light cream)
2 cups milk
salt and pepper to taste
1/3 cup butter
1 carrot for garnish, grated

Lobster Bisque

1/4 cup butter
1/4 cup diced onion
4 tablespoons all-purpose flour
1/2 teaspoon salt
dash of pepper (preferably white)
3 cups milk
1 cup chicken stock
1 ½ cups chopped lobster meat (in bite-sized pieces)
1/2 cup blend (light cream)
1 teaspoon Worcestershire sauce
4 teaspoons butter (approximately)
4 teaspoons finely diced celery (approximately)
paprika

Lobster stews or chowders are best when allowed to "age" at least five hours or as long as two days in the refrigerator. This recipe is an excellent choice for a dinner party because it can be made ahead and reheated minutes before serving.

- Melt butter in large saucepan. Add onions and cook just until limp (do not brown).

- Stir in flour, salt and pepper and cook, stirring, for 2 to 3 minutes.

- Gradually add milk and chicken stock, stirring constantly until creamy and smooth.

- Add lobster, blend and Worcestershire sauce and heat thoroughly.

- Let cool and refrigerate for up to 2 days. Reheat and serve in hot bowls topped with butter, celery and paprika. Makes 4 servings.

Golden Cheese Soup

1/4 cup water
2 tablespoons butter
1 package (10 ounces/300 g) frozen corn
1 cup broccoli florets
1/2 cup thinly sliced carrot
1/4 cup chopped onion
1/4 teaspoon pepper
salt to taste
2 cans (10 ounces/284 mL each) cream of potato soup
2 cups milk
1 cup grated cheddar cheese
1 cup grated provolone cheese*

This recipe was given to me by Marie Sartori, a friend we used to meet in Florida every year. We nicknamed her husband Joe "Cheese" because he was a cheesemaker in Wisconsin.

- In a large saucepan, combine water, butter, corn, broccoli, carrot, onion, pepper and salt. Bring to boil, reduce heat and simmer for 10 minutes.

- Stir in potato soup, milk and cheeses*. Heat, stirring, until cheese melts and soup is hot but not boiling. Watch carefully to prevent sticking. Makes 7 to 8 cups.

*Provolone may be reduced to 1/4 cup or omitted. Since this was the type of cheese Joe made, it was readily available for his favourite soup.

To get the most out of today's favourite green vegetable, I started making soup from the stalks. I wash, peel, slice, and freeze them until I have enough. Six to eight stalks should make soup for six people. A chopped green apple is a more recent addition, said to be the secret of "the world's best broccoli soup."

• In heavy-bottomed saucepan, heat butter and sauté onions until limp but not brown.

• Stir in broccoli and apple. Add bay leaf, thyme and just enough chicken stock to cover broccoli. Bring to boil, reduce heat and simmer for approximately 2 hours, keeping cover ajar to allow steam to escape.

• Remove from heat and discard bay leaf. Purée in blender, a third at a time. Add flour to one batch of soup in blender.

• Return soup to saucepan and boil for a minute or so to cook flour. Season with salt and pepper.

• Reduce heat and add milk, 1/4 cup at a time, until soup is right consistency for serving. Makes 4 to 6 servings.

Variation: For curried broccoli soup, add 1 tablespoon curry powder to simmering soup.

Cream of Broccoli Soup

2 tablespoons butter,
    margarine or vegetable oil
2 onions, chopped
1 bunch of broccoli or equal
    amount of broccoli stalks
1 green apple, cored and
    chopped
1 bay leaf
pinch of thyme
4 to 6 cups chicken stock
2 tablespoons all-purpose flour
salt and pepper to taste
milk or cream

What could be nicer on a rainy day than a bowl of hearty corn chowder? Some recipes call for a tablespoon or two of flour to thicken the chowder, but the same effect may be accomplished by mashing the cooked potatoes slightly.

• Melt butter in heavy saucepan. Sauté onion and celery until limp but not brown.

• Add potatoes and water. Bring to boil and cook 10 to 15 minutes or until potatoes are tender.

• Mash potatoes slightly without draining.

• Add corn, milk, salt and pepper. Heat through for approximately 5 minutes.

• Serve hot and garnish with parsley, if desired. Makes 5 to 6 servings.

Corn Chowder

2 tablespoons butter or
    vegetable oil
1/2 cup chopped onion
1/4 cup chopped celery
    (optional)
2 cups diced raw potatoes
2 cups water or vegetable stock
1 can (19 ounces/540 mL)
    creamed corn
2 cups milk
salt and pepper to taste
minced parsley for garnish

Cream of Carrot Soup

2 tablespoons butter or
    vegetable oil
2 onions, sliced
2 pounds carrots, peeled and
    sliced
1/2 teaspoon dill seeds
5 cups chicken stock
salt and pepper to taste
1/8 teaspoon ground nutmeg
2 cups blend (light cream) or
    milk
fresh parsley sprigs for garnish

Hot or cold, this soup is a delicious way to stock up on beta-carotene which makes the vitamin A our bodies need. To lower the saturated fat content, I use oil instead of butter and two per cent milk in place of cream. It may not be as rich, but it's still an excellent soup.

• In heavy saucepan, melt butter and sauté onions until transparent.

• Add carrots, dill, chicken stock, salt, pepper and nutmeg. Cook 25 minutes or until carrots are tender.

• Purée mixture, 1/3 at a time, in blender or food processor. Add blend and reheat.

• Garnish with fresh parsley sprigs. Makes 6 servings.

Note: To serve cold, chill thoroughly. Garnish each bowl with spoonful of sour cream or yogurt and sprig of parsley, if desired.

Family Leek and Potato Soup

4 large leeks
4 tablespoons butter or
    margarine
2 medium onions, finely
    chopped
4 medium potatoes, peeled
    and cut into cubes
    (approximately 4 cups)
6 cups chicken stock
salt and freshly ground black
    pepper to taste
freshly chopped parsley for
    garnish

This is the family-style version of a delicious soup. The addition of cream dresses it up for guests but also increases fat content.

• Cut off tops of leeks, leaving on 2 inches of green. Remove coarse, outer leaves and split leeks approximately 1/2 inch from bottom to top. Wash carefully under cold running water, gently pulling leaves open to check for sand inside. Chop into small cubes.

• In large, heavy saucepan, melt butter. Add leeks and onions and cook for approximately 5 minutes, stirring frequently. Do not brown.

• Add potatoes and chicken broth and bring to boil. Reduce heat and simmer 15 minutes or until potatoes are just tender.

• Season with salt and pepper and garnish with parsley, if desired. Serve hot. Makes 8 servings.

Note: To make with milk or cream, add 1 cup to soup just before serving.

Zucchini was a latecomer to my kitchen but, because of its year-round availability, it was inevitable that some would eventually turn up in the soup kettle. This soup is also delicious served cold, especially if yogurt or sour cream replaces the blend.

- Sauté onion and garlic in butter until transparent.

- Add zucchini and toss to coat with butter.

- Add curry, salt, pepper and chicken stock and cook until zucchini is tender.

- Purée in food processor or blender.

- Whisk in cream, return to stove and heat until simmering. Makes 6 servings.

Note: Young, tender zucchini need not be peeled, but larger ones have tough skin which should be removed.

Curried Zucchini Soup

1/2 medium onion chopped
2 cloves garlic, pressed
2 tablespoons butter
2 pounds zucchini, washed and sliced (see note)
2 teaspoons curry powder
1 teaspoon salt
1/2 teaspoon pepper
3 ½ cups chicken stock
1 cup blend (light cream) or milk

This hearty soup is a meal in itself. Regular ground meat may be used, since the fat is drained after cooking.

- In large saucepan or soup kettle, brown meat. Remove meat to strainer and drain off fat.

- Return meat to pot and add onions, carrots and celery. Cook for 5 minutes, stirring.

- Add potatoes, tomatoes, tomato sauce, barley, water, bouillon, pepper, basil and bay leaf. Bring to boil, reduce heat and simmer, covered, for 1 hour.

- Remove bay leaf and serve hot. Makes 6 to 8 servings.

Hamburger Soup

1 pound (500 g) ground beef
2 cups chopped onions
1 cup diced carrot
1 cup diced celery
1 cup diced potatoes
1 can (28 ounces/796 mL) tomatoes, undrained and chopped
1 cup tomato sauce
1/2 cup pearl barley, rice or small pasta
6 cups water
2 tablespoons beef bouillon powder
1/8 teaspoon pepper
2 teaspoons dried basil
1 bay leaf

Pumpkin (or Squash) Soup

2-pound pumpkin or squash
1 cup water
2 cups diced onions (optional)
butter (optional)
3 cups milk
1 tablespoon butter or
    margarine
1 teaspoon sugar
salt and pepper to taste

Here's a delicious soup from the land where the big pumpkins grow. When boiling the pumpkin, save the water to use for future soup-making. It adds flavour and nutrients. My rule of thumb is that a pound of pumpkin, as it comes, produces 3/4 cup cooked, mashed pumpkin.

• Pare rind from pumpkin or squash. Remove seeds and cut flesh into small pieces.

• Place in soup kettle with water and bring to boil. Reduce heat and simmer for 35 minutes, until pumpkin is tender.

• Drain and put through sieve or purée in blender. Return to soup kettle.

• Sauté onions, if using, in small amount of butter.

• Mix with pumpkin.

• Scald milk and add to pumpkin mixture along with 1 tablespoon butter, sugar, salt and pepper. Bring to boiling point, stirring to prevent scorching. Makes 4 servings.

Note: An easier way to prepare purée is to cut pumpkin or squash in half after washing it, remove seeds and fibres and place halves, cut side down, on cookie sheet or directly on oven rack. Bake at 375°F for 40 minutes. Cool slightly, scrape out flesh and mash or purée in blender.

Cabbage Chowder

4 cups shredded cabbage
2 cups sliced carrots
2 cups diced potatoes
1/2 teaspoon salt
1/2 teaspoon pepper
3 cups water or vegetable stock
4 cups milk, scalded
yogurt for garnish
paprika for garnish

For those who don't like the smell of cabbage cooking, toss in a handful of chopped celery leaves. Not only will they reduce the odour, but they're also a nourishing addition to this tasty chowder.

• In large saucepan or soup kettle, combine cabbage, carrots, potatoes, salt, pepper and water. Bring to boil, reduce to medium heat and cook, uncovered, for 10 to 15 minutes or until vegetables are just tender. Do not overcook.

• Add scalded milk and return to boiling point.

• Remove from heat, ladle into bowls and garnish each with spoonful of yogurt and dash of paprika, if desired. Makes 8 to 10 generous servings.

Cream of Tomato Soup

In this recipe, canned tomatoes combine with white sauce to make a delicious soup. To prevent curdling, have both mixtures at the same temperature and combine just before serving. The tomatoes should be added slowly to the sauce.

2 tablespoons butter
2 tablespoons flour
2 cups milk
1 can (19 ounces/540 mL) tomatoes
1/4 cup chopped celery (optional)
2 tablespoons chopped onion (optional)

• Melt butter in top of double boiler or saucepan. Add flour and cook, stirring, for 2 to 3 minutes.

• Gradually add milk, stirring until sauce comes to boil and is smooth and thick. Keep hot.

• In another saucepan, combine tomatoes with celery and onion, if using. Bring to boil, reduce heat and simmer for 5 minutes.

• Slowly add tomato mixture to white sauce. Makes 4 to 6 servings.

Cream of Mushroom Soup

This soup also came late to my kitchen because fresh mushrooms were not always as available as they are today. When I think of all those cans of cream of mushroom soup that I used over the years, for everything from sauces to appetizers, I can't help wondering how we survived all that salt. There's more than 1,000 mg of sodium in a cup of canned cream of mushroom soup.

1 pound fresh mushrooms
1 onion, finely chopped
1/4 cup butter or margarine
1/4 cup all-purpose flour
3 cups chicken stock or broth
2 cups milk
1/2 teaspoon salt
1/4 teaspoon white pepper
1/2 cup dry sherry (optional)

• Clean mushrooms with damp paper towel. Slice half and chop the remainder.

• In large saucepan or soup pot, sauté mushrooms and onion in melted butter for approximately 10 minutes.

• Sprinkle flour over mushrooms, stir and cook for 1 to 2 minutes.

• Gradually add chicken stock and cook over medium heat, stirring constantly, until thickened and bubbly.

• Reduce heat to low, stir in milk, salt, pepper and sherry, if using.

• Cook until heated through, stirring occasionally. Makes 6 cups.

French Onion Soup

2 tablespoons butter
1 tablespoon oil
5 onions, thinly sliced
2 tablespoons flour
1/2 teaspoon pepper
3 cans condensed beef broth
2 soup cans water
6 slices white toast or stale
    French bread
6 thin slices Swiss cheese
4 tablespoons grated Swiss or
    Parmesan cheese

When we were first married, onion soup was all the rage. Although I have forgotten my earliest offerings, this one has long been in my file of favourites.

• Heat butter and oil in large saucepan or soup pot. Add onions and sauté over low heat until limp and translucent, stirring frequently.

• Add flour and pepper and cook, stirring, for 2 to 3 minutes.

• Gradually add broth and water, stirring constantly. Cover and cook over low heat for 30 minutes.

• Cut toast into rounds to fit soup bowls. Place round of toast in each bowl, place slice of cheese on toast and pour soup over it.

• Place under broiler for 1 minute until cheese has melted. Sprinkle with grated cheese. Makes 6 servings.

Vegetable Chowder

2 cups soup stock
2 cups corn kernels
2 cups chopped celery
1/2 green pepper, chopped
1 onion, chopped
1 cup canned tomatoes, cut up
3 tablespoons butter or
    margarine
3 tablespoons flour
2 cups milk, scalded
salt and pepper to taste
1/2 cup grated cheese (optional)

With soup stock in the freezer, and canned corn and tomatoes in the cupboard, you've got the makings of a hearty soup for lunch.

• In a dutch oven or soup kettle, bring to a boil the stock, corn, celery, green pepper, onion and tomatoes. Reduce heat and simmer for 30 minutes.

• In a saucepan, melt butter. Stir in flour and cook, stirring, for 2 or 3 minutes.

• Gradually stir in milk and cook, stirring, for 5 minutes, until mixture is smooth and thickened. Add to vegetable mixture. Add salt and pepper, if required. Add cheese, if using, stirring until melted. Makes 6 servings.

SALADS

T he molded or congealed salads popular during the 1950s and 60s were more often sweet than savoury. I'm not sure if the trend hinged on the constant pampering of the sweet tooth, or if we just liked the colour the molds added to the table.

Certainly my boys referred to their favourites by colour; Frank liked the "yellow one," Gary the "orange one," while Bob, along with his cousin David, preferred the "geen gelly" (the green one).

Because of increased numbers on cottage weekends, many meals were a variety of foods served buffet style, and emerald salad or pineapple and carrot mold usually won the popularity contest.

Other favourite buffet salads included cucumbers with sour cream (the recipe is in *Out of Old Nova Scotia Kitchens*), copper pennies (marinated carrots), and the ubiquitous potato salad that was the favourite accompaniment to cold cuts. When the Dunnets (Laurie's sister Melda, her husband Gordon and their family) came for weekends, there always had to be potato salad, especially for Gordon. He used to reach for the bowl and place it in front of him, saying, "I've got my potato salad, where's yours?"

During the season, fresh mackerel was no further away than the end of the fishing line, and I used to keep a jar of mackerel salad in the refrigerator in case I needed a quick appetizer or light meal.

With the garden producing quantities of leaf lettuce, getting it all used was a major problem. I kept bringing it to the table on a platter, sprinkled with brown sugar and vinegar—and as soon as I set the platter down, hands would reach for the pieces with the most amount of sugar.

Life B.S.S. (before the salad spinner) was not as easy as it has been since. How to get the excess water off the lettuce in order to keep it crisp and prevent a soggy salad was a problem. Patting it dry with paper toweling, no matter how gentle the touch, bruised the tender leaves. I tried the pillow case method, arranging the lettuce inside the case, twisting the ends into handles, and spinning it around as fast as I could make it go. The centrifugal force did the job in removing the water, but containing it was another thing. Not only did I get a shower, but everything around me was damp. The inexpensive little salad spinner is worth its weight in gold.

Emerald Salad

1 package (3 ounces/85 g) lime-
    flavoured gelatin
1 cup pineapple juice (reserved
    from drained pineapple; add
    water to make 1 cup)
2/3 cup chopped celery
2/3 cup chopped apples
2/3 cup well-drained, crushed
    pineapple
1/2 cup mayonnaise
1/2 cup whipping cream
lettuce

Molded salads have a way of turning ordinary cold meat loaf, ham or turkey into something special. With one in the fridge, I always feel ready for company. When my family was at home, emerald salad was everybody's favourite.

- In large bowl, dissolve gelatin in hot pineapple juice. Let set until fairly stiff.

- Stir in celery, apples, pineapple and mayonnaise.

- Whip cream and fold into gelatin.

- Pour into ring mold. Place in refrigerator until firm, then turn out on bed of lettuce. Makes 8 to 10 servings.

Pineapple and Carrot Mold

1 package (3 ounces/85 g)
    orange-flavoured gelatin
1 cup boiling water
1 cup pineapple juice (reserved
    from drained pineapple; add
    water to make 1 cup)
1 teaspoon lemon juice or
    vinegar
1/4 teaspoon salt
grated rind of an orange
1 cup well-drained, crushed
    pineapple
1 cup grated carrot
1/4 cup chopped maraschino
    cherries
lettuce

There's a little trick to removing a jellied salad from a mold. Put hot water in the sink and dip the mold quickly into the water, without submerging the top. If this doesn't release the salad, shake the mold gently back and forth. Place the serving plate on top of the mold and invert it. If necessary, give it a final little shake.

- In large bowl, dissolve gelatin in boiling water. Stir in pineapple juice, lemon juice or vinegar and salt. Let set until slightly thickened.

- Add orange rind, pineapple, carrot and cherries. Pour into mold and place in refrigerator until firm.

- Turn out on bed of lettuce. Makes 8 to 10 servings.

The recipe for cucumbers with sour cream (published in Out of Old Nova Scotia Kitchens) *may have been the favourite salad accompaniment to summer barbecues in our home, but this mold has always run a close second.*

- In large bowl, dissolve gelatin in boiling water. Let set until slightly thickened.

- Stir in cucumber, celery, mayonnaise and sour cream. Pour into mold and place in refrigerator until firm.

- Turn out on bed of lettuce. Makes 8 to 10 servings.

Cucumber Salad

1 package (3 ounces/85 g) lime-flavoured gelatin
1 cup boiling water
1 cup grated cucumber, well-drained
1 cup diced celery
1/2 cup mayonnaise
1 cup sour cream
lettuce

For colour as much as for its refreshing taste, this salad reigned over other molds during the 1950s. However, perfection salad has been around in one form or another since 1905, when a Pennsylvania woman took third prize in a cooking contest with her recipe. In doing so, she showed the world that gelatin was no longer intended just for desserts.

- In large bowl, soften gelatin in cold water, then dissolve in hot water.

- Add sugar and salt and stir until dissolved.

- Stir in vinegar and lemon juice. Cool in refrigerator.

- When mixture begins to thicken, add cabbage, celery, pimiento and green pepper. Pour into 9 x 5-inch loaf pan and chill until set.

- Unmold on bed of lettuce. Garnish with ripe olive halves, if desired. Makes 8 to 10 servings.

Perfection Salad

2 envelopes unflavoured gelatin
1/2 cup cold water
2 cups hot water
1/2 cup granulated sugar
1/2 teaspoon salt
1/2 cup vinegar
2 tablespoons fresh lemon juice
1 ½ cups finely shredded cabbage
1 cup chopped celery
1/4 cup chopped pimiento
1/2 cup chopped green pepper
lettuce
ripe olive halves for garnish (optional)

Lobster Aspic Mold

2 envelopes unflavoured
  gelatin
1/2 cup pineapple juice
  (reserved from drained
  pineapple)
1/2 cup hot water
1 cup chopped celery
1 green pepper, diced
1 ½ cups lobster meat, cut into
  bite-sized pieces
1 can (19 ounces/540 mL)
  pineapple tidbits, drained
3/4 cup mayonnaise
1 tablespoon lemon juice
generous pinch each of salt and
  paprika
lettuce

What a hit this salad used to make when it was presented in individual servings at luncheons or afternoon bridge. Do not use fresh or frozen pineapple or pineapple juice in jellied salads because it contains an enzyme which prevents the gelatin from setting.

• In large bowl, soften gelatin in pineapple juice. Add hot water and stir to dissolve.

• Chill until gelatin has the consistency of egg whites.

• In separate bowl, combine celery, green pepper, lobster, pineapple, mayonnaise, lemon juice, salt and paprika. Fold into gelatin, then pour into individual molds or a large mold. Place in refrigerator until firm.

• Turn individual molds out on lettuce cups, larger mold on bed of lettuce. Makes 10 servings.

Curried Chicken Salad

2 (3 pound/1.5 kg) chickens
1 cup slivered almonds
4 ribs celery, chopped finely
1 bunch green onions, chopped
  finely
2 cups seedless green grapes,
  halved if large
1 cup sliced water chestnuts
3/4 cup sour cream
1 cup mayonnaise
2 tablespoons curry powder
1 tablespoon lemon juice
1 tablespoon Worcestershire
  sauce
1/4 cup chopped fresh parsley

There have been many variations of chicken salad through the years. This more recent recipe surpasses all the others. I once doubled it to serve at a family gathering of 16 adults and 4 children.

• Cook chickens. When cool enough to handle, remove meat from carcasses; cut into bite size chunks. Set aside.

• Spread almonds on cookie sheet and place in oven at 250°F, shaking pan occasionally, for approximately 12 minutes or until golden. Set aside.

• In large bowl, combine celery, green onions, grapes and water chestnuts. Stir in chicken.

• In separate bowl, mix sour cream, mayonnaise, curry powder, lemon juice and Worcestershire sauce. Stir into chicken mixture and mix well. Chill.

• Just before serving, fold in 2/3 cup almonds. Spoon into glass bowl and sprinkle with remaining 1/3 cup almonds and chopped parsley. Makes 8 to 10 servings.

When the mackerel were running in St. Margaret's Bay, we used to grab our gear, pile into the boat and go after them. Then we'd fry them up for breakfast, lunch or dinner and always cook enough extra to make this delicious salad. It keeps for at least a week in a tightly covered jar.

- Soak bread in vinegar.

- Place in bowl of food processor with mackerel, onion, apple, eggs and pepper. Using chopping blade, process with on-off switch until mixture is slightly lumpy. Taste and adjust seasoning. Add more vinegar to increase tartness, if desired.

- Store in refrigerator in tightly covered jar. Serve with a mixed salad. Makes approximately 3 ½ cups or 6 to 8 servings.

Note: To mix by hand, chop ingredients in wooden bowl.

Mackerel Salad

1 slice rye bread
3 tablespoons vinegar
2 ½ cups flaked cooked
    mackerel
1 medium onion, cut into
    chunks
1 large apple, peeled and diced
3 hard-boiled eggs
dash of pepper

This salad is so sweet it could be served for dessert. It was a reliable recipe for summer parties of our past, not only because everybody wanted more but also because it could be made the day before.

- In top of double boiler over boiling water, combine beaten eggs, pineapple juice, vinegar and sugar. Beat constantly until thick and smooth.

- Remove from heat and add butter. Cool.

- Remove rind and membranes from oranges, then cut into pieces.

- Fold oranges, grapes and pineapple into cooled egg mixture.

- Whip cream. Fold cream and marshmallows into fruit mixture.

- Chill in refrigerator for 24 hours. Makes 10 to 12 servings.

24-Hour Salad

2 eggs, beaten
2 tablespoons pineapple juice
    (reserved from drained
    pineapple)
2 tablespoons vinegar
2 tablespoons granulated sugar
1 tablespoon butter
2 oranges
2 cups halved seedless green
    grapes
2 cups drained pineapple
    chunks, canned or fresh
1 cup whipping cream
2 cups small marshmallows

Potato Salad

6 medium potatoes
1 onion, chopped
4 hard-boiled eggs, sliced
1 cup chopped celery
1 teaspoon salt
1/2 cup salad dressing or
    mayonnaise

If all the potato salads we ate during our cottage years were placed side by side, I'm sure they would reach from Indian Point in St. Margaret's Bay to Halifax. Potato salad is a great dish for entertaining since it needs to be made hours ahead so that the flavours will blend. I have often doubled the recipe for a crowd.

• Boil potatoes with skins on, then peel and cube to make 4 cups.

• Combine with onion, eggs, celery, salt and dressing.

• Chill for 4 to 6 hours. Makes 8 servings.

Sour Cream Green Bean Salad

1 ½ pounds (750 g) fresh green
    beans
1 medium red onion, thinly
    sliced
3/4 teaspoon salt, divided
1 tablespoon cider vinegar
1 tablespoon granulated sugar
3/4 cup sour cream
1/4 teaspoon freshly ground
    pepper

This is another make-ahead salad that's delightfully refreshing in summer. Anyone who enjoys cucumbers in sour cream will be hard pressed to choose between the two. We can thank Nova Scotia's early German settlers for both dishes.

• Wash, trim and cut beans into 2-inch lengths. Cook in boiling salted water until tender-crisp, approximately 6 to 8 minutes.

• Drain in colander and refresh under cold running water. Drain again and turn out on paper towels to dry.

• Put onion in bowl and sprinkle with 1/4 teaspoon salt. Let sit for 15 minutes, stirring once or twice.

• In large bowl, combine 1/2 teaspoon salt, vinegar, sugar, sour cream and pepper.

• Drain onions, pressing firmly between layers of paper towels. Add to dressing along with beans.

• Toss well, cover and chill. Makes 6 servings.

Note: If fresh beans are not available, use 2 packages (10 ounces/300 g each) frozen cut green beans. Cook according to package directions, drain, refresh in cold water and dry as above.

Many hostesses have puzzled over what happened to the parsley they used to garnish a sandwich tray. When they learned I was eating it, reaction ranged from surprise to shock. Parsley is one of the best sources of vitamins A and C and a good breath freshener after eating onions or garlic. That's why I add parsley to coleslaw.

• Combine cabbage, parsley and onions in large bowl and chill.

• In a jar, combine sugar, salt, vinegar and oil. Cover; shake well to dissolve sugar.

• Just before serving, shake again; pour dressing over vegetables and toss lightly. Makes 6 servings.

Coleslaw

3 cups finely shredded crisp cabbage
3/4 cup chopped parsley
1/2 cup sliced green onions
2 tablespoons granulated sugar
1/2 teaspoon salt
1/4 cup vinegar
3 tablespoons vegetable oil

Children who balk at eating carrots may be tempted to try them in this raisin-studded slaw. The leftovers make tasty sandwiches, although it may be necessary to drain off the dressing first.

• Combine carrots and raisins.

• In separate bowl, mix together mayonnaise, yogurt and lemon juice.

• Pour over carrots and raisins and mix well. Makes 5 to 6 servings.

Carrot Raisin Slaw

2 cups shredded raw carrots
1/2 cup seedless raisins
1/4 cup mayonnaise
1/4 cup low-fat yogurt
2 tablespoons fresh lemon juice

Not just as Oscar of the Waldorf prepared it in the 1890s, but I think the addition of grapes, raisins and nuts has improved this famous salad.

• Dice apples into a bowl. Sprinkle with lemon juice or citric acid to keep them from turning brown.

• Add grapes, walnuts, celery, raisins and mayonnaise. Mix well. Serve on lettuce-lined plates. Makes 6 servings.

Waldorf Salad

2 large red apples, unpeeled
1 large green apple, unpeeled
lemon juice or citric acid
1 cup halved seedless green grapes
1/2 cup chopped walnuts
1 cup diced celery
1/3 cup raisins
1/3 cup mayonnaise

Copper Pennies

2 pounds (1 kg) carrots, peeled
   and sliced
1 green pepper, finely diced
3 medium onions, cut into
   rings
1 can (10 ounces/284 mL)
   tomato soup
salt and pepper to taste
1/2 cup vegetable oil
1/2 cup vinegar
1/2 cup granulated sugar
1 teaspoon prepared mustard
1 teaspoon Worcestershire
   sauce

This marinated carrot salad has become a popular addition to light summer meals and buffets. Summer cooks will love the fact that it can be prepared two or three days ahead.

• Cook carrots in water to cover until just tender. Drain.

• Add green pepper and onions and mix gently.

• In separate bowl, combine soup, salt, pepper, oil, vinegar, sugar, mustard and Worcestershire sauce. Pour over carrot mixture.

• Store in airtight container in refrigerator for 2 to 3 days before serving, turning frequently to improve flavour. Serve cold. Makes 10 to 12 servings.

Orange and Red Onion Salad

2 large oranges
1 small red onion
4 large lettuce leaves
French dressing

This unusual combination is simple and delicious and has been a hit every time I've served it. By overlapping alternate slices of orange and onion on top of crisp lettuce leaves, I've also had guests admiring my artistic effort.

• Peel oranges and slice crosswise into 8 slices.

• Peel onion and slice into rings.

• Arrange lettuce, orange slices and onion rings on 4 salad plates. Serve with dressing.

Apple Salad

2 apples, peeled, cored and
   sliced
2 onions, thinly sliced
1 head tender lettuce
1 teaspoon lemon juice
1 teaspoon grated lemon rind
1/4 cup French dressing
paprika

It's like comparing oranges and apples, except in this case apples work as well as oranges. I think I first tried this combination one day when I was out of oranges. I was particularly pleased with the results since I live in apple country.

• Combine apples and onion slices. Arrange on lettuce leaves in a salad bowl.

• Add lemon juice and rind to dressing.

• Pour over salad. Sprinkle with paprika. Makes 4 servings.

My husband's sister and brother-in-law, Melda and Gordon Dunnet of Toronto, leased a little cottage in Hubbards for years. It was the scene of many happy family gatherings. This salad, often doubled to accommodate us all, was one of Melda's standbys. Although she kept the salad light, I like the addition of mandarin oranges for colour.

- In large bowl, combine pineapple, oranges, coconut, marshmallows, sour cream and cottage cheese. Refrigerate for several hours.

- Serve on lettuce. Makes 6 to 8 servings.

Note: If doubling, add just enough extra coconut to thicken.

Melda's Cottage Cheese Salad

1 cup drained pineapple tidbits
1 cup drained mandarin oranges
1 cup shredded coconut
1 cup small white marshmallows
1 cup sour cream
1 cup cottage cheese

Once again there are two little boys in my life. Because my three-year-old grandson Corey lives in Edmonton, I don't have the opportunity to get to know his food preferences. But ten-year-old Craig lives close by in Indian Point and often comes for meals. Without fail, he asks if I have any of "that frozen stuff" on hand. If I do when he arrives, I don't by the time he leaves.

- Soften gelatin in cold water, then dissolve over hot water.

- Combine fruits in large bowl. Add lemon juice and dissolved gelatin. Place in refrigerator until it begins to thicken.

- Whip cream. Fold into fruit mixture with mayonnaise. Turn into metal baking pan, cover and place in freezer.

- To serve cut into squares and serve in lettuce cups, if desired. Makes 9 servings.

Frozen Fruit Salad

1 tablespoon unflavoured gelatin
1/4 cup cold water
3 cups diced fruit (peaches, pears, melon balls, canned pineapple, etc.)
1/2 cup halved seedless green grapes
1 banana, diced
3 tablespoons lemon juice
1 cup whipping cream
1 cup mayonnaise

Full Meal Salad

1/2 head cauliflower, cut into
   bite-sized florets
1 green pepper, cut into strips
1 red onion, sliced and
   separated into rings
1 pound (500 g) fresh white
   mushrooms, sliced
1 head iceberg lettuce, torn into
   bite-sized pieces
1 head romaine lettuce, torn
   into bite-sized pieces
2 cups fresh bean sprouts
2 cups alfalfa sprouts
2 tomatoes, each cut into 8
   pieces
2 carrots, sliced
2 stalks celery, sliced
3/4 cup drained and halved
   pimiento-stuffed olives
1/2 cup vegetable oil
1/2 cup red wine vinegar
pinch of oregano
pinch of garlic powder
pinch of dry mustard

In my early days in the kitchen, there were only two kinds of lettuce — leaf lettuce which we grew in the garden in summer and iceberg lettuce during the rest of the year. The salad bowl soon expanded to include a wide variety of vegetables as this large, well-loaded salad indicates. Remember to wash and drain all fresh vegetables except mushrooms, which should be wiped with a damp cloth or paper towel.

- In very large salad bowl, toss cauliflower, green pepper, red onion, mushrooms, iceberg and romaine lettuce, bean sprouts, alfalfa sprouts, tomatoes, carrots, celery and olives.

- Combine oil, vinegar, oregano, garlic powder and mustard in jar. Cover and shake well.

- Pour over salad and toss well. Makes 10 servings.

Sauerkraut Salad

1 quart (1 L) sauerkraut
1 small green pepper, chopped
1 onion, chopped
1 cup chopped celery
1 bottle (4 ½-ounce/128 mL)
   pimiento, chopped
1/2 cup vinegar
1/2 cup salad oil
3/4 cup granulated sugar

Being processed, canned sauerkraut just doesn't make it in this recipe. Use the crisp freshly-packed product that comes in litre and half-litre cartons. If you're worried about its high sodium content, refresh under hot running water before proceeding with the recipe.

- Drain sauerkraut. Combine with green pepper, onion, celery and pimientos.

- In a saucepan, combine vinegar, oil and sugar. Heat to dissolve sugar. Cool.

- Pour over sauerkraut mixture and mix well. Store, covered, in a plastic or glass container for at least 24 hours before serving. Makes 10-12 servings.

Sundays at the cottage usually started with brunch, and I particularly liked those that Laurie prepared. Not only did he turn out a mean omelet, filled with whatever the refrigerator provided, but he had a way of getting everyone to sit down at the table together. While the boys might successfully wheedle me into granting them an early escape, their father stood firm until the table was cleared.

Sometimes, brunch would centre around fried tinker mackerel just minutes out of the water. During an early morning calm on St. Margaret's Bay you could stand on the deck and watch the mackerel swimming about 100 feet below the surface.

"The mackerel are running. Let's go!" someone would yell. And off they—or we—went.

One day the bay came alive with fish jumping everywhere. We rushed to the boat but didn't even slip the mooring or use bait. Those little tinkers just kept popping up, almost asking to be caught. And we obliged.

Even more often, pancakes were the order that started the day. Armed with the old reliable basic recipe, Old Fashioned Griddle Cakes from *Out of Old Nova Scotia Kitchens*, Laurie depended on his own creativity and the fruit of the season to enhance his reputation as pancake king of Indian Point.

But oatmeal porridge had and still has its place on our breakfast table. It was the mainstay of winter breakfasts, a tradition still repeated when our grandchildren come for a visit.

Porridge was also the traditional Christmas breakfast, served after the stockings had been opened. We had first to get to the toe so the big, juicy orange could be retrieved and cut up as the appetizer before the porridge.

Never one to break with tradition, Frank still insists on oranges and porridge for Christmas breakfast.

"Let me make a strata for Christmas morning," I suggested to Sarah a few years ago before we moved in with them for the holiday.

"No way," said Frank. "It will be oranges and porridge as always."

BREAKFASTS

Great Day in the Morning Granola

8 cups old-fashioned rolled
    oats
2 cups raw wheat germ
1 cup buckwheat groats
1 cup soy flour
1 cup sesame seeds
1 cup hulled sunflower seeds
2 tablespoons flax seeds
1 cup chopped nuts
1 cup unrefined oil
1 cup honey

A small amount of this granola supplies a large amount of nutrition. I keep it in plastic bags in the freezer, since wheat germ should be stored at a cool temperature.

- In large bowl, combine oats, wheat germ, groats, flour, seeds and nuts. Add oil, mixing thoroughly.

- Add honey and mix until dry ingredients are thoroughly coated.

- Spread in large roasting pan and toast at 250°F for 1 hour or until golden. Stir frequently after the first 30 minutes.

- Cool completely before storing in tightly sealed containers or plastic bags. Makes about 4 ½ pounds.

French Toast

2 eggs
1/4 teaspoon salt
1 tablespoon granulated sugar
1/2 cup milk
1/4 teaspoon nutmeg or 1/2
    teaspoon vanilla
2 tablespoons butter or
    margarine
4 to 6 slices bread

My boys would eat French toast any day, accompanied by bacon and (much to the distress of my budgeting attempts) pure maple syrup. I can't blame them—I like French toast with my maple syrup too.

- In small bowl, beat eggs, salt, sugar, milk and nutmeg or vanilla with a fork.

- Heat electric frying pan to 380°F or heavy bottomed skillet to medium-low heat. Add butter and tilt to grease bottom. Dip slices of bread into egg mixture just until coated. Fry at once until browned on both sides, adding more butter if necessary.

- Serve hot with syrup or applesauce. Makes 4 to 6 slices.

Although the boys liked maple syrup with their French toast, they liked this fruit sauce as much or more. It was so familiar in our house that I would never have dreamed of serving it to guests. Now that I take another look at this recipe, I see that I should have.

- In small saucepan, combine jelly, cherries and lemon juice. Bring to boil, reduce heat and simmer for 10 minutes. Keep hot.

- Beat egg, milk and salt in shallow flat dish or pie plate.

- Spread cereal crumbs on waxed paper.

- In large heavy skillet, melt butter over medium–low heat. Dip both sides of bread quickly into egg mixture. Dip in cereal to thoroughly coat both sides. Place in skillet and brown well on both sides, adding more butter if necessary.

- Serve immediately with fruit sauce. Makes 2 to 4 servings.

Crispy French Toast with Fruit Sauce

1/2 cup red currant jelly
1/2 cup cut-up canned red
   cherries, drained
1 tablespoon lemon juice
1 egg
1/3 cup milk
1/4 teaspoon salt
3/4 cup coarsely crushed cereal
   flakes
2 tablespoons butter
4 slices white bread

When I started making these pancakes, they were limited to the blueberry growing season. Now, with individually quick frozen blueberries available, I can treat my family year-round to pancakes enhanced with Nova Scotia's famous little berries. To ensure that the berries don't "bleed" or get crushed, sprinkle them on top of the pancakes as they cook.

- In bowl, combine egg, milk and butter.

- Sift flour, baking powder, sugar and salt to distribute baking powder evenly.

- Gradually add dry ingredients to egg mixture, using a rotary beater.

- Drop batter on hot, lightly greased griddle, using 1/4 cup batter for each pancake. Sprinkle 2 table-spoons blueberries on each cake. When underside is golden, turn and cook other side. Makes about 8 pancakes.

Blueberry Pancakes

1 egg, well beaten
1 cup milk
1/4 cup butter or margarine,
   melted
1 cup all-purpose flour
2 ½ teaspoons baking powder
2 tablespoons granulated sugar
1/2 teaspoon salt
1 cup fresh or individually
   quick frozen blueberries

Apple Griddlecakes

1 cup milk, scalded
1 cup fresh bread crumbs
1 tablespoon butter, melted
1 egg, separated
1/2 cup all-purpose flour
1 teaspoon baking powder
1/4 teaspoon salt
1 tablespoon maple syrup
3/4 cup chopped peeled apple

Remember the bread pancakes that date back 100 years? These apple griddlecakes are a variation of that recipe. They also provide a great way to use up stale bread.

• In bowl, pour hot milk over bread crumbs. Add butter and let stand until crumbs are very soft. Mash with fork.

• Beat egg yolk and add to bread mixture.

• Combine flour, baking powder and salt and add to bread mixture. Stir in syrup.

• Beat egg white until stiff but not dry. Fold into bread mixture along with apples.

• Drop by large spoonfuls onto hot, lightly greased griddle. When bubbles form on griddlecakes, flip and brown other side. Makes 8 to 10 medium-sized griddlecakes.

Pumpkin Fritters or Pancakes

2 cups all-purpose flour
1/2 teaspoon salt
1/4 teaspoon nutmeg
2 eggs, well beaten
2 cups milk
1 tablespoon vegetable oil
1 tablespoon granulated sugar
1 ½ cups cooked mashed
    pumpkin (or use canned)
oil for deep-frying
icing sugar (optional)

We discovered pumpkin fritters in Barbados where our cook, Maureen, grew so tired of making them that she decided to give us the recipe.

• Sift together flour, salt and nutmeg.

• In separate bowl, combine eggs, milk, 1 tablespoon oil and sugar. Stir into flour mixture. Fold in pumpkin.

• Heat oil to 365°F in a deep-fryer. Drop batter by teaspoonfuls into hot oil, a few fritters at a time. Cook 2 to 3 minutes, turning once.

• Drain on paper towels. Sprinkle with icing sugar, if desired. Serve hot with syrup.

Note: Batter may also be dropped onto hot, lightly greased griddle for delicious pancakes.

In our house, everyone liked their eggs scrambled. Beating the eggs first ensured their fluffiness but often they were broken directly into the pan and stirred only slightly. When things got really busy, I turned to my own favourite method which needed almost no attention.

- Place oil and onion in top of a double boiler and cook over direct heat until onion is soft.

- Stir in tomato and green pepper. Place pot over boiling water.

- Add eggs and seasonings. Cover and cook, stirring once or twice, until eggs are creamy.

- Serve on toast, buttered or not as desired. Makes 4 servings.

Double Boiler Spanish Eggs

1 tablespoon vegetable oil
1 onion, chopped
1 tomato, peeled and chopped
1 green pepper, seeded and
    chopped
6 eggs, well beaten
salt and pepper to taste
4 slices toast

The addition of a sharp cheddar dressed up the morning eggs for weekend brunches or school day lunches. Since my son Gary always added ketchup, I tried building it into the recipe. He added more.

- In skillet, combine cheese, butter, onion, mushrooms and ketchup. Simmer for 2 minutes, stirring constantly.

- Add eggs and seasonings and stir until set.

- Serve on toast, buttered or not as desired. Sprinkle with fresh chives. Makes 4 servings.

Cheese Scramble

1/4 cup grated cheddar cheese
1 tablespoon butter
2 tablespoons chopped onion
1/2 cup chopped mushrooms
2 tablespoons ketchup
2 eggs, well beaten
salt and pepper to taste
4 slices toast
chives (optional)

Eggs in the Hole

soft butter or margarine
4 slices day-old white bread
4 eggs
salt and pepper to taste

There were many evenings when we would brings friends home after a movie or cocktail party for a bite to eat. Eggs in the hole would often be the bill of fare. My sons also loved them for breakfast or lunch and, since they liked the little circles best, I used to cut extras and fry them for seconds.

- Butter both sides of bread. With a 2 ½-inch cookie cutter or top of a tumbler, cut centres out of bread slices.

- Place bread and cut-outs in electric frying pan preheated to moderate. Brown on one side and turn.

- Break eggs into centre holes. Cover and cook about 4 minutes or until egg whites are firm.

- Sprinkle with salt and pepper. Serve with bread circles. Makes 2 to 4 servings.

Laurie's Omelet

4 eggs
1/4 cup milk
salt and pepper to taste
1 tablespoon butter

My husband Laurie started cooking omelets for a quick snack after returning home ravenous from cocktail parties that offered more liquor than food. He came to be so good at them that they were often requested for Sunday brunch.

- In bowl, beat eggs until light and fluffy. Add milk, salt and pepper and mix well.

- Heat butter in omelet pan. Add egg mixture and cook slowly over low heat until underside has set. Lift omelet slightly with spatula to let uncooked portion flow underneath and cook.

- Fold over and serve. Makes 2 servings.

Note: Before folding, omelet may be filled with chopped cooked ham, sautéed mushrooms, grated cheese or any other filling.

D uring this period in our lives, some dishes were so versatile that they made their appearance at the lunch table, as a light supper or even at breakfast. Fish cakes were a particular favourite, especially when served with homemade baked beans.

If conversation needs a little perking up at a gathering, just drop the words fish cakes and, if they're Nova Scotians, they'll take the bait. Everybody has their own idea how fish cakes should be made.

To say equal parts of fish and potatoes will get you started. So, what kind of fish? Most say salt cod.

But I had them fooled with the fish cakes I used to make from chicken haddie. Here was the original chicken of the sea—fish, usually cod or hake, or a mixture of both, salted and canned. It was so convenient and inexpensive that I always kept a 14 ounce can or two on hand.

Working with hot mashed potatoes, I'd throw in a chopped onion, a pat of butter and an egg, beating it all together before adding the drained and mashed chicken haddie. Formed into cakes and dipped in bread crumbs, they'd go into the fridge for at least a couple of hours so the crumbs would adhere and the flavours blend.

"What did you put in your fish cakes? They're delicious," someone would comment.

"Oh, this and that," I'd answer. Why spoil it by telling them it was canned fish.

But that was long ago. Chicken haddie is hard to find these days, although occasionally I see it—in 7 ounce cans. And it isn't cheap!

Back then, pasta was a little known word. There was elbow-shaped macaroni, and spaghetti, which would be cooked and served with tomato sauce, and sometimes, meatballs.

There was also rice—either fried in a not-too-authentic Chinese style, or Spanish rice. Beyond that, rice was for dessert.

Cookbooks of the period usually attached one or two pasta or rice recipes to the end of the cereal chapter. The classic dish was macaroni and cheese, baked in the oven. But what child of the 60s didn't know, and love, the first packaged macaroni and cheese dinner, which cooked in about seven minutes on top of the stove?

LIGHT MEALS, PASTA AND RICE

Corned Beef Hash

2 tablespoons butter or
   vegetable oil
1 onion, chopped
2 cups finely chopped cooked
   or canned corned beef
2 cups finely chopped cooked
   potatoes,
dash of pepper
1/4 cup milk

People who still make hash should stand up and be counted. It's an excellent dish which probably lost favour during the great depression when it appeared all too often as potatoes and onions. Children became ashamed to admit that they had hash for dinner yet again.

• Melt butter or oil in large, heavy frying pan. Sauté onion for 2 to 3 minutes.

• Combine beef, potatoes, pepper and milk and spread evenly over pan. Heat through for 40 minutes or until hash has browned.

• Fold over like an omelet and remove to hot platter. Makes 6 servings.

Variation: To make corned beef hash with eggs, shape equal portions of uncooked hash mixture into 1-inch thick patties. Place in lightly greased baking dish. Make a depression in each patty and break an egg into it. Cover and bake at 325°F for 25 minutes or until eggs are set.

Crisp Roast Beef Hash

3 cups finely diced cooked
   roast beef
3 cups finely diced cooked
   potatoes, (cold)
1/2 cup chopped onion
1/4 cup chopped green pepper
salt and pepper to taste
milk

Hash made with leftover roast beef doesn't enjoy the long culinary history of corned beef hash. But it became a customary Monday supper in homes where roast beef, not chicken, was the traditional Sunday dinner.

• In large bowl, combine roast beef, potatoes, onion, green pepper and seasonings. Add just enough milk to moisten.

• Heat lightly greased skillet to low, add hash mixture and cook until thoroughly browned on one side.

• Fold over like an omelet. Turn out and cut into 6 servings.

Tiny balls of this mixture can be rolled in flour and bread crumbs and deep-fried at 390°F for 3 minutes. Pass as appetizers.

• In a large bowl, cover codfish with cold water; let soak for several hours or overnight.

• Drain fish and discard water. Cover fish with fresh water, bring just to the boiling point, then immediately reduce heat and cook fish at a slow simmer for 5 minutes.

• Drain again and turn out on paper towels to dry. Pick cod apart into small pieces.

• In the meantime, bring potatoes to a boil and cook until tender. Drain thoroughly and mash.

• Stir in beaten egg, butter, pepper and onion. Add fish and combine well. If mixture is too soft, stir in enough bread crumbs to make it firm enough to mold. If mixture is too firm, stir in a tablespoon or two of milk to make it the right consistency.

• Using about 1/4 cup of the still-warm mixture, shape into individual patties about 1/2-inch thick. Dip both sides in dry bread crumbs. Cover and store in refrigerator for at least an hour to let flavours meld and make bread crumbs adhere better.

• Fry in hot butter or oil until golden on both sides. Makes 12 to 15 fish cakes, depending on size.

My boys liked this dish for lunch and I liked it because it was so easy to prepare. Although I sometimes substituted other cooked vegetables, tuna, leftover chicken or lobster, peas were their favourite. Today they would opt for lobster.

• Prepare medium white sauce in top of double boiler.

• Add peas and continue cooking until peas are well heated.

• Spoon over slice of unbuttered toast. Butter another slice of toast, cut into 4 triangles and lay against creamed peas on each side. Makes 3 to 4 servings.

Codfish Cakes

1 pound salt cod
6 medium potatoes, peeled and
   quartered
1 egg, beaten
1 tablespoon butter or
   margarine
1/8 teaspoon pepper
1 onion, chopped
1/2 cup dry bread crumbs, or
   more as needed
butter or oil for frying

Creamed Peas on Toast

1 cup medium white sauce (see
   index)
2 cups cooked drained peas
6 or 8 slices toast

Sautéed Mushrooms on Toast

1 pound (500 g) mushrooms, trimmed and sliced
2 tablespoons all-purpose flour
4 tablespoons butter
1/2 teaspoon grated onion
1/2 teaspoon salt
1/4 teaspoon pepper
1/2 cup boiling water
2 teaspoons lemon juice
2 teaspoons chopped parsley
12 slices toast

When I began preparing this dish, mushrooms were washed and scraped or peeled. Today we know that, because of their high water content, they should only be wiped clean with a damp paper towel or brush and then trimmed.

- Sprinkle mushrooms with flour.

- Melt butter in large frying pan, add mushrooms, onion, salt and pepper. Cook, stirring, for 5 minutes.

- Add boiling water and cook 5 minutes more.

- Add lemon juice and parsley. Serve on unbuttered toast, garnished with slice of buttered toast cut into 4 triangles. Makes 6 servings.

Mushroom Tart

1/2 pound (250 g) fresh or frozen mushrooms, sliced
1 teaspoon lemon juice
2 tablespoons butter
2 cups grated cheddar cheese
pastry for single, 9-inch pie shell
4 eggs
1 ½ cups milk
1/2 teaspoon salt
1/2 teaspoon pepper
dash of cayenne pepper

This tart is fancy enough to set before weekend guests or serve at a Sunday brunch. With crisp bacon or breakfast sausages, it makes an impressive, yet substantial meal.

- Sprinkle mushrooms with lemon juice.

- In large frying pan, melt butter. Add mushrooms and, tossing gently, sauté until golden.

- Sprinkle cheese evenly in bottom of pastry-lined pie plate. Spread mushrooms over cheese.

- Beat eggs with milk and seasonings just until blended. Pour over mushrooms.

- Bake at 375°F for about 40 minutes or until firm. Allow to cool 10 minutes before slicing. Makes 6 servings.

This is another great choice for a breakfast pie because there's no pastry to make. I sometimes save a few extra minutes in the morning by slicing the onions the night before and storing them in the refrigerator in a sealed plastic bag. Guests may enjoy a leisurely cup of coffee while the pie bakes.

- Make crust by mixing ¼ cup melted butter and 1 cup cracker crumbs. Press into 9-inch pie plate.

- In large skillet, melt 2 tablespoons butter. Add onions and sauté for 5 minutes, adding mushrooms during the last 2 minutes. Spoon mixture into cracker crust.

- Place scalded milk in medium-sized bowl and slowly add eggs, stirring constantly.

- Add salt, cayenne, curry powder and cheese and stir until blended. Pour over onion mixture. Sprinkle with 1/2 cup cracker crumbs.

- Bake at 350°F for 1 hour or until firm and golden. Garnish with crisp bacon, if desired.

Onion Pie

Crust:
1/4 cup butter, melted
1 cup cracker crumbs

Filling:
2 tablespoons butter
1 ½ cups thinly sliced onions
1/2 cup sliced canned
    mushrooms, drained (or 1
    cup sliced fresh mushrooms)
1 cup milk, scalded
2 eggs, well beaten
1/2 teaspoon salt
dash of cayenne pepper
1/4 teaspoon curry powder
1 ½ cups grated, sharp cheddar
    cheese
1/2 cup cracker crumbs
bacon slices, cooked until crisp
    (optional)

Some people may consider this recipe too simple to include. But this book is a compilation of memories and hash browns is one of them.

- Chop potatoes and season with salt and pepper.

- Heat butter or oil in heavy frying pan. Add potatoes and brown until crisp. Turn and brown other side. Makes 6 servings.

Hash Browned Potatoes

6 large boiled potatoes
salt and pepper to taste
2 tablespoons butter or
    vegetable oil

Macaroni and Cheese

1 ½ cups uncooked elbow
    macaroni
3 tablespoons butter or
    margarine
3 tablespoons flour
salt, pepper and paprika to
    taste
1 ½ cups milk
1 ½ cups grated cheddar cheese
3/4 cup soft bread crumbs
2 tablespoons butter

I often used to make macaroni and cheese the basic way—layering the two ingredients, almost covering them with milk and then dotting the top with butter. This version dresses the dish up a bit. To make it even more special, add two layers (about 1 cup for each layer) of cooked, diced chicken.

• Cook macaroni according to package directions. Drain and set aside.

• In top of double boiler over boiling water, melt butter. Add flour, salt, pepper and paprika and cook, stirring, for 3 to 4 minutes.

• Gradually add milk, stirring until thick and smooth.

• Add 1 cup grated cheese and stir until melted.

• In greased baking dish, layer half of the macaroni. Cover with half the sauce and sprinkle with 1/4 cup grated cheese. Repeat layers.

• Melt butter; mix with bread crumbs. Sprinkle buttered crumbs over top. Bake at 375°F for 20 minutes or until top is nicely browned. Makes 6 servings.

Noodles and Franks

1 pound weiners
1 tablespoon butter
1/2 cup chopped onion
1 can (10 ounces/284 mL)
    tomato soup
1 cup tomato sauce
1/2 cup water
1 tablespoon Worchestershire
    sauce
8 ounces medium noodles

Where once I used elbow macaroni to make this favourite dish for my boys, granddaughter Ashley prefers noodles.

• Cut weiners lengthwise into quarters, then crosswise into halves.

• Melt butter in a saucepan. Sauté onions until tender.

• Add soup, tomato sauce, water, Worchestershire sauce and weiners. Bring to a boil, reduce heat and simmer for 10 minutes.

• Cook noodles according to package directions. Drain. Spoon hot mixture over noodles. Makes 5 to 6 servings.

This was another favourite macaroni dish in our house, to which I added a sauce and sometimes ground beef. It occasionally got served directly from the frying pan, when the boys came tearing through the door asking, "What's for lunch?"

- Cook macaroni according to package directions. Drain and spoon into greased casserole dish. Set aside.

- In saucepan, melt butter. Add flour and cook, stirring, for 3 to 4 minutes.

- Add tomatoes and cook until thickened. Set aside.

- In frying pan, sauté mushrooms in small amount of vegetable oil. Remove mushrooms and set aside.

- Sauté onions and green pepper.

- Add beef and cook, stirring, until no pink remains.

- Return mushrooms to pan. Add tomato mixture and cheese. Pour over macaroni. Stir to blend.

- Combine bread crumbs and melted butter. Sprinkle over top of casserole and bake, uncovered, at 350°F for 30 minutes. Makes 6 servings.

Macaroni Creole

2 cups uncooked elbow macaroni
1/4 cup butter
1/4 cup flour
2 cups canned tomatoes
1 can (10 ounces/284 mL) sliced mushrooms, drained
vegetable oil
1/4 cup chopped onion
1/2 cup chopped green pepper
1/2 pound (250 g) ground beef (optional)
1 cup grated cheddar cheese
3/4 cup soft bread crumbs
2 tablespoons butter, melted

This dish may be prepared ahead and reheated in a casserole dish at 350°F for 30 minutes, if desired. With the addition of a cup of diced, cooked chicken, beef, pork, ham or shellfish, it's a complete light meal.

- In large frying pan, melt butter. Add onion, celery, green pepper and mushrooms and sauté until lightly browned.

- Stir in bouillon and soy sauce. Add rice and blend well. Makes 6 servings.

Chinese Fried Rice

2 tablespoons butter or margarine
2 onions, chopped
1 cup chopped celery
1 green pepper, chopped
1/2 pound (250 g) fresh mushrooms, chopped
2 cups chicken bouillon
1/2 cup soy sauce
6 cups cooked rice (2 cups uncooked)

Spaghetti and Meatballs

2 tablespoons vegetable oil
1 large onion, chopped
1 can (19 ounces/540 mL)
    tomatoes
2 cans (5 ½ ounces/156 mL
    each) tomato paste
2 cups water
1 tablespoon sugar
1/2 teaspoon salt
1/2 teaspoon pepper
1 bay leaf
1 pound (500 g) ground meat
    (beef and pork mixed)
1 cup fine, dry bread crumbs
1/2 cup grated Parmesan cheese
1 tablespoon finely chopped
    parsley
1 garlic clove, minced
1/2 cup milk
2 eggs, beaten
dash each of salt and pepper
vegetable oil
8 ounces (226 g) long spaghetti

I used to spend a few minutes in the kitchen, after the lunch dishes were cleared away, to get this spaghetti dinner started. With the sauce made ahead and the meatballs shaped and browned, my biggest task at dinnertime was to cook the spaghetti.

• In large saucepan over moderate heat, heat oil. Add onion and cook until golden.

• Add tomatoes, tomato paste, water, sugar, 1/2 teaspoon salt, 1/2 teaspoon pepper and bay leaf. Cook over low heat for 1 hour.

• Meanwhile, combine ground meat, bread crumbs, cheese, parsley, garlic, milk, eggs and dash each of salt and pepper in large bowl. Form into 1 ½-inch balls.

• In frying pan, heat small amount of vegetable oil. Brown meatballs.

• Add to sauce and cook over low heat for 15 minutes. Remove bay leaf.

• Cook spaghetti according to package directions. Drain and serve with sauce and meatballs. Makes 6 to 8 servings.

Spanish Rice

2 tablespoons butter,
    margarine or oil
1 cup chopped onion
1 garlic clove, crushed
1/2 cup chopped green pepper
1/2 cup chopped celery
1 can (28 ounces/796 mL)
    tomatoes
1 teaspoon sugar
1/2 teaspoon salt
3 cups cooked rice (1 cup
    uncooked)

This lunch dish varied from time to time with the addition of cubes of roast beef, cooked chicken, ham, bologna, sliced wieners or drained and flaked salmon or tuna.

• In large frying pan, melt butter over moderate heat. Add onion, garlic, green pepper and celery and cook until limp.

• Stir in tomatoes, sugar and salt. Bring to boil, reduce heat and simmer for 10 minutes.

• Stir in cooked rice, then pour into greased casserole. Bake at 350°F for 30 minutes. Makes 4 servings.

For 20 years, making sandwiches seemed to be my second vocation. If I wasn't preparing them for the boys at lunch time, I was making them for afternoon teas, coffee parties, after bridge snacks, sorority meetings, church sales, picnics, birthday parties and on evenings when friends dropped in for a visit.

While I kept trying to come up with something different from the usual chicken, ham, or egg salad, I eventually learned that kids, as might be expected, preferred the simple sandwich. What I did find disconcerting though, was that after spending a day in the kitchen cooking a chicken and cutting it up, or rolling up a few cherry cheese bites, there would invariably be someone who would carefully look the sandwiches over, and then ask if I just wouldn't make him a peanut butter sandwich. Perhaps it was occasions like this that led to that first carrot peanut sandwich, that, even today, never fails to make an impression. Wherever I serve it for the first time, somebody asks for the recipe. I like it made with a cracked wheat bread.

Another standby in my kitchen, and everyone else's, was the IODE cheese sandwich spread—the Cheese Whiz kid that went to college. Since it freezes well, one was never at a loss for something to spread on bread or crackers to serve with a cup of coffee to those drop-in friends.

When they really wanted to make an impression, hostesses of the time would put together a ribbon sandwich loaf. Although it looks like a lot of work—and it is—it's well worth the time. Since it has three types of filling (you can vary the selections), it's the only sandwich you'll have to make for an afternoon tea or any other occasion.

The sandwich-snack that our Friday night bridge partners, Helen and Bernie Sieniewicz, liked better than any other was Mushroom Soup Rolls. How easy it was to slip out when I was the "dummy," flatten bread slices, spread with mushroom soup, roll up and fasten with toothpicks, brush with a little melted butter and put them under the broiler to brown. It's a neat trick that I seldom think of any more. But when I do, I think of Bernie and Helen.

SANDWICHES

IODE Cheese Spread

4 eggs, beaten
3/4 cup granulated sugar
4 teaspoons dry mustard
1/2 cup butter
1/4 cup cider vinegar
1 pound (500 g) processed
    cheese (such as Velveeta)
1 jar (4 ounces/125 ml)
    pimiento, chopped
1 large green pepper, chopped

Local chapters of the IODE once operated a little tea room on Citadel Hill, where the cheese sandwiches were as popular as the fish chowder. Home cooks soon learned the secret of the spread and began making it to serve on bread, crackers or celery sticks.

- Put beaten eggs in top of double boiler.

- Mix together the sugar and mustard. Add to eggs, along with butter. Cook until mixture has the consistency of custard.

- Add vinegar and cheese, which has been cut into pieces. Cook, stirring, until cheese melts and mixture is thickened.

- Remove from heat. Stir in pimiento and green pepper.

- Turn into bottles or freezer containers. Will keep at least a week in the refrigerator and freezes beautifully.

Tuna Sandwich Spread

1 can (7 ounces/198 g) tuna,
    drained
1 apple, finely chopped
1 hard-boiled egg, chopped
1 small onion, finely chopped
2 sweet pickles, diced
1/2 cup finely chopped pecans
1/2 cup diced celery
1/2 cup mayonnaise (or more
    if needed)
lightly buttered bread slices

I like white, not light canned tuna for these sandwiches. I also save a few pennies by buying tuna already flaked, instead of the more costly chunks which I would then have to flake myself.

- In bowl, combine tuna, apple, egg, onion, pickles, pecans, celery and mayonnaise.

- Spread on lightly buttered bread slices. Top with second slice of bread. Makes 4 to 5 sandwiches, depending on thickness of filling.

I have never liked canned chicken in sandwiches. So, when the little broilers were on special, I would buy three or four and cook them all. I would then freeze the meat in measured amounts for sandwiches and casseroles. The bones were simmered for stock.

•   In bowl, combine chicken, green pepper, salt, celery, lemon juice and mayonnaise. Chill.

•   Spread chicken mixture between bread slices with lettuce leaves. Makes 5 sandwiches.

Note: Chopped stuffed olives may be substituted for green pepper.

Chicken Salad Sandwiches

1 ¼ cups chopped cooked
    chicken
2 teaspoons minced green
    pepper
pinch salt
1/2 cup finely chopped celery
1 tablespoon lemon juice
3 tablespoons mayonnaise
buttered bread slices
crisp lettuce leaves

It was a toss-up whether to include this recipe here or in the breakfast chapter. For breakfast, brunch, lunch or as a snack, these sandwiches fill the bill.

•   Fold ham slice in half and place between 2 slices of cheese. Place between 2 slices of bread and cut in half. Repeat to make 6 sandwiches.

•   Dip each half in beaten egg and fry in approximately 1 inch hot oil for 5 to 8 minutes or until completely puffed and golden.

•   Serve warm. Makes 6 sandwiches.

Ham and Swiss Cheese Sandwiches

1/2 pound (250 g) ham, thinly
    sliced
3/4 pound (375 g) Swiss cheese,
    thinly sliced
12 slices bread, crusts removed
3 eggs, beaten
vegetable oil

•   If using frozen lobster meat, thaw and drain well before chopping.

•   In a bowl, combine all ingredients, adding enough mayonnaise to make mixture hold together without being too wet.

•   Spread as generously as you like on lightly buttered bread and top with another bread slice. Makes 6 to 8 sandwiches, depending on thickness of filling.

Lobster Sandwiches

2 cups chopped cooked lobster
    meat, fresh or frozen
1 cup diced celery
1 teaspoon lemon juice
1/4 cup mayonnaise (or more if
    needed)
pepper, to taste

Western Sandwich

2 tablespoons butter,
    margarine or oil
2 tablespoons diced onion
2 tablespoons chopped green
    pepper
1/2 cup diced ham
dash of Worcestershire sauce
salt and pepper to taste
3 eggs, beaten
6 slices buttered toast

In the early days of family life, I used to watch for ham to be on special and buy one much larger than I needed for a meal. Although ham was not a favourite with the younger Nightingales, my husband and I shared a passion for ham with scalloped potatoes. I made it up to the boys by serving toasted Western sandwiches on the third day.

• In skillet over medium heat, melt butter. Sauté onion, green pepper and ham. Season with Worcestershire sauce, salt and pepper.

• When vegetables are soft, pour in beaten eggs and stir to blend. Cook until lightly browned, turn and cut into 3 pieces.

• Serve between slices of buttered toast. Makes 3 sandwiches.

Carrot Peanut Sandwiches

1 cup shredded raw carrot
1/2 cup diced celery
1/2 cup minced green pepper
1/2 cup chopped salted peanuts
4 tablespoons mayonnaise
1 teaspoon lemon juice
1 teaspoon minced onion
salt and pepper to taste (very
    little salt)
cracked wheat or whole grain
    bread slices

Don't get the idea that these sandwiches are just for kids. Every time I serve them to adults, someone asks, "What are these? They're delicious." As strange as this combination may seem, it's a great way to eat a healthy vegetable.

• In bowl, blend carrot, celery, green pepper, peanuts, mayonnaise, lemon juice, onion, salt and pepper.

• Spread between slices of cracked wheat or whole grain bread. Makes 6 sandwiches.

I had nutrition in mind when I first put these ingredients together between bread slices. It turned out to be a winning combination.

- In bowl, combine peanut butter, 1/4 cup of the sprouts, carrot, milk and honey.

- Spread evenly on 4 slices of bread. Top with remaining sprouts and bread slices. Makes 4 sandwiches.

Peanut Butter, Carrot and Sprout Sandwiches

6 tablespoons peanut butter
1/2 cup alfalfa sprouts, divided
1 medium carrot, shredded
1 tablespoon milk
1 tablespoon liquid honey
8 slices cracked wheat bread

These are tea sandwiches, pure and simple. Of all the ribbon, checkerboard and rolled sandwiches that I once made for sandwich trays, this filling continues to appear periodically with today's heartier combinations.

- In bowl, combine cream cheese, milk, cherry juice, lemon juice and cherries.

- Remove crusts from bread slices. Roll each slice once with rolling pin to keep bread from cracking.

- Spread lightly with softened butter, then cheese filling. Roll up and repeat with remaining filling.

- Wrap sandwiches in damp towel, then plastic wrap until ready to serve. Cut each roll in half. Makes about 16 small rolls.

Cherry Cheese Sandwiches

1 package (8 ounces/250 g)
  cream cheese, softened
1 tablespoon milk
1 tablespoon cherry juice
1 teaspoon lemon juice
1/4 cup chopped maraschino
  cherries
1 fresh loaf sandwich bread
butter, softened

Ribbon Sandwich Loaf

Ham Salad Filling:
1 ½ cups ground cooked ham
1/4 cup finely chopped sweet
   pickle
1/2 teaspoon prepared mustard
1/4 cup mayonnaise (or more if
   needed)

Parsley Butter:
1/4 cup butter, softened
1/4 cup finely chopped parsley
pinch of salt

Egg Salad Filling:
5 hard-boiled eggs
2 tablespoons chopped pickle
1/4 cup finely chopped celery
1/3 cup mayonnaise
1 teaspoon prepared mustard
1/2 teaspoon vinegar
1/2 teaspoon salt
1/4 teaspoon grated onion

Cucumber Filling:
3/4 cup finely chopped peeled
   cucumber
1/2 cup mayonnaise
dash of salt and pepper

Other:
1 loaf unsliced bread
butter, softened
3 tomatoes, sliced thinly
2 packages (8 ounces/250 g
   each) cream cheese, softened

How we did things in those days of gracious afternoon teas! The table would be covered with a lace cloth, tall candlesticks, a shining silver tea service and our very best china cups and saucers. Then the frosted sandwich loaf would be all but piped in, served with exclamations.

- To make **ham salad filling**, combine ham, pickle, mustard and mayonnaise in small bowl. Mix well and set aside.

- To make **parsley butter**, cream butter with mixer in small bowl. Add parsley and pinch of salt and blend well. Set aside.

- To make **egg salad filling**, chop eggs finely in small bowl. Add pickle, celery, mayonnaise, mustard, vinegar, salt and grated onion. Mix well and set aside.

- To make **cucumber filling**, combine cucumber, mayonnaise and dash of salt and pepper in small bowl. Mix well and set aside.

- Cut crusts from all 6 sides of loaf. Cut lengthwise into 4 uniform slices

- Spread first slice lightly with butter. Spread generously with ham filling. Spread second slice with butter and lay it, buttered side down, over ham filling.

- Spread top of second slice with thin layer of parsley butter, then generous layer of egg salad filling (same thickness as ham filling). Spread third slice of bread with thin layer of parsley butter and lay it, buttered side down, over egg filling.

- Spread top lightly with butter and cover with overlapping tomato slices. Spread cucumber filling over tomatoes. Top with fourth unbuttered slice of bread.

- Wrap loaf firmly in damp towel, then plastic wrap and place on a flat tray or board. Chill thoroughly, 4 hours or longer.

- Unwrap loaf and place on serving platter with layers of filling running horizontally or vertically, as desired. Spread softened cream cheese over top and sides of loaf.

- Cut loaf into 10 to 12 slices and serve on salad plates with forks.

FISH

I have to credit Carl "Buck" Jones with the regular inclusion of fish in our family meals, for he was the man who brought the freshest of seafoods to the door twice weekly. His arrival, usually announced by one of my toddlers calling out "the fish man's here," would send me out to the van to see what Buck had carefully packed on ice that day. Only when he rolled back the special parchment paper so his customers could choose from the day's catch, would air touch the fish that Buck took so much pride in supplying.

In June, the choice might be fresh salmon to serve with green peas and potatoes.

"Here's a good piece," Buck would say. "See those white rings in the salmon? Those are fat rings which tell you the fish is fresh."

"Fresh" was his operative word. He would go early in the morning to National Sea Products, then headquartered in Halifax, or Burns Fisheries, now extinct, and choose fish that might have been swimming in the ocean the day before. His customers knew what fresh fish was. He probably taught them. But some complained about the price.

"Dominion Stores are selling fillets for 39 cents a pound, so why are you charging 40 cents?" some fretted.

"Well, I've cleaned it and I've brought it to your door. I guess that's worth an extra penny or two, isn't it?" he would answer.

The biggest seller was fresh haddock, which he supplied either whole or filleted. Fresh cod was another favourite, although he also carried salt cod for the popular dish salt cod and pork scraps, or fish cakes.

You could buy the firmest, glistening blue-grey pound-and-a-half mackerel for about 40 cents, and scallops so fresh that you could pop a raw one into your mouth.

Oysters could be ordered and delivered, shucked and bottled, the next day. The only frozen fish Buck carried was halibut, and then only in January when storms kept the boats from venturing out to sea.

Buck sold his last pound of fillets in 1965 when he retired from the fish business to take up house painting and papering. Fishing nets, even then, were beginning to come up empty.

Seafood Casserole

1 pound scallops
1 pound haddock fillets
1 pound cooked lobster meat
    (thawed, if frozen)
2 cans (4 ounces/113 g each)
    shrimp (or use 1 pound
    frozen shrimp, thawed)
1/2 cup butter
1/2 cup all-purpose flour
1/2 teaspoon dry mustard
1/2 teaspoon salt
1/4 teaspoon pepper
4 cups milk
1/4 cup white wine or sherry
2 teaspoons Worcestershire
    sauce
2 tablespoons grated parmesan
    cheese
2 cans (10 ounces/ 284 mL each)
    sliced mushrooms, drained
1 cup soft bread crumbs
2 tablespoons butter, melted
2 tablespoons grated parmesan
    cheese

During the 1950s, when haddock went for 39 cents a pound and lobster and scallops cost little more, seafood casseroles were almost as common in Halifax as chicken dishes are today. With increased costs, this dish has since been elevated to company fare. It's great for a buffet.

• Wash scallops thoroughly and remove bitter part that attaches them to shells. If large, cut in half.

• Wipe haddock fillets with damp paper towel and cut into bite-size pieces.

• Cut lobster into chunks.

• Drain canned shrimp.

• In large saucepan, bring approximately 2 quarts water to boil. Add 1 teaspoon salt and scallops and simmer approximately 2 minutes.

• Add haddock and cook another 3 minutes or until fish turns white and flakes easily. Drain.

• Add lobster and shrimps to the drained seafood. Refrigerate.

• In top of double boiler, melt butter. Add flour and mustard. Cook, stirring, 2 to 3 minutes to remove taste of flour.

• Stir in salt and pepper. Gradually add milk, stirring constantly.

• Stir in wine and cook, stirring frequently, for 15 minutes or until thickened.

• Stir in Worcestershire sauce and 2 tablespoons parmesan cheese.

• Pour sauce over seafood. Add mushrooms. Transfer to a large lightly-greased casserole dish.

• Combine bread crumbs, 2 tablespoons melted butter and 2 tablespoons parmesan cheese. Sprinkle over casserole. Cook at 350°F until heated through, about 30 to 35 minutes. Makes 8 to 10 servings.

Note: This casserole may be prepared several hours ahead and refrigerated. Allow to stand at room temperature 30 minutes before putting in oven.

Barbecuing was at its zenith when Laurie brought home the first salmon of the season, which we simply wrapped in foil and grilled. But the fish has to be fresh, as we learned when we once settled for frozen British Columbia salmon.

- Clean fish and remove head, tail and fins. Pat dry, then rub inside with salt and pepper.

- Rub oil over double thickness of foil and lay fish on foil. Spread butter on top of fish. Bring sides of foil up, fold top over tightly and crimp ends to seal.

- Place fish on grill about 4 inches over medium-hot coals. Barbecue for 15 minutes on one side, turn and cook 12 minutes on other side. Unwrap and test for doneness. Fish should be opaque in centre. If further cooking is needed, rewrap and return to grill for another 5 minutes. Test again. Makes 6 to 10 servings.

Whole Salmon Barbecued in Foil

4 to 7 pound (2 to 3.5 kg) salmon
salt and pepper to taste
vegetable oil
butter

Back when fish was cheaper than hamburger, we bought inch-thick halibut steaks without batting an eyelash. Two pounds would serve the five of us for a meal. As the price increased, the steaks got thinner and the portions smaller. Still, when fresh halibut is on special, we sometimes treat ourselves to inch-thick steaks and try not to think about how times have changed.

- Grease broiler pan with vegetable oil and lay steaks on pan.

- In small bowl, combine onion, butter, lemon juice, salt, pepper and thyme. Baste steaks with half the sauce.

- Broil approximately 4 inches from heat for 4 to 5 minutes. Turn steaks, baste with remaining sauce and continue broiling until fish flakes easily with fork.

- Garnish with paprika and parsley, if desired. Makes 4 to 6 servings.

Broiled Halibut Steaks

vegetable oil
1 ½ pounds (750 g) halibut steaks
1 tablespoon grated onion
1/4 cup butter, melted
2 tablespoons lemon juice
1/4 teaspoon salt
dash of pepper
1/4 teaspoon thyme or tarragon
paprika and parsley for garnish

Baked Halibut with Cheese

2 pounds (1 kg) halibut,
   3/4-inch thick
1/4 cup lemon juice
1/4 teaspoon salt
dash of pepper
1/4 teaspoon thyme
1 cup grated cheddar cheese
1/2 cup fine bread crumbs
1/4 cup butter, melted

Just as Bajans consider their king fish to be the best in the sea, many Nova Scotians hold halibut in such esteem. I certainly do and I never had a problem getting my boys to eat this sweet, white fish.

• Wipe halibut with damp paper towel, lay in lightly greased 9 x 13-inch shallow baking dish and pour lemon juice over fish. Sprinkle with salt, pepper and thyme. Bake uncovered at 375°F for 20 minutes.

• Meanwhile, combine cheese and bread crumbs in small bowl. Sprinkle over fish and then drizzle with melted butter.

• Bake 10 minutes more or until fish flakes easily with fork. Makes 6 to 8 servings.

Fish Baked in Milk

1 ½ pounds (750 g) halibut or
   haddock fillets or scallops
2 onions, sliced and separated
   into rings
chives or chopped parsley
salt and pepper to taste
1 cup milk, heated
butter

Nothing could be easier to prepare than fish baked in milk. Laurie's favourite was smoked fillets done this way without the onions. Smoked fish should be first covered in water and simmered for a few minutes as the smoke in the fish would otherwise curdle the milk.

• Arrange fish in greased baking dish and cover with onion rings. Sprinkle with chives, salt and pepper. Pour milk over fish and dot with butter.

• Bake at 450°F for 20 minutes or until fish flakes easily with fork. Makes 6 servings.

We lived just a couple of minutes from the school, although the boys managed to take as long as 15 minutes to make the trip. That still gave them lots of time to come home for lunch. Although they were happiest when I served fish sticks and french fries, I often had my way with variations on the theme of fish fillets. This one was popular, probably due to the crisp coating.

- Cut fillets into serving pieces.

- Combine milk and salt in bowl and soak fish in mixture for 3 minutes.

- Remove fish, drain, sprinkle with lemon juice and dip both sides in crushed cornflakes.

- Place in lightly greased baking dish and dot with butter.

- Bake at 450°F to 500°F for 10 minutes per inch at thickest part (double time if fish is frozen) or until fish flakes easily with fork. Makes 5 to 6 servings.

Crispy Baked Fillets

1 ½ pounds (750 g) fish fillets
1/2 cup milk
1 teaspoon salt
1 teaspoon lemon juice
1 cup or more crushed
  cornflakes
1 tablespoon butter or
  margarine

It's amazing what a few almonds can do. In this case, they transform ordinary fish into a dish fit for a king, or any other dinner guest. The method keeps the fish moist inside and crisp and brown on both top and bottom.

- In broiler pan, bring 2 tablespoons butter to the sizzling point under broiler.

- Remove and place fillets in pan, cover with almonds and sprinkle with salt. Dot with 2 tablespoons butter.

- Broil for 8 to 10 minutes. Makes 6 servings.

Almond Fillets

2 tablespoons butter
1 ½ pounds (750 g) fish fillets
1 cup slivered almonds
1/4 teaspoon salt
2 tablespoons butter

Broiled Fish Fillets Mayonnaise

1 ½ pounds (750 g) haddock
    fillets, 1/2-inch thick
salt and pepper to taste
vegetable oil or melted butter
mayonnaise or salad dressing
all-purpose flour

I can't remember where this recipe came from but it was probably developed in the test kitchen of a company that produced commercial mayonnaise. It was a smart move, since everybody started making the dish and buying lots of that brand of mayonnaise.

- Line broiler pan with aluminum foil. Place fish on greased broiler rack and sprinkle with half of the salt and pepper. Brush with vegetable oil.

- Broil 2 to 3 inches from heat for 5 minutes or until browned. Turn carefully.

- Spread fish with mayonnaise and then sprinkle with a little flour and salt and pepper.

- Broil 10 minutes more or until tender and browned. Makes 6 servings.

Fillet of Sole in Foil

1 pound (500 g) frozen sole
    fillets, thawed
1 cup crab meat
1/2 cup mayonnaise
1/2 cup milk
salt and pepper to taste
1/4 cup chopped fresh parsley

The sole caught in waters off Nova Scotia is actually flounder, although the name made famous by Dover sole sounds more sophisticated in marketing the product. Whether flounder or sole, it is a very popular fish that cooks quickly in a variety of ways. We particularly like this treatment.

- Dry fillets with paper towels.

- Cut four 12-inch squares of aluminum foil, crease each diagonally and unfold. For each package, place a serving of sole on one side of crease and top with crab.

- Combine mayonnaise, milk, salt and pepper in small bowl. Lift edges of lower foil up slightly and pour sauce over each serving. Sprinkle with parsley. Fold foil over and seal securely.

- Place packages on baking sheet and bake at 400°F for 15 minutes. Makes 4 servings.

What a delightful combination of tastes are combined in this dish which comes from an old Cape Breton cookbook. The book must have been borrowed, since I copied the recipe into one of my binders without noting the source.

- In top of double boiler, melt 3 tablespoons butter. Add flour and cook, stirring, for 3 to 4 minutes. Stir in salt.

- Slowly add milk and cook, stirring, until thickened.

- In greased baking dish, arrange scallops, clams and eggs.

- Pour sauce over mixture. Sprinkle with bread crumbs and dot with 1 tablespoon butter.

- Bake at 450°F for 15 minutes. Makes 6 servings.

Cape Breton Casserole

3 tablespoons butter
3 tablespoons all-purpose flour
1/2 teaspoon salt
2 cups milk
1 ½ pounds (750 g) scallops
1 can (10 ounces/284 mL) baby clams
2 hard-boiled eggs, chopped
1/2 cup fine, dry bread crumbs
1 tablespoon butter

How I long for the days when we could eat all the fried foods we wanted with never a pang of guilt. If I needed any reassurance, I reasoned that I had to make use of the deep-fat fryer I won in a raffle. The appliance still works but it's relegated to a top shelf and is collecting dust.

- Put scallops in colander and quickly run cold water over them. Drain and dry on paper towels.

- Roll each scallop in flour, dip in egg and then roll in bread crumbs.

- Place in single layer in basket of deep-fat fryer and lower basket carefully into deep fat at 375°F. Cook 3 to 4 minutes or until golden brown.

- Drain on paper towels. Keep hot in warm oven until all scallops have been cooked.

- Serve with lemon wedges and tartar sauce (see index), if desired. Makes 6 servings.

Deep-Fried Scallops

1 ½ pounds (750 g) scallops
1/2 cup all-purpose flour
2 eggs, beaten
1 ½ cups fine, dry bread crumbs
lemon wedges for garnish

Indian Curried Shrimp

2 cups uncooked rice
1 medium onion, chopped
5 tablespoons vegetable oil
6 tablespoons all-purpose flour
1 teaspoon curry powder (or
    more or less to suit taste)
1/2 teaspoon salt
1 ½ teaspoons granulated sugar
1/4 teaspoon powdered ginger
1 chicken bouillon cube
1 cup boiling water
2 cups milk
2 cans (4 ounces/113 g each)
    shrimp
1 teaspoon lemon juice

If there was just one dish that could be singled out as the family favourite, this Indian curried shrimp would have to battle it out with the more expensive seafood casserole included in this chapter. The boys all took the recipe with them when they left home and they often ask for it when they come back for a meal. In recent years, it has become one of Laurie's specialties and he often uses frozen shrimp instead of canned.

• Cook rice according to package directions.

• Meanwhile, sear onion in oil, then simmer until lightly browned.

• Combine flour, curry powder, salt, sugar and ginger. Stir into onions and cook for 3 to 4 minutes to remove taste of flour.

• Dissolve bouillon cube in boiling water. Add to mixture in pan, stirring until smooth.

• Slowly add milk and cook over low heat until thickened, stirring occasionally.

• Add shrimp and lemon juice and heat through.

• To serve, place hot cooked rice in centre of warmed platter. Pour curry mixture all around rice, spooning a little over top. Makes 5 servings.

Tuna Casserole

1 can (10 ounces/284 mL)
    condensed cream of
    mushroom soup
1/2 cup milk
1 can (6 ½ ounces/184 mL) tuna,
    drained and coarsely flaked
1 cup drained cooked peas
1 ½ cups crushed potato chips

I wasn't planning on including this simplest of all casseroles as I expected that it would already be in everyone's recipe files. But on a recent visit from Calgary, my son Gary requested it, saying it was one of his most vivid memories of home. I guess that says it all.

• In 1 quart (1L) casserole dish, combine soup, milk, tuna, peas and 1 cup potato chips. Sprinkle remaining 1/2 cup potato chips over top.

• Bake at 350°F for 25 minutes. Makes 4 servings.

I always felt fortunate when I was able to make a family meal that everyone enjoyed. From the start, this proved to be one of those dishes and was frequently served with a salad for a light supper or with toast for a Sunday morning brunch.

- Lightly beat 2 eggs in medium-sized bowl.

- Add salmon, milk, 1/2 cup bread crumbs, salt and pepper and combine. Shape into 12 patties.

- Lightly beat 2 eggs with water. Dip patties into egg, then coat on both sides with bread crumbs.

- Sauté in butter until browned on both sides.

- Serve on hot toast with white sauce to which celery has been added. Makes 4 servings.

Salmon Patties

2 eggs
2 cans (7 ½ ounces/213 mL each) salmon, drained and flaked
2 tablespoons milk
1/2 cup dry bread crumbs
salt and pepper to taste
2 eggs
2 tablespoons cold water
dry bread crumbs for coating
butter or margarine
1 cup medium white sauce (see index)
1/2 cup finely chopped celery
4 slices toast

It's important to "freshen" salt cod before cooking with it. Soak it overnight in cold water, then drain and rinse under cold, running water. Place it in a saucepan, cover it again with cold water and bring it to the boiling point. Drain it and repeat this process two or three times until the fish is no longer excessively salty. To cook salt cod, cover it again with cold water and bring it to a boil. Reduce the heat and simmer for 18 to 20 minutes. Rinse it a final time in cold water, then shred or flake it and use it to make salt cod and pork scraps, codfish cakes, creamed codfish on toast or salt cod hash.

- In large frying pan, melt butter. Sauté onions until limp.

- Add cod and potatoes and cook 15 minutes or until browned.

- Sprinkle with parsley and serve hot. Makes 6 servings.

Salt Cod Hash

2 tablespoons butter, margarine or oil
1 cup diced onion
3 cups freshened, cooked cod (see opposite)
3 cups diced cooked potatoes
1 tablespoon chopped parsley

Scrambled Codfish

2 tablespoons butter,
  margarine or oil
2 cups freshened cooked cod
  (see introduction to
  preceding recipe)
6 eggs
1 cup milk

Salt cod has declined in popularity since fresh and frozen varieties of fish have become more accessible. There are also cooks who scorn the salt or feel that all those necessary soakings drain away the nutrients. Nevertheless, there are still "old salts" around, like me, who like the taste of a salt cod dish like this one, which is equally good for breakfast or supper.

- In large frying pan, melt butter. Add codfish and cook until browned.

- Beat eggs and then stir in milk.

- Pour over codfish and cook 5 minutes or until eggs are creamy. Makes 6 servings.

Creamed Finnan Haddie

1 ½ pounds (750 g) finnan
  haddie
1/4 cup butter or margarine
1 tablespoon grated onion
1/4 cup all-purpose flour
2 cups milk
1/8 teaspoon pepper

A story is told that in Findon, Scotland, where lines of haddock were hung out to dry, a fire raged through the village and smoked everything in its path. Those who lived by the motto "waste not, want not" sampled the fish before dumping it. And so Findon haddock or finnan haddie became a delectable new taste among the Scots.

- In heavy saucepan, cover fish with water and bring to boiling point. Reduce heat and simmer 15 to 20 minutes or until fish flakes easily with fork.

- Drain. Break fish into bite-sized pieces and remove any bones.

- In saucepan over low heat, melt butter. Add onion and cook until limp.

- Stir in flour and cook, continuing to stir, for 3 to 4 minutes.

- Remove from heat and gradually add milk, stirring constantly, until well blended.

- Return to moderate heat and cook, stirring constantly, until smooth and thickened. Add fish and pepper. Heat thoroughly. Makes 6 servings.

Lobster Wiggle

I don't know why this dish was named lobster wiggle. Perhaps somebody wanted it to stand out from the many other creamed lobster recipes that are served locally.

2 tablespoons butter
2 tablespoons all-purpose flour
1 cup milk
salt and pepper to taste
cayenne pepper to taste
1 ½ cups chopped cooked
 lobster meat
1 can (10 ounces/284 mL) small
 peas, drained
10 slices toast

• In top of double boiler over hot water, melt butter. Stir in flour and cook, stirring, for 3 to 4 minutes.

• Gradually add milk and cook, stirring, until thickened.

• Season with salt, pepper and cayenne pepper. Add lobster and peas and heat through.

• Serve on single slice of unbuttered toast, garnished with 4 points of buttered toast. Makes 5 servings.

Boiled Lobster

Some who live by the seashore like to cook lobster in sea water, with or without a piece of seaweed. Others say sea water isn't salty enough and toss in a hefty extra measure. But everyone agrees that the favourite way to cook lobster is to boil it.

salt
lobster

• Fill large kettle with enough water to cover the lobster, adding 1/4 cup salt for each quart (litre) water. Toss in 1 or 2 extra tablespoons "for the pot." Bring water to vigorous boil.

• Pick up lobster by the back and plunge it, head first, into the water to ensure death is instantaneous. Add 1 or 2 more (no more than 3 at a time).

• Cover pot and cook according to weight: 10 to 12 minutes for 1 to 1 ½ pounds (500 to 750 g), 15 to 18 minutes for 1 ½ to 2 pounds (750 to 1 kg) and 20 to 25 minutes for 2 ½ to 5 pounds (1.25 to 2.5 kg).

• Plunge cooked lobster immediately into cold water to prevent overcooking. Drain well before serving.

Steamed Clams

12 steamer clams per person
melted butter
lemon juice

Mussels, so much in demand today, were almost unheard of during the 1950s and 60s. Those were the days when clams, either steamed or deep-fried, were at the height of their popularity.

- Wash clams in several changes of water, scrubbing thoroughly to remove any sand.

- Place in large kettle with approximately 1 cup boiling water. Cover kettle and steam over low heat for 10 minutes or until shells open.

- Serve hot with individual dishes of melted butter, seasoned with a little lemon juice.

- To barbecue: Place unopened clams on an aluminum foil tray on grill over medium-hot coals. When shells pop open, they're ready to eat.

Clam Patties

2 cans (10 ounces/284 mL each)
    minced clams
2 cups mashed cooked potatoes
1 tablespoon butter or
    margarine
1/2 teaspoon salt
1/2 teaspoon nutmeg
1 tablespoon lemon juice
1 egg, slightly beaten

Whenever we visited the boys during the summers they spent at Camp Champlain, in the Digby area, the big event was to take them out for fried clams. The little Seashell Restaurant in the area laid claim to the best fried clams in Nova Scotia. At home, they settled for clam patties.

- Drain minced clams and rinse under cold running water. Drain and dry on paper towels.

- Combine with mashed potatoes, butter, salt, nutmeg and lemon juice. Add egg and mix well.

- Shape into 10 patties and fry in a mixture of hot butter and vegetable oil, until lightly browned on both sides. Makes 5 servings.

W ith only one car between us, when we lived on Retreat Avenue, I wasn't always able to "run to the store" to get something for dinner. And the only freezer I had was the tiny compartment in the top of the fridge that held little more than ice cubes.

But those were the days when you could pick up the phone and have your groceries delivered straight to the kitchen.

Studley Grocery, on Coburg Road, was not the handiest store, but owner Austin Steeves was a friend who gave good service (and we settled our account just once a month). Best of all, he knew his meat.

I never had to tell him what kind of roast to cut; if I left it up to him I knew we'd get the best. Nor did I tell him how thick to cut the steaks—unless we were barbecuing, which meant "thicker, please."

I might say something like "Pick out a good head of lettuce" or "a nice crate of strawberries." And it all happened as if by magic. Within three hours the order would be delivered and I don't ever remember being disappointed. Could this utopia really have existed? Or is it just a case of good memories outshining the mediocre?

As I think of it now, there was little variety to the orders "Steevie" scribbled in his book at the other end of the line. I wonder if I ever placed an order that didn't include two pounds of ground round steak, to be made into a savoury meat loaf, or a batch of porcupine balls with enough left over for Laurie's favourite meat crumble.

I don't think I discovered the various grades of hamburger until Steevie retired from the grocery business and I started making twice-weekly trips to the "big" new supermarkets (not so big by today's standards). It was then that I changed from ground round to regular hamburger, not only to save money (since now I had to pay before I got out of the store) but to make a moister meat loaf. As the "fat" word began to crop up more often, I learned to drain the excess liquid out of the corner of the pan. Later, I felt it wise to switch to medium ground beef, and finally to lean and extra lean—which puts me right back where I started. The story of my culinary life—all wrapped up in a couple of pounds of hamburger!

MEATS

Standing Rib Roast

4-bone rib roast
1 tablespoon vegetable oil
1 garlic clove, crushed
freshly ground pepper to taste

What do you do when family members want their beef rare but guests prefer theirs well done? This method sears the ends of the rib roast to a crusty brown while the centre remains nice and rare.

• Place roast in shallow roasting pan.

• In small saucepan, heat oil, add garlic and pepper and mix well. Brush this mixture over roast and let stand at room temperature for an hour or so (not more than 2 hours).

• Preheat oven to 450°F. Place roast in oven and cook, uncovered, for 10 minutes.

• Reduce heat to 350°F and continue roasting, 1 hour and 20 minutes for rare, 1 hour and 35 minutes for medium and 1 hour and 50 minutes for well done.

• Baste with pan drippings occasionally as meat is roasting. Makes 8 servings.

Filet Mignon

1 filet per person, cut 1-inch thick
1 slice bacon per person, partially cooked
2 tablespoons butter

When I was first married, my husband Laurie knew a butcher who had a little shop on Agricola Street. Every week this butcher saved a whole beef tenderloin for us. It cost us a dollar. Finally we begged off—we were tired of filet mignon.

• Form each filet into a neat round, wrap a slice of bacon around edge of meat and fasten firmly with a toothpick.

• Sauté in butter in preheated frying pan for 4 to 5 minutes on each side. Beef tenderloin should be served rare.

This steak recipe has served us well (and often) for more than 20 years. Now the third generation asks for it and usually demands seconds.

• Combine all ingredients except steak in small bowl.

• Remove all visible fat from steak. Put steak in a plastic bag, pour soy mixture into bag and seal. Place bag on a plate and store in refrigerator to marinate for at least 4 hours, turning bag over occasionally.

• Remove steak from bag and place on an oiled broiler pan. Broil approximately 4 inches from heat, 8 minutes on first side and 5 minutes on second or until cooked as desired. Slice steak diagonally against the grain. Makes 4 to 6 servings, depending on size of steak.

Flank Steak Oriental

1/4 cup soy sauce
2 tablespoons vinegar
2 tablespoons dried onion
    flakes
2 large garlic cloves, crushed
1 ½ teaspoons ground ginger
1 flank steak

Swiss Steak

1 ½ pounds (750 g) round steak,
    about 3/4-inch thick
1/4 cup all-purpose flour
salt and pepper to taste
2 tablespoons vegetable oil
1 can (10 ounces/284 mL)
    condensed tomato soup
1/2 cup water

Chopped onions may be added to this old-fashioned meat dish as well as chopped celery and carrots. Simply remove the meat after browning and sauté the vegetables for about eight minutes. Return the meat to the pan and pile the vegetables on top. However, if you're cooking for fussy, young palates as I once did, you may prefer to prepare the vegetables separately.

• Wipe steak dry with paper towels.

• Combine flour, salt and pepper and sprinkle over meat. Pound as much flour mixture as possible into meat with meat mallet or edge of strong saucer.

• Cut into serving-size pieces.

• In large skillet, heat oil. Add meat and brown on both sides (about 10 minutes).

• Pour in soup and water. Reduce heat to low, cover and simmer for about an hour or until meat is tender. Stir occasionally during cooking, adding more water if sauce becomes dry. Makes 6 servings.

Spicy Corned Beef

3 or 4 pounds (1.5 to 2 kg)
　　corned beef brisket
1 orange, sliced
1 large onion, quartered
2 stalks celery, cut in half
2 garlic cloves, quartered
1 teaspoon dill seed
1/2 teaspoon rosemary
6 whole cloves
3-inch cinnamon stick
1 bay leaf
2 tablespoons corn syrup for
　　glazing

This corned beef is great hot or cold, so consider buying an extra pound or two. Serve it hot with braised cabbage and mashed potatoes and cold in sandwiches. Use the leftovers to make corned beef hash.

• Place corned beef in large pot and cover with water. Add all remaining ingredients.

• Cover and bring to boiling point. Reduce heat and simmer (do not allow to boil) for 1 hour per pound of meat or until tender.

• Remove meat from liquid and, while hot, brush with corn syrup to glaze.

• Serve at once or chill to serve cold. Makes 8 to 10 servings.

Beef Stroganoff

1 pound (500 g) trimmed beef
　　sirloin, 1/4-inch thick
1/4 cup butter or margarine
2 cups sliced fresh mushrooms
1/3 cup chopped onion
1 can (10 ounces/284 mL)
　　condensed beef bouillon
2 ½ tablespoons all-purpose
　　flour
1 cup sour cream
salt and pepper to taste
hot rice or noodles

My sister-in-law Thalia introduced us to this dish. It became one of our favourites, for family or company.

• Cut sirloin into strips 1/4-inch wide (cuts easier if meat is slightly frozen).

• In large frying pan, melt butter and brown meat quickly over high heat.

• Push meat to one side and add the mushrooms and onions. Cook until tender but not brown.

• Stir in beef bouillon and heat to boiling.

• Blend flour into sour cream, then stir into bouillon. Cook, stirring constantly, until slightly thickened. Sprinkle with salt and pepper to taste.

• Serve over hot rice or noodles. Makes 4 to 6 servings.

When yogurt began to be recognized as a healthy alternative to sour cream, I added this variation of the classic dish to my growing collection of ground beef recipes.

- Melt butter in a large skillet. Brown meat with onion and garlic.

- Stir in flour, seasonings, mushrooms, soup and milk. Simmer 15 to 20 minutes.

- Stir in yogurt. Heat through but do not boil.

- Serve over noodles with a sprinkle of chopped parsley. Makes about 8 servings.

Ground Beef Stroganoff with Yogurt

3 tablespoons butter or margarine
1 ½ pounds (750 g) ground beef
1 medium onion, chopped
3 garlic cloves, minced
3 tablespoons all-purpose flour
1/2 teaspoon salt
dash of pepper
1 can (10 ounces/284 mL) sliced mushrooms
1 can (10 ounces/284 mL) condensed cream of chicken soup
1 cup milk
1 ½ cups plain yogurt (or sour cream)
12 ounces thin egg noodles, cooked and drained
chopped fresh parsley

Meat loaf recipes come and go but this one will live on forever. At our cottage, I usually made two at a time, one to serve hot and the other cold. When mixing, use a large bowl so that you will have lots of room to toss and blend the ingredients. And don't overwork the meat or it will be dense and tough.

- In large bowl, combine meat and bread crumbs. Knead well.

- Beat eggs in small bowl. Add remaining ingredients, pour over meat mixture and blend with hands.

- Turn into 9 x 5-inch loaf pan. Bake at 325°F for an hour, until well browned on top.

Savoury Meat Loaf

2 pounds (1 kg) ground beef
2 cups fine bread crumbs
2 eggs
2 tablespoons prepared mustard
2 tablespoons prepared horseradish (optional)
1 teaspoon or less salt
pepper to taste
1/2 cup ketchup
1 large onion, minced
1 garlic clove, minced

Stuffed Cabbage Rolls

1 large green cabbage
1 ½ pounds (750 g) ground beef
1/4 cup uncooked rice
1 small onion, chopped
pinch each of summer savory,
    thyme, celery salt
salt and pepper to taste
1 egg, slightly beaten
1 can (19 ounces/540 mL)
    tomatoes, cut up
1 can (10 ounces/284 mL)
    condensed tomato soup

This was another popular meal at the cottage, when we seldom knew how many would sit down for dinner. Cabbage rolls are delicious stuffed with ground lamb or pork but I more often use ground beef because of its availability.

• Remove core from cabbage. Place cabbage, cut side up, in enough boiling water to cover and let stand until the leaves begin to soften.

• In the meantime, combine ground beef, rice, onion, seasonings and egg in bowl. Moisten with about 1/4 cup of juice from tomatoes.

• When cabbage leaves can be separated, remove at least 8 large leaves. Let drain on paper towels.

• Shave thick part of leaf stems with vegetable peeler or sharp knife to make rolling easier. Place 2 or 3 tablespoons of meat filling at base of each leaf and fold leaf, envelope style, over filling. Tuck in sides while rolling up leaf.

• Chop remaining cabbage. Combine with tomatoes and tomato soup in large baking dish.

• Place cabbage rolls, seam side down, on top of the sauce and spoon a little sauce over them.

• Cover dish and bake at 350°F for an hour. Uncover and baste with sauce. Continue baking, basting occasionally, for another 30 minutes or until cabbage is tender. Makes 6 to 8 servings.

Ground Meat Crumble

1 tablespoon vegetable oil
1 large onion
1 ½ pounds (750 g) ground beef
1 teaspoon or less salt
6 tablespoons all-purpose flour
3 cups water
mashed potatoes to serve 6

Whether it's standing rib or lowly hamburger, Laurie likes simple preparations best. This recipe couldn't be easier but it is his favourite ground beef dish.

• In a large skillet, heat oil. Brown onions.

• Add meat and salt and brown well, stirring constantly.

• Sprinkle flour over meat and stir well. Add water and blend well. Continue cooking until gravy bubbles and thickens.

• Serve over mashed potatoes. Makes 6 servings.

Frank was probably right when he said I had a hundred ways of cooking hamburger. The fact that he didn't appreciate my many variations occasionally drove him to his grandmother's house for dinner. When he encountered hamburger there as well, he learned to call ahead to check the menu.

- In large bowl, combine meat, rice, egg, onion and seasonings. Mix lightly to blend. Form into 1 ½-inch balls and place in 2-quart (2 L) baking dish.

- Combine soup with warm water, blending well. Pour over meatballs.

- Cook, uncovered, at 350°F for 30 minutes. Cover and continue cooking for another 30 minutes, basting occasionally.

- To serve, spoon sauce over meatballs. Makes 6 servings.

Porcupine Balls

1 ¼ pounds (625 g) ground beef
1/2 cup uncooked rice
1 egg, slightly beaten
   (optional)
1/2 cup chopped onion
1/2 teaspoon summer savory
salt and pepper to taste
1 can (10 ounces/284 mL)
   condensed tomato soup,
   plus 1/2 can warm water

There are many variations of this famous English dish which was created to use leftovers. Traditionally, shepherd's pie was made with lamb but North Americans more often use beef. Friends have been made or lost over the ingredients—purists may permit half a cup each of chopped carrots and celery but they won't abide ground meat. I like it either way.

- Heat oil in large skillet. Brown onion.

- Add cooked or raw meat and stir over medium heat until no longer pink.

- Drain fat. Season meat with savory, salt and pepper.

- Transfer to baking dish, pour corn over meat and top with mashed potatoes.

- Bake at 375°F for 20 minutes until potatoes are beginning to brown. Makes 4 servings.

Shepherd's Pie

2 tablespoons vegetable oil
2 onions, finely chopped
2 cups chopped beef or 1
   pound (500 g) ground beef,
   uncooked
1/4 teaspoon summer savory
salt and pepper to taste
1 can (19 ounces/540 mL)
   creamed corn
4 cups mashed potatoes

Weiner Schnitzel

5 pieces boneless veal, sliced
   thinly
1/4 cup all-purpose flour
salt and pepper to taste
2 eggs, well beaten
1 cup dry bread crumbs
1/2 cup butter
1 lemon, quartered

There was a time when I used a whole cup of butter to fry these veal cutlets. With the information now available about saturated fats, it was obviously necessary to amend the recipe. It's still delicious with a smaller amount of butter (or half butter and half oil) and it's still a great way to stretch a pound of meat.

- With meat mallet, pound veal until almost paper thin.

- Dip in flour which has been seasoned with salt and pepper, then in egg and then in bread crumbs. Press crumbs into meat. If coating doesn't hold, dip a second time in egg and crumbs. Refrigerate 20 minutes to set.

- In 10-inch skillet, heat butter over medium heat. Add veal and fry, turning once, until golden on both sides.

- Drain on paper towels. Serve with wedge of lemon. Makes 5 servings.

Roast Leg of Lamb

5 pound (2.5 kg) leg of lamb
1 garlic clove
1 teaspoon rosemary
pepper to taste

The cooking of lamb has changed drastically in the last few decades. Cooking times have been reduced, from 25 or 30 minutes per pound to 12 or 18 minutes per pound, so that the meat is pinkish in colour and still tender and juicy. It is now also recommended that the papery white membrane covering the lamb, known as the fell, be removed.

- With a damp cloth or paper towels, thoroughly wipe lamb clean. Remove the fell (thin, paper-like covering).

- Cut garlic into 4 pieces. Make 4 small slits on fat side of leg, spacing them evenly, and insert a sliver of garlic into each.

- Rub leg all over with rosemary. Sprinkle with pepper. Place on small rack in an open roasting pan, fat side up.

- Cook at 325°F for 12 minutes per pound for rare, 18 minutes per pound for medium.

- Remove lamb to a warm platter and let stand 20 minutes before carving. Use drippings for gravy, if desired. Makes 6 to 8 servings.

This has long been a favourite dish of mine even though there are no other "takers" in our family. Not only do I like liver, but I also need the iron and this is a great way to get it.

- In a skillet, heat butter. Sauté onion until soft and then push to one side.

- Dredge liver in flour which has been seasoned with salt and pepper.

- Sauté liver in skillet, adding more butter if needed, until golden brown on both sides (4 minutes per side for medium). Makes 2 servings.

Liver and Onions

1 tablespoon butter
1 cup chopped onions
2 slices calf's liver, trimmed
all-purpose flour
salt and pepper to taste

Young and tender Nova Scotian lamb is now available fresh all year long. It makes a delicious change from beef, pork and poultry and this recipe couldn't be easier.

- Use a sharp knife to slash fatty edges at intervals so that chops will lie flat during broiling.

- Place meat on rack of a broiler pan and brush with Italian dressing.

- Broil 4 inches from heat for approximately 8 minutes. Turn chops, brush again and broil 4 to 5 minutes longer. Be careful not to overcook. Makes 5 servings.

Broiled Lamb Chops

5 shoulder lamb chops, 1/2 to
    3/4-inch thick
bottled Italian dressing

Pork is leaner than it was 30 years ago and doesn't require as much cooking. We are no longer afraid of a hint of pink, which often used to result in dry, overcooked meat. I've adjusted the cooking time of this old favourite to apply to today's pork.

- Wipe pork chops with damp paper towel. Place in single layer in baking pan.

- Put 1 slice of lemon and 1 tablespoon brown sugar on each chop.

- Combine soup, water, salt and pepper. Pour over chops.

- Cover and bake at 350°F for 1 hour. Uncover during last 15 minutes. Makes 6 servings.

Sweet and Sour Pork Chops

6 pork chops with fat trimmed
6 slices lemon
6 tablespoons brown sugar
1 can (10 ounces/284 mL)
    condensed tomato soup,
    plus 1/2 can water
salt and pepper to taste

Pork and Sauerkraut

1 quart (1 L) sauerkraut
6 loin pork chops
pepper to taste
paprika to taste
2 tablespoons vegetable oil
1 onion, chopped
2 cups sour cream

Living in Nova Scotia, I just had to find ways to serve the wonderful sauerkraut that is produced along the South Shore. Our family likes it boiled with corned beef, baked under spare ribs or served with pork and sour cream. Sauerkraut should always be refreshed, by soaking it in cold water for 15 minutes or by pouring boiling water over it. Either way, drain the sauerkraut well before using it.

- Drain sauerkraut, cover with fresh, cold water and allow to stand for 15 minutes.

- Drain again.

- Meanwhile, sprinkle pork with pepper and paprika. Heat oil in large skillet and brown chops. Drain on paper towels.

- Add chopped onion to skillet and stir until limp.

- Add sauerkraut and sauté until golden.

- Stir in sour cream.

- In bottom of 2-quart (2 L) baking dish, layer half the sauerkraut mixture. Arrange pork chops on top and cover with remaining sauerkraut.

- Cover and bake at 300°F for 1 hour. Makes 6 servings.

Oven Barbecued Spareribs

4 to 5 pounds (2 to 3 kg)
    meaty spareribs
1 cup ketchup
1 ½ cups water
2 tablespoons Worcestershire
    sauce
1 teaspoon chili powder
1/4 cup lemon juice
1 large onion, sliced
1 tablespoon brown sugar
1/2 teaspoon salt

Although I have several recipes for spareribs, this has always been my boys' choice. I also like to brown them and then bake them over sauerkraut in a covered dish at 350°F for a couple of hours.

- Wipe ribs with damp paper towel and cut into serving portions. Place, meaty side up, in shallow pan and bake at 450°F for 30 minutes.

- Meanwhile, combine ketchup, water, Worcestershire sauce, chili powder, lemon juice, onion, brown sugar and salt in saucepan. Quickly bring to boiling point, reduce heat and simmer 20 minutes.

- Pour over ribs. Bake at 350°F for 45 minutes to an hour or until tender. Baste every 15 minutes during cooking. Makes 5 to 6 servings.

When my boys came home for lunch, they loved to find these frankfurters waiting for them. Sometimes I served them in a bun, other times I'd slip a few raw vegetables on the plate. The vegetables didn't always get eaten, but the franks certainly did.

Stuffed Franks

12 wieners
4 ounces (125 g) cheddar cheese
12 slices bacon
12 wiener rolls (optional)

• Split each wiener lengthwise but not through. Cut fingers of cheese the length of the slit. Place a piece in each wiener, pushing it in firmly.

• Wrap a strip of bacon diagonally around each wiener and fasten each end with a toothpick.

• Place, split side down, on broiler pan and broil until bacon is crisp, about 4 to 5 minutes. Turn and broil 5 minutes longer, until bacon is crisp and cheese has melted.

• Serve in wiener rolls, if desired. Makes 6 servings.

A tender, centre-cut ham slice, served with scalloped potatoes, is what comfort food is all about. In this recipe, the cooking is easy too.

Ham Steak with Orange

1 ½ pounds (750 g) centre-cut
   ham steak
whole cloves
1 tablespoon brown sugar
1 teaspoon liquid honey
4 tablespoons pineapple juice
2 tablespoons orange juice
pinch of cinnamon
4 orange slices

• Score fatty edges of ham and insert cloves into fat.

• Place brown sugar, honey, pineapple juice, orange juice and cinnamon in cold skillet or electric frying pan large enough to hold ham. Turn heat to low and cook, stirring until mixture is bubbling.

• Add ham steak, cover and simmer for 15 minutes. Turn steak, place orange slices on top, cover and cook for 10 minutes more.

• Remove steak to hot platter. Turn heat to high, let sauce boil for 1 or 2 minutes.

• Pour sauce over steak or serve separately. Makes 6 servings.

Baked Ham

1 whole or half ham
whole cloves
1 cup packed brown sugar
3/4 cup thoroughly drained,
    crushed pineapple
2 teaspoons dry mustard

Most hams sold today are tenderized or partially cooked. In general, they should be baked, uncovered, in a moderate oven. Even the more costly, full baked or ready-to-eat hams benefit from further baking (to an internal temperature of 130°F). Although I've used many glazes over the years, Laurie always felt cheated if there wasn't pineapple on his ham.

• Wipe ham all over with damp cloth. With rind still on, place on rack in a roasting pan (fat side up for whole ham, cut side down for half ham).

• Bake, uncovered, at 325°F, for 18 to 24 minutes per pound or until meat thermometer registers 160°F. As a rule, shorter baking time is required per pound for whole ham, longer time for half.

• About 30 minutes before meat is done, remove from oven and drain off pan drippings. Remove rind by cutting with sharp knife and lifting off gently. Score fat in large crisscross pattern, making cuts about 1/8-inch deep. Insert whole cloves at points of diamond cuts.

• Combine brown sugar, pineapple and mustard and spread thickly over fat side of ham. Return to oven to finish baking.

• For browner glaze, raise oven temperature to 425°F for final 15 minutes.

Leftover Ham

• Leftover ham is a meal-maker's treasure. Apart from sandwiches, it can be mixed with chopped cooked potatoes in a hash. It can be added to a white sauce and served over toast. It can be folded into omelets and pancake batters or stuffed into buns.
• But no matter how you serve it, try to save 2 cups of the chopped ham to combine with 1 cup of chopped cooked broccoli, 3 cups of cooked noodles, and a can of cream of mushroom soup, thinned with 1/2 cup of milk. Mix together, pour into a baking dish, sprinkle with grated cheese and bake at 350°F for 20 minutes. Makes 4 servings.

POULTRY

W hen my husband's mother was alive, we always had Christmas and New Year's dinners at her house. That just left the Thanksgiving bird for me to cook. We often spent this October holiday at our cottage, where we sometimes barbecued the turkey on the spit. However, as I am so often asked how to roast a turkey, I will explain the steps. They haven't changed much in 40 years.

Before cooking a turkey, you must decide what to buy. As a guide, a 14 pound turkey will serve six people, an 18 pound bird will serve eight and a 22-pounder will feed 10 to 12 people. With all sizes there should be leftovers for the next day. Make sure your refrigerator can handle the turkey you buy, since a fresh turkey must be refrigerated until cooking time and a frozen bird should thaw in the fridge.

There are varying grades of turkey available, all of which are acceptable. Canada Grade A is meaty with a good covering of fat and is well shaped and free from defects. Canada Grade B may be slightly less meaty, have less fat and may have a crooked keel bone as well as minor discolourations or tears. A turkey bearing the Canada Grade Utility marker is at least grade B in quality but may be missing a part, such as a wing or leg, or an area of skin.

If the bird is to be carved in the kitchen, there are no disadvantages to buying a utility bird, and the lower cost is certainly a bonus.

There is also the injected turkey, which may be labelled "deep-basted" or "self-basting." It usually contains vegetable oils, which increases the juiciness of the cooked bird. However, the fat content and cost are higher. If appearance is important, these birds are a good choice since they are usually well shaped.

You will also need to choose between fresh and frozen. It's important to be sure of the freshness of a turkey which has never been frozen. It should be ordered well ahead but left in the store cooler as long as possible.

If you choose a frozen turkey, take care when thawing it. To thaw it in the refrigerator, leave on the original wrap, place the turkey on a tray to catch any drippings and put it in the fridge, allowing five hours per pound for thawing. A 12 pound bird, for

example, requires two and a half days to thaw and a 20 pound turkey will need four days.

If there is no room in your refrigerator, it's possible to put the wrapped turkey in a sink filled with cold water and change the water every half hour or so. Allow 30 minutes thawing time for every pound. Before using the sink again, it should be washed with a chlorine solution disinfectant. Hands and any surfaces that come in contact with raw turkey should also be washed thoroughly with disinfectant.

To prepare the turkey for cooking, examine the body cavity for any unpalatable parts, such as the lungs or windpipe, and remove them. Run your hand over the skin, feeling for hair and pin feathers. Pin feathers may be removed with tweezers and hair may be singed with a lighted match. Be sure to remove the giblet bag, which is often found in the neck cavity.

Rinse and dry the bird thoroughly before stuffing it. Sprinkle both the neck and body cavity with salt and then loosely pack in the stuffing, bearing in mind that it will expand during cooking.

Although stuffing ingredients may be prepared early and stored in separate containers in the refrigerator, they should not be combined until the bird is almost ready for the oven. A bird should never be stuffed ahead since bacteria can grow quickly in this environment.

After trussing the turkey, place it on a rack in an open roasting pan. Rub it with oil, cover it with a loose tent of aluminum foil (making sure the thighs and neck are well shielded) and roast at 325°F according to the timetable at left.

Remove the aluminum foil during the last half hour of roasting in order to brown the turkey nicely. It's at this time that a meat thermometer should be inserted into the centre of the stuffing for approximately five minutes. The turkey is done when the stuffing temperature reaches 165°F, the drumstick and breast meat feel soft and the leg moves easily when twisted. The juices should run clear.

The cooked turkey should not be allowed to stand at room temperature for more than two hours. Dressing should be removed and stored separately. The leftover meat generally may be stored, covered, in the refrigerator for three or four days.

Roasting Time

for Stuffed Turkey

6 to 8 pounds • 3 ½ to 4 hours
8 to 10 pounds • 4 to 4 ½ hours
10 to 12 pounds • 4 ½ to 5 hours
14 to 16 pounds • 5 ½ to 6 hours
18 to 20 pounds • 5 ¾ to 6 ½ hours
20 to 24 pounds • 6 ¼ to 7 hours

The first time I roasted a turkey, in a tiny kitchen in the little cottage we rented on Retreat Avenue, I was faced with a dilemma. Should I stuff it with the potato dressing my grandmother made or should I switch to the bread stuffing preferred by my husband's family? The Nightingales outnumbered me and so their tradition continues.

- Melt butter in skillet. Sauté onions and celery for approximately 5 minutes.

- In large bowl, combine bread cubes, summer savory, salt and pepper.

- Add onion mixture and enough stock to make stuffing hold together when squeezed between thumb and index finger.

- Makes enough stuffing for a 10 to 12 pound turkey.

*Since heat brings out the flavour of summer savory, it's hard to gauge how much to use. It's better to use too little than too much.

Although they had their favourites, my boys could be talked into trying different recipes. This was one of them and was noted in my files as "delicious."

- Combine flour, nutmeg, celery salt and garlic salt in plastic bag. Shake chicken pieces in bag until well coated.

- In frying pan, heat butter and brown chicken on both sides. Remove to large casserole dish.

- In bowl, combine juice from pineapple, lemon juice, soy sauce and brown sugar. Pour over chicken, cover casserole and put in refrigerator to marinate for 2 to 3 hours or overnight.

- Unless dish can withstand extreme temperature changes, allow to stand at room temperature for 30 minutes before putting in oven.

- Bake at 350°F for 1 ½ hours.

- Remove from oven, sprinkle with pineapple and allow to heat through or run pineapple under broiler.

- Serve with rice. Makes 5 servings.

Basic Bread Stuffing

1/4 cup butter
2 onions, chopped
2 stalks celery, chopped
8 cups cubed day-old bread, (1/2-inch cubes)
1/2 to 1 teaspoon dried summer savory*
1/2 teaspoon salt
1/4 teaspoon pepper
1/3 to 1/2 cup chicken stock or water

Pineapple Chicken

1/2 cup all-purpose flour
1/2 teaspoon nutmeg
1 teaspoon celery salt
1/2 teaspoon garlic salt
2 to 3 pound (1 to 1.5 kg) chicken, cut up
2 tablespoons butter or vegetable oil
juice from drained can of pineapple
2 tablespoons lemon juice
3 tablespoons soy sauce
2 tablespoons brown sugar
1 can (19 ounces/540 mL) pineapple rings or tidbits

Southern Oven-Fried Chicken

2 cups crushed potato chips
1/4 teaspoon garlic salt
dash of pepper
2 to 3 pound (1 to 1.5 kg)
    chicken, cut up
1/3 cup butter, melted

This was my boys' absolute favourite chicken dish when they were growing up. The potato chips may be replaced with crushed cornflakes or a cup of each may be used. I've also sometimes brushed the chicken with vegetable oil instead of melted butter. These changes were permitted by those who ruled the roost, as long as I kept that southern oven-fried chicken coming.

• Combine crushed potato chips, garlic salt and pepper in shallow dish.

• Dip chicken in melted butter, then roll in chip mixture.

• Place pieces in greased shallow pan, making sure they don't touch and are skin side up.

• Bake at 350°F for 1 hour or until tender. Do not turn. Makes 5 servings.

Curried Chicken with Almond Currant Rice

1/2 cup slivered or chopped
    blanched almonds
1/2 cup butter or margarine
1 ⅓ cups chopped onions
1 cup diced green pepper
1 cup all-purpose flour
6 cups chicken broth
1/2 teaspoon salt
2 tablespoons curry powder
4 cups diced cooked chicken
2 cups uncooked rice
6 tablespoons currants
2 tablespoons butter

Here is a delicious recipe that Pat Becker, a friend of mine from Sudbury, Massachusetts, shared with me many years ago. For those worried about the amount of curry powder, start with less and adjust the measure until the "heat" is right for you and your family.

• In frying pan, sauté almonds in 1/2 cup butter until golden. Remove from pan and set aside.

• To pan, add onions and green pepper. Sauté until tender but not brown.

• Stir in flour and cook, stirring, for 1 or 2 minutes to cook flour.

• Gradually add broth, stirring to blend thoroughly.

• Add salt and curry powder and cook until thickened, stirring occasionally.

• Add chicken and continue cooking until heated.

• Meanwhile, cook rice according to package directions, adding currants and 2 tablespoons butter to boiling salted water with rice.

• When cooked, stir in sautéed almonds. Spoon onto plates and top with curried chicken. Makes 6 servings.

It was at the end of the 60s that people were beginning to become fat-conscious, although the winds of change were barely a tropical breeze. Women's magazines were taking up the issue but dieting took aim at calories more than fat. In the June, 1969 issue of Woman's Day, *a makeover was done on chicken tetrazzini. Butter and egg yolks were omitted, skim milk replaced cream, cheese was reduced and skinless chicken breasts replaced dark meat. The result was a healthy but tasty dish.*

- Arrange drained spaghetti in 6-cup broilerproof baking dish.

- Drain mushrooms and blend 1/4 cup of the liquid with flour in small bowl.

- In 3-quart (3 L) saucepan, bring milk and evaporated milk to boil. Stir in flour mixture and cook, stirring, until thickened.

- Add mushrooms, sherry, green pepper, salt, pepper, Worcestershire sauce and pimiento. Mix well.

- Fold in chicken. Pour mixture over spaghetti and sprinkle with cheese.

- Bake at 300°F for approximately 45 minutes. When finished cooking, place under broiler to brown lightly. Makes 6 servings.

Chicken Tetrazzini

6 ounces (180 g) thin spaghetti, cooked
1/2 cup sliced canned mushrooms, (reserve liquid)
3 tablespoons all-purpose flour
1 cup skim milk
1 cup undiluted evaporated skim milk
2 tablespoons sherry
1 small green pepper, slivered
2 teaspoons salt (may be reduced to 1/2 teaspoon)
1/8 teaspoon white pepper
1 teaspoon Worcestershire sauce
1/4 cup drained and sliced pimiento
4 cups diced, cooked white chicken meat, (no skin)
2 tablespoons grated parmesan cheese

My mother used to smother her chicken with onions. I found my family preferred mushrooms, once they became more readily available.

- In plastic bag, combine flour, salt, pepper and ginger. Add chicken pieces and shake to coat well.

- Heat oil in deep, heavy frying pan. Brown chicken. Remove to baking dish, arranging in single layer. Sprinkle mushrooms on top.

- Heat milk and pour over chicken and mushrooms.

- Cover and bake at 350°F for 1 hour or until chicken is tender. Makes 4 to 6 servings.

Note: Sour cream may be used in place of milk or in combination with milk.

Smothered Chicken

1/2 cup all-purpose flour
1/2 teaspoon salt
1/4 teaspoon pepper
1/4 teaspoon ground ginger
6 to 8 chicken breasts, legs or combination
1/4 cup vegetable oil
1/4 pound (125 g) mushrooms, cleaned and sliced
2 cups milk

Cranberry Glazed Chicken

1/2 cup all-purpose flour
1/2 teaspoon salt
dash of pepper
3 pound (1.5 kg) chicken, cut
   up
2 to 3 tablespoons butter or
   margarine
1 ½ cups fresh or frozen
   cranberries
1 cup packed brown sugar
3/4 cup water
1 tablespoon wine vinegar
1 tablespoon all-purpose flour
1/2 teaspoon ground cinnamon
1/4 teaspoon ground cloves
1/4 teaspoon ground allspice
1/4 teaspoon salt

Before we had a freezer to store our supply of cranberries from the bogs of Nova Scotia, we had to content ourselves with enjoying this dish between October and January only, when fresh cranberries were available.

•   Combine 1/2 cup flour, 1/2 teaspoon salt and pepper in plastic bag. Add chicken pieces and shake well to coat.

•   In skillet, melt butter. Slowly brown chicken (approximately 30 minutes). Remove chicken from pan.

•   Add cranberries, brown sugar and water to drippings in pan. Cook for 5 minutes or until cranberry skins pop.

•   In small bowl, mix vinegar with 1 tablespoon flour, cinnamon, cloves, allspice and 1/4 teaspoon salt. Add to cranberry mixture. Cook, stirring constantly, until mixture thickens.

•   Return chicken to skillet and simmer for 30 minutes. Makes 4 to 6 servings.

Chicken with Almonds

6 chicken breasts, legs or
   combination
2 tablespoons vegetable oil
1 green onion, diced
1 can (10 ounces/284 mL)
   condensed cream of chicken
   or mushroom soup
3/4 cup milk
1/4 teaspoon thyme
pinch of nutmeg
1/3 cup slivered almonds
2 tablespoons butter
3/4 cup soft stale bread crumbs
1/4 cup sherry (optional)

In reading through my old recipes, I find it hard to believe how universally canned soups were used in the 1950s and 60s. Even this company dish has a sauce that is made from a can.

•   In skillet, sauté chicken pieces lightly on both sides in hot oil. Arrange in single layer in shallow baking pan.

•   In bowl, combine green onion, soup, milk, thyme and nutmeg. Pour over chicken.

•   Bake at 350°F for 45 minutes.

•   Meanwhile, sauté almonds in butter until lightly browned. Stir in bread crumbs. Sprinkle mixture over chicken and then sprinkle with sherry, if using.

•   Bake 20 minutes longer. Makes 4 to 6 servings.

It wasn't until the 1970s that we became "sophisticated" enough to enjoy a glass of wine. In previous years, sherry was served at the coffee parties that were a regular Saturday morning social event for the ladies. Sherry also makes a nice change from the traditional red wine in this easy to make coq au vin.

- Wash and dry chicken thoroughly.

- In large frying pan, melt butter. Brown chicken on both sides. Remove to paper towels to drain.

- In same skillet, lightly brown onions, garlic and carrots.

- Push vegetables to one side, sprinkle flour over oil and cook, stirring, for 2 to 3 minutes.

- Gradually stir in 2 cups sherry. When well mixed with vegetables, add bay leaf, parsley, thyme and mushrooms. Sprinkle with salt and pepper.

- Reduce heat, add browned chicken and allow to simmer, covered for 45 minutes. Add more sherry, if needed. Discard bay leaf and serve. Makes 6 servings.

Easy Coq au Vin

4 pounds (2 kg) chicken, cut up
2 tablespoons butter
3 large onions, quartered
1 garlic clove, crushed
6 medium carrots, scrubbed or peeled
2 tablespoons all-purpose flour
2 cups or more sherry
1 bay leaf
1 tablespoon chopped fresh parsley
1/4 teaspoon thyme
1/2 cup chopped fresh mushrooms
salt and freshly ground pepper to taste

There were times when we had to be elegant, especially if our niece Tammy Dunnet was around. Cherry anything was her favourite, even when she wore braces. The braces are gone now and Tammy's a judge of the Supreme Court of Ontario. I wonder if she remembers the chicken jubilee.

- Place chicken in large bowl and marinate with French dressing for an hour, turning once.

- Drain chicken and place in casserole.

- In saucepan, melt orange juice. Add drained cherries and jelly and heat thoroughly.

- Pour hot sauce over chicken, cover and bake at 400°F for 1 hour. If sauce appears watery, uncover casserole for last 30 minutes of cooking.

- Just before serving, heat brandy in ladle and light on fire. Pour over chicken dish. Makes 6 servings.

Chicken Jubilee Flambé

6 boneless chicken breasts
1 cup French dressing
1 can (6 ounces/178 mL) frozen orange juice concentrate
1 can (14 ounces/398 mL) pitted black cherries, drained
1/2 cup currant jelly
2 tablespoons brandy

Sweet and Sour Chicken Wings

8 or more chicken wings or
    drumsticks
1/2 cup all-purpose flour
1/2 teaspoon salt
1/4 teaspoon pepper
2 tablespoons vegetable oil
1 small onion, chopped
2/3 cup orange juice
1/3 cup ketchup or chili sauce
1 tablespoon brown sugar
1 teaspoon soy sauce
1/4 teaspoon ground ginger
garlic to taste (optional)

There's a note on this recipe which says simply "a favourite with all." Chicken wings were cheaper when I wrote that note so this meal would have had the added bonus of being economical. It's also delicious with drumsticks.

- Snip off wing tips and discard.

- In plastic bag, combine flour, salt and pepper. Add wings or drumsticks and shake to coat well.

- In frying pan, brown slowly on both sides in hot oil. Remove chicken pieces to baking dish.

- To frying pan, add onion, orange juice, ketchup or chili sauce, brown sugar, soy sauce, ginger and garlic, if using. Bring to boil, stirring to dissolve flour particles.

- Pour sauce over chicken in baking dish, cover and bake at 350°F for 25 minutes. Turn chicken over, cover again and continue baking for 30 minutes or until very tender.

- Serve with fried or steamed rice, spooning sauce over each serving. Makes 4 servings.

Chicken à la King

1/4 cup butter or margarine
1/4 cup all-purpose flour
2 cups milk
1 ½ cups chicken broth or
    bouillon
1/8 teaspoon cayenne pepper
1/8 teaspoon dry mustard
1/8 teaspoon salt
4 cups diced cooked chicken
1/2 pound (250 g) sliced fresh
    mushrooms or 1 can (10
    ounces/284 mL) sliced
    drained mushrooms
1 large green pepper, chopped
1/2 cup pimiento, cut into strips

Taking shortcuts was a way of life for cooks in the 60s and, at the time, I was always busy with volunteer work. But I liked to take the time to make my own tea biscuits instead of using puff pastry shells with this quick and easy, family-style meal.

- Melt butter in large saucepan. Add flour and cook, stirring, over medium heat until bubbly.

- Gradually stir in milk, then bouillon, cayenne pepper, mustard and salt. Continue cooking, stirring frequently, until mixture is smooth and thick.

- Stir in chicken, mushrooms, green pepper and pimiento and cook until heated through.

- Serve over tea biscuits. Makes 6 servings.

I love double-duty recipes like this one. It only takes a little longer to make a second meal for the freezer. If freezing, it's best to use a dish that will withstand extreme temperature changes so the pie can go directly from freezer to oven. To cook from frozen state, cut a few slits in the top and bake at 375°F for 50 minutes (40 minutes for individual servings) or until it has browned.

- In saucepan, melt butter. Blend in flour, salt and pepper.

- Gradually add broth, stirring constantly until it boils. Continue cooking over low heat for 5 minutes. Cool.

- When cooled, stir in chicken, peas, mushrooms and carrots.

- Divide mixture between two 6-cup baking dishes or ten 1 ½-cup baking dishes (to make individual servings).

- Roll out pastry and cut to fit tops. Place over chicken mixture and seal edges well. To cook, cut several slits in top and brush with milk.

- Bake at 425°F for 35 minutes for large pie or 25 minutes for small or until browned. Each pie makes 5 servings.

Chicken or Turkey Pies

6 tablespoons butter or margarine
6 tablespoons all-purpose flour
1/2 teaspoon salt
1/2 teaspoon pepper
3 cups chicken broth
4 cups diced cooked chicken or turkey
2 cups cooked green peas
2 cups sliced mushrooms, sautéed
2 cups sliced cooked carrots
pastry for 2-crust pie
milk

Chicken Vermouth

- You can get a meal into the oven as quick as a wink. Place 4 whole boned and skinned chicken breasts in a baking dish. Sprinkle over the chicken 1 envelope of Knorr Onion Soup mix. Combine 1/2 cup of dry vermouth with 1/2 cup of water; pour over chicken. Cover and bake at 350°F for 1 hour.

My Favourite Chicken Casserole

2 chicken bouillon cubes
1 cup hot water
1/4 cup butter or margarine
1/4 cup all-purpose flour
1 ⅔ cups evaporated milk
1/2 cup water
1/2 teaspoon salt
3 cups cooked rice
2 ½ cups diced cooked chicken
2 ½ cups sliced fresh
　　mushrooms
1/4 cup chopped pimiento
1/3 cup chopped green pepper
1/2 cup slivered and toasted
　　blanched almonds

This old stand-by has seen me through many occasions. Paired with a seafood casserole, it often took centre stage when I was serving a buffet to a crowd.

- Dissolve bouillon cubes in 1 cup hot water.

- In large saucepan, melt butter. Add flour and cook, stirring, for 2 to 3 minutes.

- Gradually add bouillon mixture, milk and 1/2 cup water, stirring constantly. Cook over low heat, stirring, until mixture thickens.

- Stir in salt, cooked rice, chicken, mushrooms, pimiento and green pepper.

- Pour into large, greased casserole and bake at 350°F for 30 minutes or until heated through.

- Sprinkle with almonds. Makes 8 to 10 servings.

Turkey Hash

2 cups diced cooked turkey
1 cup leftover stuffing
salt and pepper to taste
2 tablespoons butter,
　　margarine or oil
1/2 cup chopped green pepper
1/2 cup chopped onions
1/2 cup leftover turkey gravy

"There's no recipe for hash," my mother used to say as she turned out a memorable dish from leftovers. Because it was served so often in the years following the depression, hash became associated with hard times. However, a renewed interest in the comfort foods of our youth has returned it to favour and to its rightful place on family menus.

- In bowl, combine turkey and stuffing. Season with salt and pepper.

- In large frying pan, melt butter. Sauté green pepper and onion until limp and beginning to brown.

- Add turkey mixture and gravy and stir well. Cook over low heat for 15 minutes. Increase heat and cook 10 minutes longer or until browned and nicely crusted. Shake pan occasionally during cooking to prevent sticking. Makes 4 servings.

I f ever there was an overused mealtime phrase in our house, it had to be "eat your vegetables." Our boys tried every trick in the bag to avoid eating even the smallest helpings I served as a come-on.

Things changed dramatically, however, when we started growing our own vegetables in the ambitious garden we planted a year after the cottage was built. That first garden would have been planted in 1959.

Laurie called on our favourite neighbourhood farmer, Clifton Daupinee to "ready the ground" for us. This entailed all the hard work. First, Clift carefully removed the sods to be used elsewhere, then he spent days digging out the biggest rocks. After tilling, he spread the plot with manure and used a pitch fork to turn it under. More rocks were turned up and the raking seemed endless. But eventually, the virgin ground was ready to accept the seed.

Finally, everything was underground, with little signs marking the rows of lettuce, radishes, beans, peas, carrots, beets, spinach, Swiss chard, turnips, corn, potatoes, and off to the side, cucumbers, pumpkins and squash.

We waited and weeded, and excitedly watched the little shoots as they appeared. Then more weeding and thinning, hoeing, hilling, and raking.

And so the garden grew, promising wonderful taste experiences, some even anticipated by those same boys who "hated vegetables."

Then one dark night, I happened to look out of the window to see a face staring back at me. It was a cow. But we didn't have cows.

Disaster had struck. Clifton's cows had gotten out of the pasture and found their way to our garden.

"Oh, no! Not my beans!" I cried, as, putting fear behind me, I "shooed" those "giant" animals out of my garden, while Laurie went for Clift.

Never was anyone more devastated and apologetic than that big-hearted man. He stood, wringing his hands, offering me anything I wanted from his own garden, while I cried, "But this was ours. These were my beans—our peas. We grew them ourselves. Nothing else would mean the same."

How many times we have since laughed at my Sarah Bernhardt performance out there in the garden, trying to replant the beans which had been up-rooted—in the dark of night.

VEGETABLES

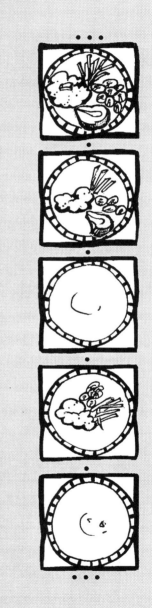

Braised Cabbage

2 tablespoons vegetable oil
6 cups coarsely shredded green cabbage
1 onion, thinly sliced
2 red apples, coarsely diced
1 teaspoon caraway seed
1/2 teaspoon salt
2 tablespoons water

The old way of cooking cabbage was to boil it for hours until it was mush. It responded to this mistreatment by filling the house with an unpleasant odour. Today, we know cabbage is a highly nutritious and tasty vegetable that requires only brief cooking. Braising has become a favourite method in my kitchen.

• In large frying pan, heat oil until very hot. Add cabbage, onion, apples, caraway seed and salt. Stir fry 3 to 5 minutes.

• Lower heat and add water. Cover and cook 5 minutes longer. Makes 4 servings.

Cauliflower Casserole

1 can (10 ounces/284 mL) cream of mushroom soup
1 cup grated cheddar cheese
1 egg, well beaten
1 cup mayonnaise
2 tablespoons grated onion
salt and pepper to taste
1 head cauliflower, broken into florets

Dressing vegetables with sauces was one way of getting the boys to eat them. This sauce could be called "bribe" sauce, since it accompanied several vegetables, including broccoli and Swiss chard, to the table.

• Combine soup, cheese, egg, mayonnaise, onion, salt and pepper.

• Briefly cook cauliflower (5 minutes). Drain well and gently combine with sauce.

• Turn into a greased baking dish and bake at 400°F for 20 minutes, until top is lightly browned. Makes 6 to 8 servings.

Roast Corn on the Cob

corn on the cob
butter
salt and pepper (optional)

Sweet corn on the cob was one vegetable the boys couldn't refuse. During its brief season, if we weren't having a corn boil, we were barbecuing it.

• To roast corn in the husk, remove only the outer leaves. Fold back the inner husks, being careful not to split them. Remove silks. Spread corn with butter, and sprinkle with salt and pepper, if desired. Pull husks back up over ears. Tie tips with string to keep corn covered and moist. Place on grill over gray coals. Roast 15 to 25 minutes, according to corn's maturity, turning several times for even cooking.

Broccoli hadn't been "invented" when I stepped into my first kitchen. In fact, I think our sons made it to their teens before they found these little trees on their plates. It was during the 70s that broccoli came into its own. Now available year round, it is probably the most popular green vegetable.

• Discard tough end of broccoli stem. Peel off outside skin. Make 1/2 inch slit through bottom of each floret to ensure even cooking.

• Steam or boil in as little water as possible, keeping the lid off for the first 5 minutes of cooking to preserve the fresh green colour. Cook 10 minutes or until just tender crisp. Drain.

• Meanwhile, melt butter in small saucepan. Add bread crumbs and sauté for 1 to 2 minutes.

• Stir in lemon juice.

• Spoon over broccoli on plates. Makes 4 servings.

Broccoli with Lemon Crumbs

1 head broccoli
2 tablespoons butter
2 tablespoons fine bread
  crumbs
2 teaspoons lemon juice

This recipe may change the thinking of those who have always considered cabbage too mundane to serve to guests.

• In large saucepan, dissolve bouillon in water. Add cabbage, carrots and onions. Sprinkle with salt and pepper and toss to mix.

• Cover and cook over medium heat for 5 to 10 minutes or until tender, stirring once during cooking. Drain, if necessary.

• Combine butter, nuts and mustard. Pour over vegetables and toss to mix.

• Spoon into warmed serving dish and sprinkle with paprika. Makes 6 to 8 servings.

Company Cabbage

1 teaspoon beef bouillon
  granules
1/4 cup water
5 cups coarsely shredded
  cabbage
1 cup coarsely shredded carrots
1/2 cup sliced green onions
salt and pepper to taste
2 tablespoons butter or
  margarine, melted
1/3 cup chopped walnuts or
  pecans
1 teaspoon prepared mustard
paprika

Celery and Corn

3 tablespoons butter or
   margarine
2 cups diagonally sliced celery
2 cups whole kernel corn,
   canned or frozen
2 tablespoons sliced or
   chopped pimiento
1/2 teaspoon salt

In a 1991 study, it was shown that eating two ribs of celery a day over a four-week period can lower both blood pressure and cholesterol significantly. Researchers believe the reductions are caused by an unusual chemical compound found in celery.

• In large skillet, melt butter. Add celery, cover and cook for 5 minutes.

• Meanwhile, cook corn according to directions on packaging.

• Drain and add to celery in skillet. Stir in pimiento and salt.

• Cook until heated through. Makes 4 servings.

Scalloped Corn

2 cans (19 ounces/540 mL)
   cream-style corn
4 eggs, beaten
1 cup crushed soda crackers
2 tablespoons butter or
   margarine, melted
1/2 cup milk
1/2 cup finely shredded carrot
1/2 cup chopped green pepper
2 tablespoons chopped celery
1 tablespoon chopped onion
several shakes of Tabasco
   sauce
1 teaspoon granulated sugar
1/2 teaspoon salt
1/2 cup shredded cheddar
   cheese (optional)

Although corn fresh from the cob is a fleeting thing, frozen kernels and canned cream-style corn are available year round. Scalloped corn makes a nice accompaniment to ham, sausages and other meats.

• In large bowl, combine corn, eggs, crackers, butter, milk, carrot, green pepper, celery, onion, Tabasco sauce, sugar and salt.

• Turn into greased, shallow 9 x 9-inch baking dish. Sprinkle with cheese, if using.

• Bake at 350°F for 1 hour until set and top is golden. Makes 8 servings.

Carrots cooked this way are not only dressed for company, but they also retain most of their valuable nutrients. New carrots need not be peeled—just scrubbed or scraped.

- Peel and cut carrots into thin 2-inch strips.

- In saucepan with tight-fitting lid, combine water, lemon juice, butter, nutmeg, sugar, salt and pepper. Add carrots, cover and cook very gently until tender. Since all liquid will be absorbed, check frequently to prevent scorching.

- Toss in generous amount of chopped parsley. Serve. Makes 4 to 5 servings.

Carrots Vichy

8 medium carrots
2 tablespoons water
1 tablespoon lemon juice
4 tablespoons butter, melted
dash of nutmeg
dash of sugar
dash each of salt and pepper
chopped parsley

This casserole will make a wonderful impression on a buffet table. It's also a good choice for a pot luck supper. Use fresh green beans, if available, and long, narrow potatoes. I've sometimes "lightened" this casserole by using milk instead of cream.

- Melt butter in small frying pan over medium heat. Add onion, red pepper and garlic. Sauté just until vegetables are tender-crisp.

- Stir in flour, continue stirring and cook 1 minute longer.

- Spread half of mixture evenly over bottom of greased 9 x 13-inch baking dish. Layer with half of potatoes and green beans and 1 cup cheese. Top with remaining onion mixture, then remaining potatoes and green beans.

- Combine blend with rosemary, salt and pepper. Pour over vegetables.

- Cover and bake at 375°F for 1 hour or until potatoes are tender.

- Sprinkle with remaining 1 cup cheese, then criss-cross red pepper strips over top. Return to oven for 5 minutes. Makes 8 to 10 servings.

Garden Casserole

3 tablespoons butter or
    margarine
1 large onion, sliced
1 medium sweet red pepper,
    cut into strips
2 cloves garlic, minced
1/4 cup all-purpose flour
6 medium potatoes, unpeeled
    and sliced
2 cups fresh cut green beans or
    1 package (10 ounces/300 g)
    frozen, thawed
2 cups (8 ounces/250 g)
    shredded Swiss cheese
1 cup blend (light cream) or
    milk
1/2 teaspoon dried rosemary
1/2 teaspoon salt
1/4 teaspoon pepper
16 strips sweet red pepper

Green Beans with Celery

1 ½ pounds (750 g) fresh green
    beans
2 tablespoons butter
1 tablespoon finely minced
    onion
1 rib finely diced celery
salt and pepper to taste

Fresh green beans are tasty when simply cooked to the crisp-tender stage and served unadorned. But, occasionally, it's fun to dress them up. This is one of my favourite dressed-up combinations.

• Wash beans quickly in cold water (soaking leaches valuable vitamins). If fresh and tender, leave whole. Otherwise, trim and snap in half.

• Put in saucepan with small amount of water and bring quickly to boil. Reduce heat, keep cover ajar so steam will escape and simmer 15 to 20 minutes or until just tender-crisp (less if beans are very young).

• Drain and place beans in warm serving dish.

• Meanwhile, melt butter in small skillet. Add onion, celery, salt and pepper and sauté over low heat, stirring until celery is tender.

• Spoon over beans and toss lightly to coat. Makes 6 servings.

Green Beans with Almonds

1 ½ pounds (750 g) fresh green
    beans
2 tablespoons butter or
    margarine
1/2 cup slivered or sliced
    almonds
salt and pepper to taste

Keep the cover off green beans and other green vegetables for the first few minutes of cooking to allow certain gases to escape and to preserve their bright green colour.

• Prepare and cook beans (see Green Beans with Celery). Drain.

• While beans are cooking, melt butter in small skillet over low heat. Add almonds and sauté until golden brown.

• Spoon over beans and toss gently to mix. Season with salt and pepper. Makes 6 servings.

Janet Hotstetter of Pittsburgh gave me this recipe years ago when we met in Florida. It's a pleasant change from scalloped potatoes.

- In large pot with small amount of salted water, cook potatoes, onion and green pepper until tender. Drain.

- Meanwhile, melt butter in top of double boiler. Add flour and cook 2 to 3 minutes, stirring almost constantly. Add salt and pepper.

- Gradually add milk and stir constantly until thickened.

- Add cheese and stir until blended.

- Mix sauce with potatoes in greased casserole dish and bake at 350°F until it bubbles, 20 to 25 minutes. Makes 6 servings.

Coal Miners' Potatoes

4 cups peeled and cubed
   potatoes
1 small onion, finely diced
1/2 cup diced green pepper
2 tablespoons butter
3 tablespoons flour
1 teaspoon salt
1/2 teaspoon pepper
2 cups milk
1 cup grated cheddar or Swiss
   cheese

Scalloped potatoes have seen many changes over the years but I'm not sure that the old-fashioned combination of sliced potatoes, onions and milk can be topped. However, during the 50s, when canned creamed soups were so popular, a deluxe version of scalloped potatoes came into being with a can of cream of mushroom soup and half a cup of milk. This more recent rendition calls for chicken broth and Swiss cheese instead of milk.

- In large saucepan, combine potatoes, broth, salt and pepper and bring to boil. Cover, reduce heat and simmer for 5 minutes.

- Drain, reserving broth.

- In lightly greased 2-quart (2 L) baking dish, layer half the potatoes, then half the cheese. Repeat layers. Pour broth over top.

- Cover and bake at 350°F for 45 minutes. Remove cover and bake 15 minutes more or until potatoes are tender and top has browned. Makes 6 servings.

Swiss Scalloped Potatoes

5 to 6 large potatoes, peeled
   and sliced
1 ½ cups chicken broth or
   vegetable stock
1/2 teaspoon salt
1/4 teaspoon pepper
1 cup shredded Swiss cheese

Sweet Potato Casserole

8 medium sweet potatoes
1/3 cup raisins
3/4 cup packed brown sugar
1 tablespoon cornstarch
1/2 teaspoon salt
1/2 teaspoon grated orange rind
1 cup orange juice
1/4 cup butter or margarine
1/4 cup chopped walnuts

It wasn't until Southern belle Sarah came north to marry our son Frank that sweet potatoes became an item on our Thanksgiving table. At first, we celebrated both the Canadian and American Thanksgiving with only Sarah and I eating sweet potatoes topped with marshmallows. Now the holidays are comfortably melded into one and this recipe has replaced the overly sweet marshmallow-topped dish.

• Scrub sweet potatoes. Place in large pot and cover with boiling, salted water. Cook just until tender.

• Drain, peel and slice. Arrange in greased 9 x 13-inch baking dish. Sprinkle with raisins.

• In saucepan, combine brown sugar, cornstarch and salt. Blend in orange rind and juice. Cook, stirring, over medium heat until slightly thickened and bubbly. Cook 1 minute longer.

• Add butter and nuts, stirring until butter has melted. Pour mixture over potatoes.

• Bake, uncovered, at 325°F for 30 minutes, basting occasionally. Makes 10 to 12 servings.

Turnip with Apples

1 turnip, approximately 2 pounds
3 tart apples, peeled and thinly sliced
salt and pepper, to taste
freshly grated nutmeg
2 tablespoons butter

Years ago, I found myself wondering if I would ever find a way to get my youngest son Bobby to eat turnip. Persistence paid off. By adding apples and a little grated nutmeg, the hated vegetable became as appealing as apple pie.

• Pare and cut turnip into 1-inch cubes. Cook in boiling salted water for 15-20 minutes, or until almost tender.

• Add apple slices and cook 5 minutes longer, or until both turnip and apples are soft.

• Drain and mash. Add salt, pepper, nutmeg and butter to taste. Makes six servings.

I never thought of pumpkin as a vegetable until I tried this casserole. It was impressive enough to find a permanent place in my "make often" file.

The easiest way to cook the pumpkin is to halve it, scoop out the seeds and strings, place cut-side down on a baking sheet and bake at 400°F for 1 hour, or until tender. Scoop pulp into a bowl and mash. If preparing ahead for this casserole, cool, cover, and store pumpkin in refrigerator until needed.

- Melt butter in top of double boiler. Add flour and cook, stirring, for 3 minutes.

- Gradually add milk, stirring constantly, and cook until mixture thickens. Season with salt and pepper. Set sauce aside.

- Hard boil eggs. Cool, peel and slice.

- Combine pumpkin, sauce, raisins and 1 cup grated cheese.

- Place half of mixture in large greased baking dish. Arrange sliced eggs over mixture and top with remaining pumpkin. Sprinkle with crackers and remaining 1/2 cup cheese. Dot with butter and bake at 350°F for 30 minutes. Serve hot. Makes 6 servings.

Pumpkin Casserole

3 tablespoons butter or
    margarine
3 tablespoons flour
1 cup milk
1/4 teaspoon salt
1/8 teaspoon pepper
3 eggs
4 cups cooked and mashed
    pumpkin
1/2 cup seedless raisins
1 ½ cups grated cheddar cheese
1/2 cup coarsely crumbled soda
    crackers
2 tablespoons butter

Until I found this recipe, I usually pickled beets or cooked them Harvard-style with a sweet and sour sauce. Sometimes I'd stir in a little orange juice. Beets with pineapple are particularly nice with lamb or pork.

- Drain pineapple and reserve juice. Add enough water to juice to make 1 cup. Set pineapple aside.

- In saucepan, combine pineapple juice with sugar, cornstarch, salt and lemon juice. Heat to boiling and cook, stirring, until sauce thickens.

- Fold in beets and pineapple. Heat thoroughly, then stir in butter. Makes 6 to 8 servings.

Beets with Pineapple

1 can (14 ounces/398 mL)
    pineapple tidbits
1 cup pineapple juice
2 tablespoons brown sugar
1 tablespoon cornstarch
1/4 teaspoon salt
2 tablespoons lemon juice or
    vinegar
2 cups cooked or canned sliced
    beets
1 tablespoon butter

Joan's Spinach Ring

2 packages (10 ounces/300 g each) frozen chopped spinach, thawed
1 package (8 ounces/250 g) cream cheese, softened
1 tablespoon chopped fresh chives
1 can (10 ounces/284 mL) condensed cream of mushroom soup
2 eggs
cooked carrots (optional)

I don't think I can blame my babies for refusing to eat spinach but I know I got tired of wearing it as they spit back my puréed offerings. Since then I've learned to cook it properly, with no more water than what is left on after rinsing and steaming it only until it is deep green (not black) and still slightly firm. I've named this recipe after my friend Joan who tested it for me some years ago. She liked it so much that it began making regular appearances on her table.

• Squeeze spinach until dry.

• In blender or food processor, combine spinach, cream cheese, chives, mushroom soup and eggs and mix well.

• Pour into greased 4-cup ring mold. Place mold in larger pan and fill with enough hot water to come halfway up side of mold.

• Bake at 350°F for 50 minutes or until knife inserted in centre comes out clean.

• Remove mold from water and let stand 5 minutes before inverting onto serving plate.

• Fill centre with cooked carrots, if desired. Serve immediately. Makes 6 servings.

Turnip Loaf

2 small turnips, diced (approximately 6 cups)
1/8 teaspoon pepper
1/8 teaspoon nutmeg
1/2 cup blend (light cream) or milk
2 eggs, lightly beaten
1/4 cup soft bread crumbs
1 tablespoon butter, melted

I grew up on turnips, the yellow kind that, along with carrots, kept us going through the winter. When they started calling them rutabagas, I never adapted. To me, it smacked of putting on airs or a marketing ploy, like calling a flounder "sole." This is Laurie's favourite turnip dish.

• Cover turnips with boiling water and cook 15 to 20 minutes or until tender.

• Drain and mash. Season with pepper and nutmeg. Add blend and eggs.

• Spoon into greased 9 x 5-inch loaf pan.

• Toss bread crumbs with melted butter and sprinkle over turnip.

• Bake at 375°F for 1 hour. Makes 6 to 8 servings.

A large squash can be difficult to cut but I've found a method that works. Remove the stem, then score the squash with a large knife all the way around the middle. Insert the knife into the squash slightly and tap it several times with a hammer. The squash will split apart along the scored line.

- Cut squash in half and remove seeds and strings. Place cut side down in pan with small amount of boiling water.

- Bake at 400°F for 1 hour or until soft but not mushy. Peel and cut into cubes. Set aside.

- In large skillet, heat 2 tablespoons butter or margarine. Add apple slices, sprinkle with sugar and nutmeg and simmer until barely tender.

- Spread apples on bottom of round 8-inch casserole dish. Spoon squash over apples.

- Combine bread cubes with 2 tablespoons melted butter or margarine. Spoon evenly over squash.

- Cook at 350°F for 30 minutes. Makes 6 to 8 servings.

Squash and Apple Casserole

1 acorn or buttercup squash
(approximately 2 pounds/
1 kg)
2 tablespoons butter or
margarine
6 apples, peeled and sliced
1/4 cup brown sugar
1/4 teaspoon nutmeg
2 slices bread, cubed
2 tablespoons butter or
margarine, melted

Whenever I used to need something to accompany a quick meal of fish cakes or cold cuts, I would reach for a can of tomatoes.

- After measuring 1/2 cup juice from tomatoes, empty remaining tomatoes into saucepan and heat until almost boiling.

- In frying pan, sauté celery, onion and green pepper in butter until nearly tender.

- Add to tomatoes.

- Blend flour into butter remaining in frying pan to form a smooth paste. Add reserved tomato juice and stir until smooth. Season with pepper.

- Stir flour mixture into tomatoes and blend thoroughly.

- Pour into greased baking dish and bake at 350°F for 35 minutes. Makes 4 to 6 servings.

Scalloped Tomatoes

1/2 cup juice from tomatoes
1 can (28 ounces/796 mL)
tomatoes
1/2 cup chopped celery
1 onion, thinly sliced
1/4 green pepper, cut in strips
3 tablespoons butter
3 tablespoons all-purpose flour
1/8 teaspoon pepper

Zucchini and Walnuts

3 tablespoons butter or
    margarine
1/2 cup coarsely chopped
    walnuts
1 ½ pounds zucchini (6 to 8
    inches in length)
1/2 teaspoon salt
freshly ground pepper

Zucchini is another recent addition to the expanding vegetable basket. Although they'll grow to almost any length, the skin becomes tough and peeling difficult. After peeling and seeding the larger zucchinis, grate them for use in breads, muffins and cakes. Keep the smaller ones, which do not need to be peeled or seeded, for vegetable dishes like this one.

- Heat 1 tablespoon butter in skillet. Stir in walnuts and toss for 8 minutes or until lightly browned. Remove from skillet.

- Wash zucchini and trim ends. Slice crosswise into 1/2-inch slices.

- Sauté in remaining 2 tablespoons butter until slices begin to soften.

- Add walnuts and stir. Season with salt and pepper. Makes 4 to 5 servings.

Zucchini Soufflé

3 cups grated or chopped
    zucchini
1/2 teaspoon salt
1/2 teaspoon pepper
1 cup crushed soda crackers
1 small onion, finely chopped
3 eggs, beaten
1 cup grated Swiss cheese
1 cup milk
2 tablespoons butter, melted

Gardeners are always looking for new ways to make use of those large zucchinis that are in abundance by summer's end. I peel and grate them, seal them in airtight freezer bags and store them in the freezer for up to a year. After thawing and pressing out the excess water, I make this zucchini souffle.

- In large mixing bowl, combine zucchini, salt, pepper, crackers, onion, eggs, cheese, milk and butter.

- Pour into buttered souffle dish.

- Bake at 350°F for 45 minutes to an hour or until souffle has puffed and top has lightly browned. Makes 4 to 6 servings.

Q uick breads were to the 1950s and 60s what muffins have been to the 80s and 90s. While established homemakers were content with their tried and true favourites, novices like me were busy trying to find the best of each variety. Since practice made perfect, we soon learned the technique of creaming the shortening, sugar and eggs before adding the dry ingredients alternately with the liquid and folding in the fruit and nuts last. It took us longer to realize that we need not be ashamed of the characteristic crack which appeared along the top of the bread.

When I began baking 40-something years ago, quick breads meant more than loaves. They included the flaky biscuits that generations of women took pride in making as well as scones, corn breads, coffee cakes, dumplings, pancakes, waffles, popovers, muffins and even doughnuts.

Homemade scones are still being turned out today, especially by those of Scottish descent. Pancakes appear for weekend breakfasts and as the main meal on Shrove Tuesday. Coffee cakes are currently making a bit of a comeback, and the sale of muffins has soared with specialty shops featuring muffins springing up everywhere.

It's safe to say that millions of muffins are being made in Nova Scotia kitchens today. Usually smaller than the creations of the muffin shops, they come in many varieties, from the basic cake-like muffin to those chock-full of bran and rolled oats. Sometimes, I think it's become ridiculous. I feel I can live without cappuccino chocolate chip or bacon cheddar boursin cheese muffins and, if I'm paying the price of a papaya, I'm not going to mush it up to make muffins.

Yeast breads never played a major part in my kitchen, except for porridge or rolled oats bread which my boys fondly remember as "Mom's bread." Since the recipe appears in *Out of Old Nova Scotia Kitchens*, I haven't repeated it. However, I have updated some of the yeast rolls and buns which have changed slightly since active dry yeast replaced the yeast cakes of my mother's day. With the recent appearance of quick-rise instant yeast which is mixed into the dry ingredients, we have advanced even further in the interest of speed and convenience. But that's another story.

SWEET BREADS

Banana Bread

1/4 cup butter or margarine
1 cup granulated sugar
1 egg
1 ½ cups all-purpose flour
1 teaspoon baking soda
1/4 teaspoon salt
3 large ripe bananas, mashed

This recipe for an old favourite is so easy it could never be replaced. Besides, without banana bread what would we ever do with all those overripe bananas?

- Cream butter and sugar in large mixing bowl.

- Add egg and beat well.

- Combine flour, baking soda and salt.

- Add to butter mixture alternately with mashed bananas, beginning and ending with dry ingredients. Do not overbeat.

- Pour into greased 9 x 5-inch loaf pan and bake at 350°F for 50 to 60 minutes or until tester inserted in centre comes out clean.

Lemon Bread

6 tablespoons butter, softened
1 cup granulated sugar
2 eggs
2 teaspoons grated lemon rind
1 ½ cups all-purpose flour
1/4 teaspoon salt
1 teaspoon baking powder
1/2 cup milk

Topping:
1/4 cup granulated sugar
3 tablespoons lemon juice

If you don't like the sweet topping of this bread, try the more innovative granola streusel. Either way it's a comforting treat.

- Cream butter and sugar together until light and fluffy in large bowl.

- Add eggs, one at a time, beating well after each addition.

- Stir in lemon rind.

- Combine flour, salt and baking powder. Add to butter mixture alternately with milk, beginning and ending with dry ingredients. Do not overmix.

- Pour into greased 9 x 5-inch loaf pan and bake at 350°F for 50 to 60 minutes or until tester inserted in centre comes out clean.

- Combine sugar and lemon juice and drizzle over hot bread.

- Let pan stand 10 minutes on a rack before turning out loaf. Cool completely before slicing.

Variation: To make granola streusel topping, combine 1 tablespoon all-purpose flour with 1 tablespoon granulated sugar and 1 ½ teaspoons soft butter or margarine. Stir in 2 tablespoons granola and spread evenly over batter in pan before baking.

When sweet breads appeared on afternoon tea tables in the 1950s, the favourites were banana, lemon and cherry-pineapple. Zucchini was unknown as a vegetable let alone as an ingredient for one of today's most popular breads.

- In large mixing bowl, beat eggs until foamy. Slowly add oil, beating continuously.

- Add sugar and beat until creamy and light.

- Stir in zucchini, lemon rind and vanilla.

- Combine flour, salt, cinnamon, ginger, baking powder and soda. Add to batter a cup at a time, stirring just enough to blend.

- Fold in nuts.

- Pour into greased and floured 9 x 5-inch loaf pan.

- Bake at 350°F for an hour or until tester inserted in centre comes out clean.

- Cool bread in pan on wire rack for 15 minutes before turning out to cool completely.

Note: If pan seems too full, make a couple of muffins with the excess batter.

Here's another oldie but goodie.

- Cream butter and sugar until light and fluffy in large bowl.

- Add eggs and continue beating until smooth.

- Combine flour, baking powder, soda and salt in separate bowl.

- Add dry ingredients to butter mixture alternately with pineapple juice, beginning and ending with dry ingredients.

- Stir in vanilla.

- Combine pineapple, cherries and orange rind. Fold into batter.

- Pour into greased 9 x 5-inch loaf pan. Bake at 350°F for an hour or until tester inserted in centre comes out clean.

Zucchini Bread

3 eggs
3/4 cup vegetable oil
1 ½ cups granulated sugar
2 cups peeled, coarsely
    shredded zucchini
1 teaspoon finely grated lemon
    rind
1 teaspoon vanilla
3 cups all-purpose flour
1/2 teaspoon salt
1/2 teaspoon ground cinnamon
1/4 teaspoon ground ginger
2 teaspoons baking powder
1 teaspoon baking soda
1/2 cup chopped walnuts or
    pecans

Pineapple– Cherry Bread

1/2 cup butter or margarine
3/4 cup granulated sugar
2 eggs, well beaten
2 cups all-purpose flour
3 teaspoons baking powder
1/4 teaspoon baking soda
1/2 teaspoon salt
1/2 cup drained crushed
    pineapple
1/2 cup of juice from crushed
    pineapple
1 teaspoon vanilla
1/2 cup drained and chopped
    maraschino cherries
1 teaspoon grated orange rind

Cinnamon Bread

2 cups all-purpose flour
1 teaspoon baking powder
1/2 teaspoon baking soda
1/2 teaspoon salt
1/4 cup shortening
1 cup granulated sugar
2 eggs
1 teaspoon vanilla
1 cup sour milk*

Topping:
2 tablespoons granulated sugar
1 tablespoon ground cinnamon

Cinnamon toast used to be a common snack after an evening of bridge. This loaf captures the same flavour and can be made ahead so that it's ready to slice and spread lightly with butter or cream cheese.

• Combine flour, baking powder, soda and salt in small bowl and set aside.

• Cream shortening. Gradually add sugar, blending well.

• Add eggs and beat until light and fluffy.

• Stir in vanilla.

• Add dry ingredients alternately with milk, beginning and ending with dry ingredients and mixing well after each addition.

• Spoon half the batter into greased 9 x 5-inch loaf pan.

• Make **topping** by mixing sugar and cinnamon. Sprinkle half this mixture over batter, cover with remaining batter and top with remaining cinnamon mixture.

• Bake at 350°F for 50 minutes or until tester inserted in centre comes out clean.

*Fresh milk can be soured by adding 1 tablespoon vinegar per cup of milk. Allow to stand 5 or 10 minutes before using.

There was a time when pumpkins were either cooked in pies or destined to become jack-o'-lanterns. Today we're smart enough to use this nutritious gourd in many different ways. The trick is to buy pumpkins in the fall, cook and mash the flesh and freeze it in plastic bags or containers. When you're ready to make this delicious pumpkin bread, thaw and drain the mashed pumpkin and reserve the liquid for soups or other uses.

- In large bowl, cream shortening and sugar thoroughly.

- Beat in eggs, one at a time, until light and fluffy.

- Stir in pumpkin.

- Combine flour, baking powder, soda, salt, cinnamon and nutmeg. Stir into creamed mixture.

- Mix in vanilla, water and nuts.

- Spoon batter into greased 9 x 5-inch loaf pan and bake at 350°F for 45 to 55 minutes or until tester inserted in centre comes out clean.

- Cool and, if possible, allow to stand for 24 hours before slicing.

Pumpkin Nut Bread

1/3 cup shortening
1 ⅓ cups granulated sugar
2 eggs
1 cup mashed, pureed or canned pumpkin
1 ⅓ cups all-purpose flour
1/4 teaspoon baking powder
1 teaspoon baking soda
1/2 teaspoon salt
1/2 teaspoon ground cinnamon
1/2 teaspoon grated nutmeg
1/2 teaspoon vanilla extract
1/3 cup water
1/2 cup chopped pecans or walnuts

One of the most popular quick breads of the 50s was date bread. There were many variations—dates with lemon, dates with bran, dates with pineapple, dates with nuts or just plain dates. This one is flavoured and darkened with coffee. If you don't have a pot on the go, boil a cup of water and stir in a tablespoon of instant coffee.

- Pour coffee over dates and set aside.

- Combine flour, baking powder, soda and salt in a large bowl. Stir in brown sugar.

- In a small bowl, mix together egg, butter, apple, nuts and date mixture. Add to dry ingredients and stir just until moistened.

- Turn mixture into a greased 9 x 5-inch loaf pan. Bake at 350°F for 60 to 65 minutes or until tester inserted in centre comes out clean.

Date Nut Loaf

1 cup hot strong coffee
1 ¼ cups snipped dates
2 ¼ cups all-purpose flour
2 teaspoons baking powder
1/2 teaspoon baking soda
1/2 teaspoon salt
3/4 cup packed brown sugar
1 egg, beaten
2 tablespoons butter or margarine, melted
1 cup peeled and shredded apple
1/2 cup chopped nuts

Carrot Prune Bread

2 cups all-purpose flour
1 cup granulated sugar
2 teaspoons baking powder
2 teaspoons ground cinnamon
1/2 teaspoon nutmeg
1/2 teaspoon salt
1 cup coarsely chopped prunes
1/2 cup shredded coconut
1/2 cup chopped nuts
2 cups shredded carrots
1 cup vegetable oil
3 eggs, beaten
2 teaspoons vanilla

Carrot bread was often found in my kitchen in the 60s. The recipe which appears in Out of Old Nova Scotia Kitchens *helped my sons Frank, Gary and Bobby earn their Cub badges for baking. Recently I have been combining fibre-rich prunes with carrots for this unusually good quick bread. If you don't like coconut, replace it with another half cup of carrots or prunes.*

• In a large bowl, combine flour, sugar, baking powder, cinnamon, nutmeg and salt.

• Add prunes, coconut and nuts. Toss to blend thoroughly.

• Add carrots, oil, eggs and vanilla. Mix just until blended.

• Turn into greased and floured 9 x 5-inch loaf pan and smooth top.

• Bake at 350°F for approximately 1 hour or until bread is springy to the touch and begins to pull away from sides of pan.

• Cool 15 minutes before turning out onto rack. Wrap in plastic wrap or foil while slightly warm. Store 24 hours before slicing.

Corn Bread

1 cup all-purpose flour
1/4 cup sugar
4 teaspoons baking powder
1/2 teaspoon salt
1 cup cornmeal
2 eggs
1 cup milk
1/4 cup soft shortening

Corn bread hot from the oven was always a favourite. It perked up even the simplest of casseroles.

• In large bowl, sift together the flour, sugar, baking powder, salt and cornmeal.

• Add eggs, milk and shortening. Beat for 1 minute, just until smooth.

• Pour into a greased 9-inch square pan and bake at 425°F for 20 minutes. Cut into 16 pieces.

Apricot bread is another sweet from my past which is now enjoying a revival. This older version has stood the test of time. I found it in Tatamagouche Kitchens, *prepared by a Tatamagouche church group. The date is lost.*

- If using dried apricots, soak in cold water for half an hour and then drain.

- Squeeze orange juice and add boiling water to make 1 cup.

- Put orange rind, apricots and raisins through food chopper and then mix with juice in large bowl.

- Stir in baking soda, sugar, melted butter and vanilla. Add egg.

- Combine flour, baking powder and salt and stir into batter along with nuts.

- Pour into greased 9 x 5-inch loaf pan and bake at 350°F for 50 minutes or until tester inserted in centre comes out clean.

Note: To give loaf a smooth top, invert a second pan on top of bread for first 20 minutes of baking.

Apricot Bread

1/2 cup dried apricots or well-drained canned apricots
juice and rind of a large orange
boiling water
1/2 cup raisins
1 teaspoon baking soda
1 cup granulated sugar
2 tablespoons butter, melted
1 teaspoon vanilla
1 egg, well beaten
2 cups all-purpose flour
2 teaspoons baking powder
1/4 teaspoon salt
1/2 cup chopped nuts

Buttermilk is a good substitute for sour milk or yogurt. It's particularly high in potassium. Freeze any leftover buttermilk. Just give it a good shake when thawed.

- In large mixer bowl, combine flour, baking powder, soda, salt, cinnamon and nutmeg. Blend in brown sugar.

- Combine beaten egg, buttermilk and melted butter. Stir into flour mixture. Add nuts.

- Pour into a greased 9 x 5-inch loaf pan and bake at 350°F for 50 minutes, or until tester inserted in centre comes out clean.

Butter Pecan Bread

2 cups all-purpose flour
2 teaspoons baking powder
1/2 teaspoon baking soda
1/2 teaspoon salt
1 teaspoon cinnamon
1/4 teaspoon nutmeg
1 cup packed brown sugar
1 egg, beaten
1 cup buttermilk
2 tablespoons butter, melted
1 cup broken pecans

Apple Oatmeal Bread

3 cups peeled and chopped
    apples
1/2 cup water
1 cup packed brown sugar
2 cups all-purpose flour
1 teaspoon baking powder
1 teaspoon baking soda
1/2 teaspoon salt
1 teaspoon ground cinnamon
1/2 teaspoon ground allspice
1 cup rolled oats
1/2 cup raisins
1/2 cup chopped nuts
2 eggs, beaten
1/4 cup vegetable oil

This delicious bread, so generously packed with apples and with the added goodness of rolled oats, makes too much batter for a regular loaf pan. I've given the bread a new shape by baking it in a 10-inch tube pan. If you prefer a conventional loaf, bake the extra batter in a tiny loaf pan or muffin cups. Watch the cooking time, however, as the smaller bread or muffins will bake much more quickly.

• In saucepan, combine apples, water and 1/2 cup of the brown sugar. Cook until apples are almost tender (about 5 minutes). Set aside to cool.

• In large bowl, combine flour, baking powder, soda, salt, cinnamon and allspice.

• Add remaining brown sugar along with rolled oats, raisins and nuts and mix.

• Add cooled apple mixture, eggs and oil, stirring just until moistened.

• Pour into greased 10-inch tube pan and bake at 350°F for 40 minutes or until tester inserted in centre comes out clean.

• Allow bread to cool in pan on a rack for 15 minutes before turning out to cool completely.

Grapenuts Bread

1 ¾ cups all-purpose flour
1 cup sugar
2 ½ teaspoons baking powder
1 teaspoon salt
3/4 cup Grapenuts cereal
1 cup milk
1 egg, well beaten
2 tablespoons butter or
    margarine, melted

About a century ago, Dr. C.W. Post invented a breakfast cereal which he named Elijah's Manna. Grocers, however, didn't like the use of the biblical name and changed it to Grapenuts. The cereal doesn't contain either grapes or nuts but it does make a good sweet bread.

• Combine flour, sugar, baking powder and salt in medium-sized bowl. Fold in cereal.

• In large bowl, combine milk, egg and butter.

• Add flour mixture, stirring only enough to dampen flour.

• Pour into greased 9 x 5-inch loaf pan and bake at 350°F for 1 hour or until tester inserted in centre comes out clean.

• Cool in pan on a rack for 15 minutes before turning out to cool completely. For easier slicing, store bread overnight in plastic wrap or foil.

Although "little muffs" have been around for centuries, it wasn't until of the 1980s that muffins became a mania. Their popularity was tied to a new, widespread interest in nutrition. But, like many things that taste great, muffins can be loaded with fat and salt. Why not make your own and control the ingredients? Most muffins freeze well, so make several batches on the weekend, store them in the freezer and then pop them in the microwave to defrost.

- In large bowl, beat together egg, milk and oil.

- Stir in bran and banana and let stand for 5 minutes.

- Combine flour, baking powder, salt, sugar and cinnamon.

- Add to bran mixture, stirring just until dry ingredients are moistened.

- Spoon into greased muffin cups, filling 2/3 full, and bake at 400°F for 25 to 30 minutes or until tester inserted in centre comes out clean. Makes 12 muffins.

The first bran muffins probably appeared, along with all-bran cereal, around the turn of the century. But it was in the early 70s that I first encountered the refrigerator muffin that kept, uncooked and ready to pour, for as long as 6 weeks. Since I seldom have the refrigerator room, I usually bake the entire batch and freeze them in bags of four or six. To put extra fibre and B vitamins in these muffins, use 3 cups all-purpose flour mixed with 1 ½ cups whole wheat flour and 1/2 cup wheat germ.

- In large bowl, pour boiling water over raw bran. Add raisins and set aside to cool.

- In very large bowl, beat eggs.

- Gradually beat in brown sugar. Add oil, molasses and buttermilk.

- Sift together flour, baking soda and salt and add to buttermilk mixture.

- Stir in raw bran and raisins. Fold in bran flakes (if necessary, divide batter into 2 bowls).

- Spoon into greased muffins cups, filling 2/3 full. Bake at 375°F for 20 to 25 minutes. Makes 5 ½ dozen muffins.

Banana Bran Muffins

1 egg
1 cup milk
3 tablespoons vegetable oil
1 cup 100 per cent bran cereal
1 large banana, mashed (to equal 1/2 cup)
1 cup all-purpose flour
2 teaspoons baking powder
1/2 teaspoon salt
1/3 cup granulated sugar
1/4 teaspoon ground cinnamon

Refrigerator Bran Muffins

2 cups boiling water
2 cups raw bran
1 to 2 cups raisins
4 eggs
1 ½ cups packed brown sugar
1 cup vegetable oil
1/4 cup molasses
1 quart (1 L) buttermilk (or milk soured with 1/4 cup vinegar)
5 cups all-purpose flour
3 scant tablespoons baking soda
1 teaspoon salt
4 cups bran flakes

Leftover Porridge Muffins

1 cup milk
2 tablespoons vegetable oil
1/4 cup granulated sugar
1 egg
1/2 teaspoon salt
1 cup leftover cooked porridge
2 cups all-purpose flour
5 teaspoons baking powder
grape or apple jelly or any jam

Topping:
2 tablespoons sugar
1 teaspoon ground cinnamon

Ever wonder what to do with the porridge that's left from breakfast? Here's the best answer I've found. It may even make your family want to have porridge for breakfast, just so they can have muffins for lunch. If you wish to lower the sugar content, omit the topping.

- Combine milk, oil, 1/4 cup sugar, egg and salt in large bowl. Add porridge and blend thoroughly.

- Sift together flour and baking powder. Add to porridge mixture, stirring just until flour is moistened. Do not overmix.

- Spoon about 2 tablespoons batter into greased muffin cups.

- Drop a teaspoon of jam or jelly on top, then top with another 2 tablespoons batter.

- For **topping**, mix 2 tablespoons sugar and cinnamon. Sprinkle on top of muffins.

- Bake at 400°F for 30 to 35 minutes or until tops are golden brown and spring back lightly when touched. Makes approximately 15 muffins.

Apple Date Muffins

1 ¾ cups all-purpose flour
2 ½ teaspoons baking powder
1/2 teaspoon salt
1/4 cup granulated sugar
2 eggs
3/4 cup milk
2 tablespoons butter, melted
3/4 cup chopped walnuts
3/4 cup chopped dates
1 cup peeled and grated raw
    apple

Topping:
1 teaspoon ground cinnamon
4 teaspoons granulated sugar
2 apples, peeled and sliced
additional chopped walnuts

I've adapted this recipe from one I copied out of an American cookbook during a trip to Florida in the 60s. These tasty and attractive muffins were prize winners at the Wood County Fair in West Virginia.

- Combine flour, baking powder, salt and 1/4 cup sugar in large bowl.

- In separate bowl, beat eggs. Add milk combined with melted butter.

- Quickly stir into dry ingredients. Add walnuts, dates and grated apple.

- Spoon batter into greased and floured muffin cups, filling each 2/3 full.

- **Topping**: combine cinnamon and 4 teaspoons sugar in small bowl. Dip apple slices into cinnamon sugar and place one on top of each muffin. Fill hole in centre with chopped walnuts.

- Bake at 425°F for 25 minutes. Makes 15 muffins.

When it's difficult to find good, fresh fruit in winter, I often turn to crushed pineapple canned in its own juice. In this recipe, it's combined with wheat germ that has been lightly toasted to impart a nutty flavour.

• Toast wheat germ in non-stick pan over low heat, keeping pan moving to prevent burning. Set aside.

• In large bowl, beat egg lightly with fork.

• Beat in milk, molasses and oil.

• Stir in pineapple, bran and wheat germ.

• Combine flour, soda and salt in a small bowl.

• Add to egg mixture and stir just to blend.

• Spoon into greased muffin cups, filling each 2/3 full. Bake at 400°F for 15 to 20 minutes or until muffin springs back when touched lightly. Makes 12 muffins.

Blueberries now rank as Nova Scotia's top fruit crop, displacing the apple which once enjoyed a much larger harvest. Picking blueberries is still a favourite August pastime for many. Others prefer to leave the bending to professional rakers and head to the fields to pick the high-bush, cultivated varieties which are easily gleaned. When it comes to muffins, however, the hands-down choice is the smaller, low-bush berry. If you're making these muffins in winter, prevent "bleeding" by using frozen blueberries directly from the freezer.

• In large bowl, combine flour, 1/2 cup sugar, baking powder and salt. Make a well in centre of mixture.

• Combine egg, milk and oil in smaller bowl. Add all at once to dry ingredients and stir just to moisten. Set aside.

• Toss blueberries with 2 tablespoons sugar and lemon rind. Fold berries into batter.

• Spoon batter into greased muffin cups, filling 2/3 full. Bake at 400°F for 18 minutes or until golden brown. Remove from pans.

• Combine melted butter and lemon juice. Dip tops of warm muffins in lemon mixture, then in sugar. Makes 12 muffins.

Pineapple Muffins

1/2 cup wheat germ
1 egg
1 ¼ cups milk
1/2 cup molasses
2 tablespoons vegetable oil
3/4 cup well-drained crushed
    pineapple
1 ½ cups natural bran
1 cup whole wheat flour
1 teaspoon baking soda
1/2 teaspoon salt

Lemon-Dipped Blueberry Muffins

1 ¾ cups all-purpose flour
1/2 cup granulated sugar
2 ½ teaspoons baking powder
1/2 teaspoon salt
1 egg, slightly beaten
3/4 cup milk
1/3 cup vegetable oil
1 cup fresh or frozen
    blueberries
2 tablespoons granulated sugar
2 teaspoons grated lemon rind

Topping:
2 tablespoons butter or
    margarine, melted
1/4 teaspoon lemon juice
sugar for dipping

Baking Powder Biscuits

2 cups sifted all-purpose flour
4 teaspoons baking powder
1/2 teaspoon salt
1/2 teaspoon cream of tartar
2 teaspoons granulated sugar
1/2 cup shortening
2/3 scant cup milk (add 1
   tablespoon if needed)

The secret to perfect biscuits lies not only in using exact measurements, but also in light handling. If you're not happy with your previous efforts (or even if you are), try this recipe for delicious hot biscuits served straight from the oven. Cut them larger and you'll have an excellent base for strawberry shortcake.

• Measure sifted flour, then sift again into large bowl with baking powder, salt, cream of tartar and sugar. This distributes baking powder evenly to prevent tiny freckles on biscuits.

• Add shortening and cut in with pastry blender or 2 knives until mixture resembles coarse crumbs.

• Make deep well in centre of crumb mixture and add milk all at once. Stir gently with fork until flour is dampened. Then stir vigorously just until dough follows fork around bowl. Overmixing will result in tough biscuits.

• Turn dough onto lightly floured surface and, handling as if made of fragile bubbles, knead with 15 to 20 gentle punches. The more delicate the touch, the lighter the biscuits will be.

• Gently pat dough to 1/2-inch thickness. Using straight up and down motion, cut into rounds with a 2 ½-inch cookie cutter. Be careful not to twist. Reroll scraps and cut more biscuits.

• Place on greased cookie sheet and bake at 400°F for 12 to 15 minutes. Makes about 10 biscuits.

Other variations:

Herb Biscuits: add 1/4 teaspoon each of powdered sage and thyme to dry ingredients.

Cheese Biscuits: add 1/2 cup of grated cheese.

Cinnamon Spirals: Roll out dough to 1/2-inch thickness, spread with a mixture of 2 tablespoons soft butter, 1/3 cup brown sugar, 1/2 teaspoon cinnamon and 1/3 cup currants or raisins. Roll as a jelly roll and cut into 3/4-inch slices.

My friend Marion has been turning out these scones for more than 30 years. By cutting them into diamond shapes, she saves herself the trouble of rerolling the dough. Although Marion prefers currants, raisins may also be used.

- Soak currants in enough cold water to cover until softened. Drain.

- In large bowl, sift together flour, baking powder, soda, sugar and salt. Cut in butter until mixture resembles coarse crumbs.

- Stir in drained currants. Add egg and sour cream and stir into flour mixture with a spatula just until dough gathers easily into a ball.

- Turn dough onto lightly floured surface. Handling lightly, knead 5 or 6 times with fingertips.

- Pat dough gently into a circle 1/2-inch thick. Cut into strips about 1 inches wide, then cut on an angle to form diamonds. Sprinkle lightly with sugar.

- Bake on ungreased cookie sheet at 400°F for 8 to 10 minutes or until lightly browned. Makes 18 to 20 scones.

Marion's Sour Cream Scones

1/4 cup currants
2 cups all-purpose flour
2 teaspoons baking powder
1/2 teaspoon baking soda
1/4 cup granulated sugar
1/2 teaspoon salt
1/3 cup butter
1 egg, beaten
3/4 cup sour cream
granulated sugar for sprinkling

Making a Yorkshire Pudding to serve with roast beef presents a challenge in getting everything to the table hot. With Laurie carving the roast as the pudding finished baking, we occasionally managed to pull it off.

- Have all ingredients at room temperature. In large mixer bowl, combine flour and salt. Gradually add milk, stirring constantly until smooth. Add beaten eggs. Add water and beat until batter is light and bubbly.

- Cover, and let stand at room temperature for at least 1 hour.

- In an 8 x 12-inch or 10-inch square pan, pour hot beef drippings to 1/4-inch deep. Put in a 425°F oven to get sizzling hot.

- Beat batter once more until bubbly, then pour into hot pan. Return to 425°F oven for 20 minutes. Reduce heat to 350°F and continue baking for 15 minutes longer, until pudding is puffed and browned. Cut in slices or squares and serve at once with roast beef.

Yorkshire Pudding

7/8 cup flour
1/2 teaspoon salt
1/2 cup milk
2 eggs, beaten
1/2 cup water
beef drippings

Cinnamon Buns

Sweet Bread Dough:
1 cup milk, scalded
1/2 cup shortening
1/3 cup granulated sugar
1/2 teaspoon salt
1 package active dry yeast
1/2 cup lukewarm water
1 teaspoon sugar
1 egg, beaten
4 to 4 ½ cups all-purpose flour

Filling:
1/2 cup raisins
2 tablespoons butter, melted
1/2 cup granulated sugar
1/2 cup firmly packed brown
    sugar
1 tablespoon ground cinnamon
1/3 cup chopped walnuts
    (optional)
melted butter

My mother made wonderful cinnamon buns. As a child, I loved to slather butter on every bite. These delicious buns are rich enough to eat as they are.

- Place scalded milk in large bowl and add shortening, 1/3 cup sugar and salt.

- Dissolve yeast in water with 1 teaspoon sugar according to package directions. Add dissolved yeast to milk mixture.

- Beat in egg. Add 2 cups flour and continue beating. Combine as much of remaining flour as needed to make a soft, not sticky dough.

- Turn dough onto lightly floured surface and knead for about 5 minutes. Form dough into a ball and place in greased bowl. Grease top of dough lightly. Cover with damp towel and let rise until doubled in bulk, about 1 ½ hours.

- Soak raisins in enough water to cover until softened. Drain.

- Punch down dough and turn onto lightly floured surface. Roll dough into a rectangle, about 23 x 14 inches.

- Brush with 2 tablespoons melted butter and then sprinkle with raisins.

- In small bowl, combine 1/2 cup granulated sugar, brown sugar, cinnamon and walnuts. Sprinkle over dough.

- Roll dough into a cylinder shape, starting with long edge. Press edges to seal and then roll so that join is on bottom.

- Using a sharp, wet knife, slice into 12 rolls. Arrange on greased 10 x 15-inch jelly roll pan, spacing slightly apart with cut side down.

- Cover with damp towel and let rise in warm place until doubled in bulk, about 30 to 45 minutes.

- Brush with melted butter. Bake at 350°F for 20 to 25 minutes or until browned. Remove from pan and cool on rack. Makes 1 dozen.

Bakery produced hot cross buns used to make a fleeting appearance several weeks before Easter and then were gone. Today, they're out sooner and last a little longer. But, bite for bite, these traditional Good Friday buns beat the bakery versions hands down. I cross my heart!

• Dissolve yeast in water according to package directions.

• Combine scalded milk, oil, sugar and salt in large bowl. Cool to lukewarm.

• Sift together 1 cup flour and cinnamon. Stir into milk mixture.

• Add eggs and beat well.

• Stir in dissolved yeast and currants.

• Add remaining flour or enough to make a soft dough, beating well.

• Cover with damp towel and let rise in bowl in warm place until doubled in bulk, about 1 ½ hours.

• Punch down dough and turn onto lightly floured surface. Cover and let rest for 10 minutes.

• Then roll or pat dough to 1/2-inch thickness and cut into rounds with a floured 2 ½-inch biscuit cutter. Shape buns so that tops are rounded and edges are tucked under.

• Placed on greased baking sheets about 1 ½ inches apart. Cover and let rise again in warm place until almost doubled in size, about 1 hour.

• If desired, snip shallow cross in each bun with sharp scissors or knife. Brush tops with egg white to glaze. Bake at 375°F for 15 minutes or until done. Cool on rack. Makes about 2 dozen.

Note: Buns may be piped with a cross of icing while still warm, if desired. Mix approximately 3/4 cup sifted icing sugar with egg white left from glaze or small amount of water. Spoon into piping bag fitted with small, round tip and make crosses.

Hot Cross Buns

2 packages active dry yeast
1/2 cup warm water
1/4 cup milk, scalded
1/2 cup vegetable oil or melted shortening
1/3 cup granulated sugar
1/2 teaspoon salt
3 ½ to 4 cups all-purpose flour
1/2 to 1 teaspoon ground cinnamon (to taste)
3 eggs, beaten
2/3 cup currants
egg white for glazing

Barb's Three-Hour Rolls

2 ½ cups milk or hot water
2 tablespoons butter
1 tablespoon granulated sugar
1 teaspoon salt
2 packages active dry yeast
1/4 cup lukewarm water
4 cups all-purpose flour (or
    more as required)
1 egg, beaten

It was a toss-up whether to include my sister Betty's overnight buns or my friend Barbara's three-hour rolls. Both are excellent choices. In the end, I opted for this recipe, from which rise years of warm family memories, as well as a wonderful batch of fine-textured rolls.

• Scald milk and pour into large bowl.

• Add butter, sugar and salt and stir to dissolve. Allow to cool to lukewarm.

• Dissolve yeast in warm water according to package directions. Add to lukewarm milk mixture.

• Add 2 cups flour and beat until smooth.

• Set in warm place to rise for 1 hour.

• Stir in beaten egg, then remaining flour. Mix well.

• Set to rise in warm place for another hour.

• Turn dough onto well-floured surface and knead well. Make into desired shapes. For round rolls, divide dough into pieces the size of small lemons and roll over work surface to form into balls. For oblong rolls, divide dough as above, roll into balls, then roll back and forth under fingers to form oblong shapes.

• Place well apart on greased baking sheets. Cover with damp cloth and set in warm place to rise for another hour.

• Bake at 400°F for 10 to 15 minutes or until lightly browned. Cool on rack. Makes about 2 dozen rolls.

My mother-in-law was a good cook. But when it came to Christmas cookies, she sometimes deferred to me.

"I can't make cookies—not like yours," she would say. So one day I determined to find out why this woman, so completely at home in the kitchen, claimed to be inefficient at such a simple task as baking cookies.

"OK, let's do it together," I said one day in her kitchen. "Where's your recipe?"

"What recipe? Who needs a recipe for making cookies?" she responded with not a little disdain.

The mixing went well enough, though I encouraged a little more creaming of the butter before adding the sugar—"And not so much sugar at a time! The dough will be too hard to manage, and it won't be properly mixed."

"Don't be so fussy," she countered. "I haven't got all day."

As she rolled the dough into uneven balls, and I started placing them about two inches apart on the cookie sheet, I ventured to no avail that, "The balls should be all the same size, for even cooking."

"Come on, you can get a lot more on the pan," she admonished moving the balls closer together.

I'm sure she didn't even hear my explanation that if she wanted a crisp, yet chewy, cookie, like the ones she always said she liked so much, you have to give them space. Otherwise, they'll join together as they spread, and the result will be soft and cake-like.

But there was still the job at hand, so I placed a filled cookie sheet on the centre rack of the oven and closed the door.

"What! Only one pan! We can get two pans on the top shelf if we overlap one of them slightly, like this, and at least one on the bottom. Then we can sit down and enjoy a cup of coffee," she said while maneuvering additional pans into the oven.

When the cookies came out, unevenly browned, some dark and crisp around the edges, others joined together without so much as a hint as to where one began and the other ended, she seemed a little surprised.

But not wanting to hurt my feelings, she gently said, "It must be my oven. It's been acting up lately. Come on, let's have a cup of coffee."

COOKIES

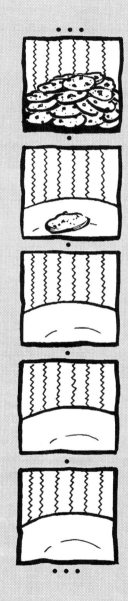

Peanut Butter Cookies

1 cup peanut butter
1/2 cup butter
1 cup packed brown sugar
1 cup granulated sugar
2 eggs, well beaten
2 cups sifted cake flour
2 teaspoons baking soda

Each of my sons had his own special cookie while growing up, although they did justice to them all. This was Gary's favourite. I consider it an everyday cookie but he insisted we also have a supply in the freezer for holiday munching.

- Cream peanut butter and butter together thoroughly in large bowl.

- Gradually add sugars, beating until light and fluffy.

- Add eggs and beat well.

- Combine flour and baking soda in separate bowl. Add to creamed mixture, stirring well.

- Roll into 1 ¼-inch balls. Place 2 inches apart on greased cookie sheets and press with fork in crisscross pattern.

- Bake at 375°F for about 12 minutes. Makes 5 to 6 dozen cookies.

Note: If substituting all-purpose flour, use 2 tablespoons less flour for each cup to allow for the greater firmness of all-purpose flour.

Forgotten Cookies

2 egg whites, at room
    temperature
1/8 teaspoon cream of tartar
1/8 teaspoon salt
3/4 cup granulated sugar
1/2 teaspoon vanilla
1 cup chocolate chips
1/4 cup chopped walnuts
    (optional)

Meringues of one kind or another have been around for years, but I can't remember when we started adding the chocolate chips. These have become a speciality of Laurie's sister, Phyllis.

- In small mixer bowl, beat egg whites with cream of tartar and salt until soft peaks form. Gradually add sugar and beat until stiff peaks form.

- Gently fold in vanilla, chocolate chips and walnuts if using.

- Drop by teaspoonfuls onto greased cookie sheets.

- Place in a 375°F oven, then immediately turn off oven. "Forget" cookies for at least 6 hours or overnight, without opening oven door.

- Store in airtight container. Makes about 30 cookies

My Grandmother Johnston's weekly baking sessions always included a batch of these old-fashioned cookies. After mixing the dough, Nanna would wrap it and store it in the icebox. The cookies turned up again during the 50s when we engaged a housekeeper to take care of the boys while Laurie and I took a holiday. She made them almost daily and passed them out to any child who came looking for them. No wonder the neighbourhood kids kept asking when we were going away again.

- Cream butter thoroughly in large bowl. Gradually add sugar and cream well.

- Add egg and vanilla and continue beating.

- Combine flour, baking soda and salt in separate bowl. Gradually add to creamed mixture and stir just until combined.

- Stir in nuts.

- On waxed paper, shape dough into rectangle about 1 ½ inches high by 2 ½ inches wide or into a roll 2 inches in diameter. Wrap and place in refrigerator to chill for several hours or until firm.

- Remove from fridge and slice 1/8-inch thick. Place cookies 1 inch apart on ungreased cookie sheet and bake at 350°F for 8 to 10 minutes. Remove and cool on rack. Makes 4 to 5 dozen cookies.

Here's another treat that Pearl, the housekeeper, made for the boys during our absences. Frank liked them so much he asked for the recipe.

- Combine rolled oats, coconut, nuts, cocoa, salt and vanilla in large bowl.

- In a saucepan, combine sugar, milk and shortening. Bring to a boil. Pour over rolled oats mixture.

- Working quickly while mixture is warm, drop by teaspoonfuls onto cookie sheets lined with waxed paper. Let cool. Makes 4 dozen cookies.

Icebox Cookies

1/2 cup butter
1 cup brown sugar
1 egg
1 teaspoon vanilla
1 ¾ cups all-purpose flour
1/2 teaspoon baking soda
1/2 teaspoon salt
1/2 cup chopped nuts

Uncooked Chocolate Cookies

2 ½ cups rolled oats
1 cup coconut
1/2 cup chopped nuts
6 tablespoons cocoa powder
1/2 teaspoon salt
1 teaspoon vanilla
2 cups granulated sugar
1/2 cup milk
1/2 cup shortening

Snickerdoodles

1 cup butter or margarine
1 ½ cups granulated sugar
2 eggs
2 ¾ cups all-purpose flour
2 teaspoons cream of tartar
1 teaspoon baking soda
1/2 teaspoon salt

Topping:
2 tablespoons granulated sugar
1 teaspoon cinnamon

Perhaps more than any other cookie, snickerdoodles heralded the Christmas season for us. They were almost as important as the cookie house which was brought down from the attic every Christmas for 14 years. There were real tears, even from my 12-year-old, when the old house finally went out with the garbage. However, the snickerdoodles remain.

• Thoroughly cream butter in large bowl. Gradually add sugar and cream well.

• Add eggs, beating well.

• In separate bowl, combine flour, cream of tartar, baking soda and salt. Add to creamed mixture and stir until blended.

• Turn dough onto large piece of waxed paper. Wrap and place in refrigerator to chill for about an hour.

• Combine sugar and cinnamon.

• Remove dough from fridge and roll into 1-inch balls. Roll balls in cinnamon sugar. Place on ungreased cookie sheets 2 inches apart.

• Bake at 400°F for 8 to 10 minutes or until lightly browned but still soft. Cookies will puff at first, then flatten out with crinkled tops. Makes about 5 dozen cookies.

Browned-Eyed Susans

1 cup butter or margarine
3 tablespoons granulated sugar
1 teaspoon almond extract
2 cups all-purpose flour
1/2 teaspoon salt

Frosting:
1 cup sifted icing sugar
2 tablespoons cocoa
2 tablespoons hot water
1/2 teaspoon vanilla
almond halves

Another "keeper" from the past, these delicious cookies were first made by my husband's Aunt Mame.

• Thoroughly cream butter in large bowl. Gradually add sugar and cream well. Add almond extract.

• Combine flour and salt in separate bowl.

• Gradually add to creamed mixture.

• Form level tablespoons of dough into balls. Place on greased cookie sheets and flatten slightly.

• Bake at 375°F for 10 to 12 minutes. Cool.

• Combine sugar and cocoa in small bowl. Add water and vanilla and stir. Frost each cookie with 1/2 teaspoon of frosting and top with almond. Makes 3 dozen cookies.

This recipe, which I haven't come across in recipe books or magazines in years, was probably created by the Kellogg's test kitchen when the cereal first appeared on the market. It may be free advertising, but Special K does make a nice cookie.

Special K Cookies

1 cup all-purpose flour
1/2 teaspoon baking soda
1/2 teaspoon salt
1/2 cup soft butter or margarine
2/3 cup granulated sugar
1 egg
1 teaspoon vanilla
3 cups Special K cereal

• Combine flour, baking soda and salt in small bowl. Set aside.

• In large bowl, thoroughly cream butter. Gradually add sugar and beat until fluffy.

• Add egg and vanilla, beating well.

• Stir in dry ingredients, then 1 cup cereal.

• Drop dough by teaspoonfuls into remaining cereal and roll to coat. Place 2 inches apart on ungreased cookie sheets.

• Bake at 350°F for 10 minutes or until lightly browned. Makes approximately 40 cookies.

These cookies, which have no peanut butter in them, were favourites of the men in Laurie's bridge club during our early years of marriage. Although they were avid card players, the men seemed more disappointed if the cookies were not served than if they had bad cards.

Peanut Cookies

1/2 cup shortening
1/2 cup brown sugar
1/2 cup granulated sugar
1 egg, well beaten
1 teaspoon vanilla
1 cup all-purpose flour
1/2 teaspoon baking soda
1/2 teaspoon salt
1 cup rolled oats
1 cup salted peanuts

• In large bowl, thoroughly cream shortening. Gradually add sugars and continue beating.

• Add egg and vanilla and cream well.

• In separate bowl, combine flour, baking soda and salt. Add to creamed mixture.

• Stir in oats and peanuts.

• Roll into 1-inch balls and place 2 inches apart on lightly greased cookie sheets. Flatten with fork.

• Bake at 375°F for 10 to 12 minutes or until golden brown. Makes about 4 dozen cookies.

Neapolitans

Dark Dough:
3 cups all-purpose flour
1/4 teaspoon salt
1 teaspoon baking soda
1/2 teaspoon ground cinnamon
1/2 teaspoon ground cloves
1 cup shortening, softened
1 ½ cups packed brown sugar
2 eggs
1 cup coarsely chopped nuts
1 cup well-chilled, finely
   ground chocolate chips

Light Dough:
2 cups all-purpose flour
1/2 teaspoon salt
1/4 teaspoon baking soda
1/2 cup shortening, softened
3/4 cup granulated sugar
1 egg
1 teaspoon vanilla
1/2 teaspoon almond extract
2 tablespoons water
3/4 cup finely chopped sultana
   raisins
12 candied cherries, snipped

Here's another once-a-year cookie that I used to make for Christmas. It was my son Bob's favourite, perhaps because it looked like three cookies in one, and he always liked to get his penny's worth. Although the ingredient list makes these neapolitans look difficult, they aren't. The end product is dozens of delicious cookies which freeze beautifully.

- For **dark dough**, sift together flour, salt, baking soda, cinnamon and cloves.

- Thoroughly cream shortening and sugar in separate bowl.

- Add eggs, beating until very light and fluffy.

- Stir in flour mixture, then nuts and chocolate. Set aside.

- For **light dough**, sift together flour, salt and baking soda.

- Thoroughly cream shortening and sugar in separate bowl.

- Add egg, vanilla, almond extract and water, beating until very light and fluffy.

- Stir in flour mixture, then raisins and cherries.

- Line a 10 x 5-inch loaf pan with waxed paper. Press half of dark dough into loaf pan, then all of light dough, then remaining dark dough. Refrigerate for 24 hours.

- At baking time, cut dough lengthwise into thirds. Slice crosswise into 1/4-inch slices. Place 1 inch apart on cold, ungreased cookie sheets.

- Bake at 400°F for 8 to 10 minutes. Makes 8 to 9 dozen cookies.

These Chinese almond cookies are near the top of my list of favourites. I also like the fact that they keep well.

- In small bowl, sift together flour, sugar, salt and baking powder. Set aside.

- In large bowl, thoroughly cream shortening and egg. Mix in 2 tablespoons water and almond extract.

- Gradually add flour mixture, stirring with fork until mixture draws away from sides of bowl.

- Knead to blend. Refrigerate dough until chilled.

- Form dough into 1-inch balls. Using palms of hands, flatten each to 1/4-inch thickness. Place 1/2-inch apart on greased cookie sheets. Press almond into each cookie.

- Beat together egg yolk and 1 tablespoon water and brush tops of cookies with mixture.

- Bake at 350°F for 25 minutes or until golden. Makes 3 dozen cookies.

My Nanna Johnston made these, my favourite cookies, every week when I was growing up. I continued the tradition, and love to serve them with ice cream. Sometimes, I dip one end of the cookies into melted chocolate and think of them as mock Florentines.

- Combine butter and sugar; pour over rolled oats in large bowl. Let stand overnight or several hours to allow oats to absorb butter mixture.

- Next morning, add salt, flour, egg and vanilla, stirring well.

- Drop by level teaspoonfuls two inches apart on well-greased cookie sheets (bake only 12 cookies on a sheet—they spread).

- Bake at 350°F for 10 to 12 minutes, or until edges are slightly browned. Leave on cookie sheet for one or two minutes until firm, then remove quickly with a spatula. Cool on wire racks. Makes 6 dozen cookies.

Hang Yen Bang

2 ½ cups all-purpose flour
3/4 cup granulated sugar
1/4 teaspoon salt
1 teaspoon baking powder
3/4 cup shortening, softened
1 egg
2 tablespoons water
1 teaspoon almond extract

Topping:
1/3 cup blanched almonds
1 egg yolk
1 tablespoon water

Lace Cookies

1 cup butter or margarine,
  melted
1 ½ cups packed brown sugar
2 ¼ cups quick-cooking rolled
  oats
1/2 teaspoon salt
3 tablespoons all-purpose flour
1 egg, slightly beaten
1 teaspoon vanilla

Big Batch Chocolate Chip Cookies

2/3 cup shortening, softened
2/3 cup butter or margarine, softened
1 cup granulated sugar
1 cup packed brown sugar
2 eggs
2 teaspoons vanilla
3 cups all-purpose flour
1 teaspoon baking soda
1/2 teaspoon salt
1 cup chopped nuts (optional)
2 cups semisweet chocolate morsels

Since Ruth Wakefield of the Toll House Inn near Boston accidently invented the chocolate chip cookie, in 1930, it has become one of North America's most popular cookies. Everybody has their favourite recipe—some like them crispy, others chewy. My family liked them in quantity.

• In large mixing bowl, thoroughly cream shortening and butter.

• Gradually add sugars, beating well.

• Add eggs and vanilla and beat until creamy.

• Combine dry ingredients. Add to creamed mixture. Stir in nuts and chocolate chips.

• Drop dough by rounded teaspoonfuls, about two inches apart, on ungreased cookie sheets.

• Bake at 350°F for 10 to 12 minutes until lightly browned. Cool slightly before moving from cookie sheets. Makes 7 dozen cookies.

Molasses Crinkles

5 cups all-purpose flour
1/2 teaspoon salt
4 teaspoons baking soda
1 teaspoon ground cloves
2 teaspoons ground cinnamon
2 teaspoons ground ginger
1 ½ cups butter or margarine
2 cups packed brown sugar
2 eggs
1/2 cup molasses
granulated sugar

These molasses crinkles are another of my old, personal favourites. I like the crispness of the cookie and the flavour of the ginger.

• In small bowl, sift together flour, salt, baking soda, cloves, cinnamon and ginger. Set aside.

• Cream butter and brown sugar in separate bowl until light and fluffy. Add eggs and molasses and beat thoroughly.

• Carefully mix dry ingredients into the creamed mixture.

• Chill dough for at least an hour.

• Shape dough into 1-inch balls. Dip top of each ball into granulated sugar. Place on lightly greased cookie sheets, sugared side up. Press top of each ball with thumb to make small indentation. Drop 2 or 3 drops of water into the indentation.

• Bake at 375°F for 12 to 15 minutes. Makes about 5 dozen cookies.

This is probably the first shortbread I ever made. Although some cooks may not consider it a true shortbread, this cookie has melt-in-the-mouth quality and is very easy to make.

Shortbread Cookies

1/2 cup cornstarch
1/2 cup icing sugar
1 cup all-purpose flour
1 cup butter, at room
    temperature

- In large bowl, sift together cornstarch, icing sugar and flour.

- With wooden spoon, blend butter into dry ingredients until soft dough is formed. If dough is very soft, wrap and chill for 30 minutes.

- Shape into 1-inch balls and place 1 ½ inches apart on ungreased cookie sheets. Flatten cookies with floured fork.

- Bake at 300°F for 20 to 25 minutes or until edges of cookies are lightly browned. Makes about 2 dozen cookies.

Since I happen to be very fond of shortbread, especially during the holiday season, I have turned to this simple recipe. I make two pans at a time to share the oven heat. Use fruit sugar for a finer texture, if it is available.

Scottish Shortbread

1 cup butter, softened
1/2 cup granulated sugar (or
    fruit sugar)
2 cups all-purpose flour
granulated sugar for topping

- In large bowl, thoroughly cream butter and 1/2 cup sugar until light and fluffy.

- Add flour, stirring just until blended.

- Press firmly into an ungreased 8 or 9-inch square pan. Prick through in several places with floured fork. Lightly sprinkle sugar over top.

- Bake at 250°F for 1 ½ hours. Turn off oven and let pans remain in oven until completely cool. Cut in oblong shapes and store in airtight container. Makes 24 pieces.

Holiday Apricot Balls

8 ounces (250 g) dried apricots
2 ½ cups flaked coconut
3/4 cup sweetened condensed milk
1 cup finely chopped nuts

In our house, these no-cook treats turn up at holidays, weddings, parties or whenever there's an excuse to celebrate. They add colour and variety to a plateful of sweets and are rich enough to be served as confection in a candy dish. Although they may be stored uncovered at room temperature for 3 or 4 days, I often make them ahead and freeze them in plastic bags.

• Finely cut apricots with scissors.

• In small bowl, blend apricots with coconut and condensed milk.

• Shape into small bowls and roll in chopped nuts. Let stand 2 hours to firm. Makes 4 to 5 dozen balls.

Candy Cane Cookies

1/2 cup butter, softened
1/2 cup shortening, softened
1 cup sifted icing sugar
1 egg
1 teaspoon almond extract
1 teaspoon vanilla
2 ½ cups all-purpose flour
1 teaspoon salt
1/2 teaspoon red food colouring
1/2 cup crushed peppermint candy
1/2 cup granulated sugar

As the holidays approached, worried voices would ask "Have you made the candy cane cookies yet?" Often the last to be made, these were the first to disappear from the cookie tins. Bless you, Betty Crocker, for bringing such joy to our Christmases.

• Thoroughly cream butter and shortening in large bowl. Gradually add sugar and cream well. Add egg, almond and vanilla. Beat well.

• Combine flour and salt. Add to creamed mixture and stir until blended.

• Divide dough into equal halves. Blend food colouring into one half.

• Roll 1 teaspoonful of each colour dough into separate strips, about 4 inches long. Place strips side by side, press lightly together, and twist like a rope.

• Place on ungreased cookie sheet. Curve top down to form a cane. Bake at 375°F about 9 minutes or until lightly browned. Remove to wire racks and while still warm, sprinkle with mixture of peppermint candy and 1/2 cup of sugar. Makes about 4 dozen cookies.

W hile cookies, cakes, sweet breads and coffee cakes figured prominently in the baked goods that were regularly turned out of home ovens during the 1950s and 60s, we now come to the serious side of baking. Squares. These ever-so-sweet little cakes were the heart and soul of women's gatherings, held either in the afternoon or evening.

It was the squares by which a woman's baking prowess was measured. She was forever trying to find a new variety which would garner compliments from her friends—the same friends who would insist that they just *had* to have that recipe. However, once the recipe was shared the search would begin again for another new treat.

Some of these recipes circulated so thoroughly that the original sources became obscure.

Although I am *sure* that my sister-in-law Thalia was the source of the Beef Stroganoff recipe which I've used for years (and which appears in the meat chapter), she thought I had given it to her. There is also controversy between us as to who gave the other the recipe for Indian Curried Shrimp (see the fish chapter). I thought she gave it to me.

Such was the way of the recipe exchange. The search for new ideas was so keen that one might forget its origin. And here I am, 30 to 40 years later, trying to remember what I might not have remembered at the time. Even with those sources I feel certain about, I wouldn't want to stake my life on any of them.

I think I'm safe in saying, however, that most of the "new" recipes that circulated during this period, came from magazine ads. Home economists were paid by food companies to develop recipes that would sell their products. Among these were graham wafers, coconut, chocolate chips, sweetened condensed milk, maraschino cherries, cocoa and walnuts. Chalk it up to good marketing.

But taste has a way of returning to its roots. Take date squares, for instance. Our grandmothers made these sweet treats when we were young, as did our mothers. But, as surely as clothes fashions went out of style, so did foods. The date squares were put aside, as we constantly searched for the "new." Now, we want them again. Not only for the taste, but the memories that the taste invokes.

SQUARES

Cheese Squares

Base and Topping:
4 cups cornflakes
1/2 cup butter, melted
1 cup packed brown sugar
1 cup all-purpose flour
1 teaspoon baking soda

Filling:
2 (8 ounces/250 g each)
    packages cream cheese
1/2 cup sugar
4 tablespoons flour
1/2 cup milk
2 eggs, separated
1 teaspoon vanilla

I never served these squares that someone didn't ask for the recipe. A forerunner of the popular cheesecake, it's best to cut them small to make an attractive addition to a tray of sweets.

• Prepare **base and topping mixture**: roll cornflakes to fine crumbs. Combine with melted butter, brown sugar, flour and baking soda.

• Press 2/3 of mixture into a 9-inch square pan. Set remaining mixture aside.

• Prepare **filling**: in large bowl of electric mixer, thoroughly cream the cream cheese. Gradually add sugar, blending well.

• Stir in flour.

• Slowly add milk, then add beaten egg yolks and vanilla.

• Fold in beaten egg whites.

• Spread over base in pan. Sprinkle remaining crumb mixture over filling.

• Bake at 350°F for 30 minutes, or until set.

No-bake Mocha Dreams

1 cup graham wafer crumbs,
    divided
1/3 cup butter
1 ½ cups sifted icing sugar
1 tablespoon instant coffee
2 eggs
2 ounces (60 g) unsweetened
    chocolate
1/2 cup chopped nuts

It's convenient to make these delicious squares the night before they're needed. Or, if you're an early riser, whip them up in the morning before leaving for work. With no baking required, they'll be ready to serve when you get home.

• Sprinkle 1/4 cup graham wafer crumbs on bottom of 8-inch square pan.

• Thoroughly cream butter. Combine icing sugar and coffee; add a little at a time to creamed butter, blending well.

• Add eggs, one at a time, beating thoroughly.

• Melt chocolate over hot water; cool slightly and add to mixture.

• Stir in nuts and 1/2 cup graham wafer crumbs.

• Spread over crumbs in pan; sprinkle with remaining 1/4 cup crumbs. Chill, preferably overnight. Cut into squares.

These squares were around in the 1940s and are still in demand today. They have been called rich coconut squares, condensed milk squares, chocolate graham wafer squares, delicious squares and Breton squares, which I think gives them the touch of class they deserve.

• To make **base**, combine wafers, butter and sugar until crumbly. Press into greased 8-inch square pan.

• Bake at 325°F for 15 to 20 minutes or until set. Cool.

• For **topping**, stir together condensed milk, coconut and vanilla and spread over cooled base.

• Bake at 325°F for about 25 minutes, watching carefully towards end so as not to overcook. Squares should be golden brown about 1/2 inch around the edge. Top with chocolate icing and cut into 25 squares.

Variation: Add 1/2 cup chopped, drained maraschino cherries to topping and replace vanilla with almond extract.

Breton Squares

Base:
22 graham wafers, crushed
1/2 cup butter
2 tablespoons brown sugar

Topping:
1 can (300 mL) sweetened
    condensed milk
2 cups desiccated coconut
1/2 teaspoon vanilla
chocolate icing (see following
    recipe)

• Cream butter in small bowl.

• Sift together icing sugar and cocoa, and gradually add to butter.

• Add milk gradually, using just enough to make a spreading consistency.

• Stir in vanilla.

Chocolate Icing

3 tablespoons butter or
    margarine
2 cups sifted icing sugar
1/4 cup cocoa
3 tablespoons milk
1/2 teaspoon vanilla

Turn stale bread into a delectable treat.

• Remove crust from bread slices. Cut into inch-wide strips. • Dip in sweetened condensed milk and then in shredded coconut. • Place on a cookie sheet and bake at 400°F until golden brown.

Coconut Fingers

Peanut Butter Nanaimo Bars

Base:
1/3 cup chocolate chips, melted
    and cooled
1/2 cup butter, softened
2 tablespoons cocoa
2 tablespoons sugar
1 teaspoon vanilla
1 egg
2 cups graham wafer crumbs
1 cup desiccated coconut
1/2 cup chopped nuts

Filling:
2 tablespoons butter, softened
2 tablespoons peanut butter
3 tablespoons milk
2 tablespoons custard powder
2 cups icing sugar

Glaze:
2/3 cup chocolate chips
1 tablespoon butter

Nobody knows why these are called Nanaimo Bars. Many a food writer has attempted to find the origin, but came up wanting. One thing for sure, it's a great Canadian favourite. In the U.S. they've even been called Canadian squares. So raise the flag and serve them on Canada Day. I like the addition of peanut butter in this version.

• Prepare **base**: combine chocolate, butter, cocoa, sugar, vanilla, and egg; mix well. Add crumbs, coconut and nuts. Mix well. Press into a 9-inch square pan. Chill.

• Prepare **filling**: combine butter, peanut butter, milk and custard powder. Blend in icing sugar. Spread over base. Chill for 15 minutes.

• Prepare **glaze**: partially melt chocolate with butter over hot water. Remove from heat; stir until completely melted. Spread over custard layer. Chill; store in refrigerator.

Mocha Cakes

1 hot milk cake or small bakery
    pound cake cut into small
    cubes (no more than
    1-inch)
1 cup icing sugar
small amount of strong coffee
1/4 teaspoon vanilla
chopped peanuts

Many a Moir's pound cake became the base for these popular little cakes. Moirs is gone now, and we don't see as many mocha cakes. But the memory lingers on.

• Combine icing sugar with enough coffee to make a thin icing. Stir in vanilla.

• Dip cubes in icing mixture to coat all sides. Let excess icing drip off, then roll coated cubes in chopped peanuts. Set on wire racks to dry.

A taste of lemon ranks high on the list of comfort foods, whether in the form of a sugar-topped loaf, a saucy pudding, a meringue pie or one of the many lemon-flavoured squares that were so popular at the time. This was one of my favourite lemon treats.

- For **crust**, combine graham wafers, 1/2 cup sugar and 1/2 cup butter and mix until crumbly.

- Reserve 1/2 cup for topping. Pat remaining mixture into ungreased 9-inch square pan and bake at 350°F for 10 minutes.

- To make **filling**, combine egg yolks, 1/2 cup sugar, cornstarch, 1 tablespoon water, lemon juice and rind and 1 tablespoon butter in top of double boiler. Cook over hot water until thick, stirring frequently.

- Beat egg whites with 2 teaspoons cold water until stiff. Fold into hot lemon mixture.

- Spread over baked crust and sprinkle with reserved crumb mixture.

- Bake at 350°F for 10 to 15 minutes, until set and delicately browned. Cut into 36 squares.

Lemon Graham Squares

Crust:
18 graham wafers, rolled into
   fine crumbs
1/2 cup granulated sugar
1/2 cup butter, softened

Filling:
3 eggs, separated
1/2 cup granulated sugar
1 ½ tablespoons cornstarch
1 tablespoon water
juice and rind of 1 lemon
1 tablespoon butter
2 teaspoons cold water

These little no-bake treats had a long run during the 1950s and 60s, adding colour and a different shape to afternoon and after-meeting sweet trays.

- Combine butter, icing sugar, coconut and almond extract, mixing well.

- Using about 1 teaspoon of the mixture for each, form into balls. Make a hole in the centre of each ball and insert a cherry, working mixture around it to cover completely. Roll in graham wafer crumbs. Store in refrigerator. Makes approximately 30 balls.

Cherry Balls

1/2 cup butter, softened
1 ½ cups sifted icing sugar
1 ½ cups desiccated coconut
1/2 teaspoon almond extract
approximately 30 maraschino
   cherries, well drained
graham wafer crumbs

Fudge Squares

1/4 cup butter
1 cup packed brown sugar
1 egg
1 cup all-purpose flour
1 teaspoon baking powder
1/4 teaspoon salt
1/2 cup chopped walnuts
1/2 teaspoon vanilla

Icing:
1 ½ cups packed brown sugar
1/2 cup milk
pinch of cream of tartar
2 tablespoons butter
1/2 teaspoon vanilla

These are every bit as decadent as fudge. In fact, the icing is fudge and should never be attempted on a rainy or humid day when the dampness tends to crystallize the sugar and makes it hard to manage.

• In saucepan, melt 1/4 cup butter and 1 cup brown sugar together. Remove from heat.

• Stir in egg.

• Combine flour, baking powder and salt and stir into mixture along with walnuts and 1/2 teaspoon vanilla.

• Spread into greased 8-inch square pan and bake at 350°F for 15 to 20 minutes.

• To make **icing**, cook 1 ½ cups brown sugar, milk, cream of tartar and 2 tablespoons butter in heavy-bottomed saucepan until soft ball stage is reached (285°F on candy thermometer). Remove from heat and cool. To hasten the cooling, place the pan containing mixture in cold water in the sink.

• Add 1/2 teaspoon vanilla. Beat until mixture is creamy and begins to lose its gloss.

• Pour over cooled squares in pan, spreading evenly. Cut into 25 squares while still warm.

Easy Pecan Squares

For the easiest sweet treat you'll ever need, line a 10 x 15-inch jelly roll pan with graham wafers.

• Boil together, for 1 minute, one cup each of butter, brown sugar and chopped pecans. • Pour evenly over wafers and bake in a 350°F over for 8 minutes.
• While still warm, cut between wafers. Remove immediately to cool on wire racks. Voila! Little pecan pies.

These oh-so-rich squares were relegated long ago to my file on the way things were. I include them here in memory of my dear friend Barbara, who loved them so.

- For **base**, mix 1/2 cup butter, icing sugar and flour until crumbly. Pat into greased 8-inch square pan. Bake at 350°F for 15 minutes. Cool.

- To make **filling**, cream 1/2 cup butter and granulated sugar in small mixing bowl. Beat in chocolate and vanilla.

- Add eggs, one at a time, beating until fluffy (about 10 minutes).

- Spread evenly over cooled base. Place in refrigerator for 30 minutes to set.

- For **topping**, whip cream and sweeten with a teaspoon of sugar and 1/4 teaspoon vanilla.

- Spread a thin layer over squares. Cut into 25 squares and store in refrigerator.

Chocolate Whipped Cream Squares

Base:
1/2 cup butter
2 tablespoons icing sugar
1 cup all-purpose flour

Filling:
1/2 cup butter
2/3 cup granulated sugar
2 squares unsweetened chocolate, melted
1 teaspoon vanilla
2 eggs

Topping:
1/2 cup whipping cream
1 teaspoon granulated sugar
1/4 teaspoon vanilla

What! Not include the recipe that shook a continent and has been bringing sticky smiles to millions for more than 40 years! I would never be forgiven.

- Melt butter in large saucepan. Add marshmallows and cook over low heat, stirring constantly, until marshmallows are melted and mixture is well blended.

- Remove from heat and stir in vanilla.

- Add Rice Krispies and stir to coat well.

- While warm, press mixture into a lightly buttered 9 x 13-inch pan. When cool, cut into 2 dozen 2-inch squares.

Rice Krispie Squares

1/4 cup butter
4 cups miniature marshmallows (or 40 regular, cut up)
1/4 teaspoon vanilla
5 cups Rice Krispies cereal

Pineapple Squares

Base:
2 ½ cups vanilla wafer crumbs
1/2 cup butter, melted

Filling:
1/2 cup butter, at room
    temperature
1 ¼ cups icing sugar
1 egg
1 can (19 ounces/540 mL)
    crushed pineapple
1 cup whipping cream

In the early 1950s, no sweet tray was complete without one or more varieties of pineapple squares that were then going the rounds. Some versions were baked but the favourite was spread over a baked base and chilled. Could there be a food more comforting than this one?

- Reserve 1/4 cup wafer crumbs for topping. Combine remaining crumbs with 1/2 cup melted butter and press into 9-inch square pan.

- Bake at 325°F for 12 to 15 minutes. Cool.

- For **filling**, cream 1/2 cup butter and icing sugar.

- Add unbeaten egg and beat lightly.

- Spread over vanilla wafer mixture. Chill well.

- Drain pineapple. Beat whipping cream until stiff and fold in pineapple.

- Spread over squares and sprinkle with the reserved wafer crumbs. Chill for several hours before serving. Makes 36 squares.

Date Squares

Filling:
2 cups pitted, cut-up dates
3/4 cup water
1/2 cup granulated sugar
1 tablespoon lemon juice

Base and Topping:
1 ½ cups all-purpose flour
1/2 teaspoon baking soda
1 ½ cups quick-cooking rolled
    oats
1 cup firmly packed brown
    sugar
1/2 cup butter or margarine

Is it because some dates lead to matrimony that caused these old favourites to be called matrimonial squares? Or was it simply because they were always served at weddings?

- In a saucepan, combine dates, water, granulated sugar, and lemon juice. Bring to a boil, reduce heat, and simmer until dates are soft and mixture is thickened. Set aside to cool.

- In large bowl, combine flour and baking soda. Stir in rolled oats and brown sugar until well blended.

- Cut in butter, rubbing between fingers until mixture resembles coarse crumbs.

- Pack half of mixture into greased 9-inch square pan. Cover with date filling, then remaining topping, gently pressing mixture evenly into place.

- Bake at 350°F for 30 minutes or until top is golden brown. Cool and cut into 36 squares.

In the land where big pumpkins grow, this recipe should be in everyone's files for the harvest season. It makes a lot of bars—serve some now and put the rest in the freezer. My husband likes them so much that he eats them from the freezer without even waiting for them to thaw. He says the frozen bars taste like pumpkin ice cream.

- In large bowl, beat together eggs, sugar and oil until lemon coloured. Blend in pumpkin.

- Combine flour, baking soda, cinnamon and salt.

- Add to pumpkin mixture, a little at a time, beating well after each addition.

- Pour into greased and floured 10 x 15-inch jelly roll pan and bake at 350°F for 25 to 30 minutes or until done. Cool.

- To make **icing**, thoroughly blend cream cheese and margarine. Stir in vanilla.

- Add icing sugar, a little at a time, beating well until mixture is smooth.

- Spread over bars and cut. Store in refrigerator or freezer. Makes 4 dozen squares.

Pumpkin Bars

4 eggs
1 ⅔ cups granulated sugar
1 scant cup oil
2 cups mashed, cooked
    pumpkin
2 cups all-purpose flour
2 teaspoons baking soda
1 teaspoon ground cinnamon
3/4 teaspoon salt

Icing:
1 package (4 ounces/125 g)
    cream cheese, softened
4 tablespoons margarine,
    softened
1 teaspoon vanilla
1 ½ cups sifted icing sugar

So easy to make, these squares taste almost like candy. This is an easy way to get kids to eat their oats.

- Combine oats, baking powder, salt and brown sugar and mix well.

- Add margarine and vanilla. Blend thoroughly.

- Spread into ungreased 8-inch square pan, pressing down slightly.

- Bake at 300°F for approximately 25 minutes or until golden brown. Let stand 5 minutes before cutting into squares. Makes 25 squares.

Variation: Drizzle with melted semi-sweet chocolate before cutting into squares.

Butterscotch Oat Squares

2 cups rolled oats
1 teaspoon baking powder
1/8 teaspoon salt
1 cup packed brown sugar
1/2 cup margarine, melted
1/2 teaspoon vanilla

Napoleons

graham wafers
1 package (6 ounces/170 g)
    vanilla pudding mix
milk
1 cup whipping cream
1 tablespoon granulated sugar
1 teaspoon vanilla

Glaze
2 cups sifted icing sugar
4 tablespoons hot milk
1/2 teaspoon vanilla
1/2 square unsweetened
    chocolate

Why pay the price for bakery Napoleons when it's so easy to make these delicious imposters?

• Line bottom of an 8 X 12-inch pan with whole graham wafers.

• Cook pudding mix according to package directions, using whole milk. Let partially cook and spread over wafers.

• Whip cream with 1 tablespoon sugar and 1 teaspoon vanilla. Spread over pudding. Place layer of whole graham wafers on top.

• Make **glaze** by combining icing sugar, hot milk and 1/2 teaspoon vanilla. Pour over wafers.

• Melt chocolate. Dip point of knife in chocolate and draw criss-cross lines about 2 inches apart on glazed surface. Draw knife diagonally each way through lines.

• Chill well (3-4 hours) before serving. Store in refrigerator. Makes 15 Napoleans.

Chocolate Arrowroot Squares

1 cup butter or margarine
4 tablespoons granulated sugar
4 tablespoons cocoa powder
2 eggs, beaten
30 Arrowroot biscuits
1/2 cup chopped walnuts
1 teaspoon vanilla
chocolate icing (see recipe
    page 133)

With Arrowroot biscuits always on hand for babies to nibble, young mothers treasured this no-cook recipe.

• In top of a double boiler, melt butter, sugar and cocoa together. Add eggs, and stirring constantly, cook until mixture is of custard consistency.

• Remove from heat. Break each biscuit into 8 or 10 pieces. Add to mixture, along with nuts. Stir in vanilla.

• Press into an 8-inch square pan. Spread with icing. Store in refrigerator at least 24 hours before cutting. Makes 25 squares.

I don't remember the first cake I ever made—not what it was nor its success or failure. But I do know that early cake mixes found little space in my cupboard. I tried them but, like the packaged pancake mix, they just didn't work for me.

Although many cakes have been tried over the years, there are a few favourites which have stayed on as "keepers."

Pound cake is one of these. While I've tried several versions, including everything from yogurt to 7-Up, the one that outlasts them all was a first prize winner at a county fair in North Carolina.

The recipe, belonging to a Mrs. Oscar McCollum of Rockingham County, N.C., turned up in a *New York Times* cookbook, published during the 1970s.

There were also, over the years, many attempts to find "the perfect" fruitcake. Although my family have other preferences, I maintain that dark fruitcake should make appearances during the Christmas holidays and at weddings. One of my early favourites was a recipe from *McCall's* magazine which achieved fame many years ago. Another was one preferred by a friend, Lorna Berringer, now deceased, who was an excellent cook.

It wasn't until 1987, when I stumbled upon a recipe in *Southern Living* magazine, that my search was finally ended. Marty Aronowitz of Fort Worth, Texas, had been making this fruit cake for 34 years, giving them to friends and to church auctions, where enthusiastic bidders had gone as high as $175.

When I ran the recipe on the food pages of *The Chronicle-Herald* and *The Mail-Star* I received several calls from readers asking if there had been an error. "There's no fat—no butter, shortening, or oil," they pointed out.

That's right, the recipe contains no fat—only fruit and nuts held together with a minimum of batter. It's an excellent fruitcake.

But fruitcake isn't the family favourite. For them, the holiday season means cherry cake—the same cake that Mildred Byrne has been turning out so successfully for years. The problem for me is that Gary and Bob still expect a cherry cake from home to brighten their holidays in Calgary and Edmonton. It isn't making the cake that I mind—it's the $20 postage.

CAKES

Pecan Fruitcake

1 pound (500 g) pitted dates, chopped
1 pound (500 g) pecans, chopped
1/4 pound (125 g) red candied cherries, chopped
1/4 pound (125 g) green candied cherries, chopped
1/2 pound (250 g) sliced candied pineapple, chopped
1 cup granulated sugar
1 cup all-purpose flour
2 teaspoons baking powder
1 teaspoon ground nutmeg
1/2 teaspoon salt
4 eggs, beaten
1 teaspoon vanilla

When is a fruitcake not a cake? This recipe is 3 pounds of fruit and nuts held together with a little batter. Now that's a FRUIT cake.

• Combine dates, pecans, cherries and pineapple in large mixing bowl. Set aside.

• Combine sugar, flour, baking powder, nutmeg and salt. Add to fruit mixture and stir well.

• Stir in eggs and vanilla.

• Grease an 8 x 8 x 3-inch square pan and line with brown paper. Spoon batter into pan and bake at 250°F for 2 ½ hours or until tester inserted in centre comes out clean. Cool cake completely in pan. Remove from pan and peel off brown paper.

Note: Cake may also be baked in two 8-inch loaf pans for approximately 1 hour and 20 minutes.

Mildred's Cherry Cake

1 ½ cups butter
2 cups granulated sugar
6 eggs
4 cups drained and chopped glazed cherries
3 ½ cups all-purpose flour
1/2 teaspoon salt
1 teaspoon baking powder
1 teaspoon vanilla

This is the family's favourite Christmas cake. We can make do without fruitcake or pound cake, but never without Mildred Byrne's cherry cake. After the boys left home, I began cutting the cake into quarters, wrapping each piece well and storing it in the freezer. This way the cake stays fresh much longer and we can still enjoy it after the holidays have passed.

• Cream butter thoroughly in large bowl. Add sugar very gradually, creaming well after each addition.

• Add eggs, one at a time, beating well after each addition.

• Dredge cherries with some of the flour.

• Combine remaining flour with salt and baking powder. Mix into creamed mixture.

• Stir in cherries and vanilla.

• Place pan of water on lower oven rack to keep cake moist while baking. Pour batter into well-greased, paper-lined tube pan and bake at 300°F for approximately 2 hours.

A few years ago, I issued an appeal for a light fruitcake recipe. Norah Stephen of Halifax responded with this one. At that time she was making 60 of these cakes every year to send to friends all over the world.

- In large bowl, thoroughly cream butter. Gradually add sugar, beating well after each addition.

- Add eggs, one at a time, beating well.

- In medium bowl, combine raisins, coconut, mixed fruit and cherries. Dust with 1 cup of the flour. Set aside.

- In small bowl, combine remaining flour, baking powder and salt.

- Remove 1/4 cup of the pineapple and save for another use. Add the remaining undrained pineapple to the creamed mixture, stirring well.

- Add dry ingredients and beat for at least 200 strokes.

- Stir in lemon extract and vanilla.

- Add floured fruit, mixing well.

- Grease 3 small round pans (Norah uses 5 ½-inch pans that are 3 inches deep). Line sides and bottoms with 3 thicknesses of brown paper (or heavy-duty waxed paper if brown paper not available). Pour batter into pans and poke down any exposed fruit. Place a pan of water on lower oven rack to keep cake moist.

- Bake at 350°F for approximately 1 hour and 20 minutes. Watch carefully. When tops of cakes are golden brown, lay sheet of heavy foil loosely over pans and continue baking until tester comes out dry.

Norah's Light Fruitcake

1 cup butter
1 ½ cups granulated sugar
3 eggs
2 ½ cups light raisins
1 cup desiccated coconut
8 ounces (250 g) glazed mixed fruit, cut
8 ounces (250 g) glazed red and green cherries, cut in half
3 cups all-purpose flour
1 teaspoon baking powder
3/4 teaspoon salt
1 can (19 ounces/540 mL) crushed pineapple, not drained
1 teaspoon lemon extract
1 teaspoon vanilla

Anna's Gumdrop Cake

1 pound (500 g) gumdrops
   (omit black ones)
3 cups all-purpose flour
1 cup butter (or 1/2 cup butter
   and 1/2 cup margarine)
2 cups granulated sugar
3 eggs
1 teaspoon baking powder
1/2 teaspoon salt
1 cup milk
1/2 teaspoon vanilla
1/2 teaspoon lemon extract

Another holiday favourite is gumdrop cake, which is said to have originated in the Maritimes during the early 1930s. This excellent recipe is from Anna Lanigan, who has been making it every Christmas for as long as she can remember.

• Cut gumdrops into small pieces with wet scissors. Dredge with about 1/3 cup of the flour. Set aside.

• In large bowl, thoroughly cream butter. Gradually add sugar, beating well after each addition.

• Add eggs, one at a time, beating well after each addition.

• Combine remaining flour with baking powder and salt. Blend into creamed mixture alternately with milk, beginning and ending with dry ingredients.

• Stir in vanilla, lemon extract and gumdrops.

• Grease an 8 x 8 x 3-inch cake pan and line with heavy brown paper. Grease again. Turn batter into pan and bake at 350°F for 1 to 1 ½ hours or until tester inserted in centre comes out clean.

Leftover Fruitcake

Here's a wonderful way to use up leftover fruitcake.

• Cut dark fruitcake into 1-inch cubes. • Spread each with glaze made by mixing 1 cup sifted icing sugar, 2 teaspoons softened butter and 1 tablespoon lemon juice. • Decorate with halved, glazed red cherry and a small piece of green cherry or citron.

The key to a good pound cake is the preparation. Ingredients should be at room temperature, the butter well creamed and the sugar added gradually, a couple of tablespoons at a time. Mixing can take as long as 30 minutes. Baking time will depend on the oven (all ovens are not created equal) and the size of the pan used. In an 8-inch fruitcake pan, this cake took 3 hours to bake in my oven, while in a 10-inch tube pan, it took only an hour and 20 minutes. By covering the cake with a towel as soon as it comes out of the oven and again when removed from the pan, it will not form a hard crust.

• Sift together flour, baking powder, salt and nutmeg. Set aside.

• In large bowl, cream butter until very light and fluffy.

• Add sugar gradually, creaming well after each addition.

• Add eggs, one at a time, beating after each addition just enough to mix.

• Combine milk and extract.

• Add sifted dry ingredients to creamed mixture alternately with milk mixture in 4 or 5 additions, beginning and ending with dry ingredients.

• Pour into well-buttered and floured 10-inch tube pan and bake at 300°F for approximately 1 hour and 20 minutes or until cake begins to pull away from sides of pan and a finger pressed gently on top of cake leaves a print that vanishes slowly.

• Cool cake upright in pan on wire rack for 10 minutes, then turn out on rack and cool to room temperature before cutting. Dust with icing sugar to garnish.

Note: This cake is also nice when iced with lemon glaze. • Blend together 3/4 cup icing sugar and the juice of 1 lemon. • Pour over cake as soon as it has been removed from pan and is still warm

Blue Ribbon Pound Cake

4 cups all-purpose flour
1 teaspoon baking powder
1/2 teaspoon salt
pinch of grated nutmeg
2 cups unsalted butter (or regular), at room temperature
3 cups sugar
6 large eggs, at room temperature
1 cup milk, at room temperature
2 teaspoons lemon extract or vanilla (or 1 teaspoon of each)

Carrot Pineapple Cake

Cake:
2 cups granulated sugar
1/2 cup packed brown sugar
1 ½ cups vegetable oil
3 eggs
1 cup crushed pineapple, not
    drained
3 cups all-purpose flour
2 teaspoons baking soda
3/4 teaspoon salt
2 teaspoons cinnamon
2 cups grated raw carrots
1 cup raisins
1 cup chopped walnuts
2 teaspoons vanilla

Cream Cheese Frosting:
8 ounces (250 g) cream cheese
1/4 cup butter or margarine
4 ½ cups sifted icing sugar
1 teaspoon lemon extract

Carrot cake became popular in the 1960s, when it began turning up at coffee parties, birthday parties and even weddings. Several variations exist. Some are made with junior baby food carrots, others add crushed pineapple, coconut, walnuts or pecans. Cream cheese frostings are popular but I've also tasted orange glaze and a baked coconut topping. This is my favourite combination.

• To make cake, cream granulated sugar, brown sugar and oil in large bowl.

• Add eggs, one at a time, beating after each addition.

• Stir in pineapple.

• Combine flour, baking soda, salt and cinnamon. Add gradually to creamed mixture.

• Stir in carrots, raisins, walnuts and vanilla.

• Pour into well-greased 10-inch tube pan and bake at 350°F for approximately 1 ½ hours. Watch cake carefully after first hour. Remove from oven and let cool in pan on a rack for 15 minutes. Turn out and cool completely.

• To make **frosting**, thoroughly cream the cream cheese and margarine. Blend in icing sugar, beating until smooth. Add lemon extract. If frosting is too thick to spread, add hot water, a teaspoon at a time. Spread over cooled carrot cake.

Marmalade Glaze

3/4 cup packed brown sugar
1/4 cup orange marmalade
3 tablespoons orange juice
1/2 cup coconut

Although it's hard to top cream cheese frosting on a carrot cake, there were times when things had to be hurried along. This was a good alternative.

• In a heavy-bottomed saucepan, combine brown sugar, marmalade, orange juice and coconut.

• Bring to a boil and cook for 2 minutes.

• Pour over warm cake which has been turned out of the pan.

Local gardeners discovered zucchini about 15 years ago and, soon after, realized that it was a prolific producer. The question soon became, how to use all the zucchini they were growing? Since carrots, beets, sauerkraut and pumpkin had already been used in cakes, there was no reason not to try zucchini. This delicious cake is large enough for a crowd. Try it for a summer celebration, when local zucchini is easy to find. If you are using small and tender zucchini, there's no need to peel it.

- In small bowl, thoroughly beat eggs.

- In large bowl, combine oil and sugar. Add zucchini and beaten eggs.

- Dust nuts and raisins with 1/2 cup of the flour.

- Combine remaining flour with baking powder, soda, cinnamon and salt. Add to zucchini mixture.

- Stir in nuts and raisins.

- Pour into well-greased and floured 10-inch tube pan and bake at 350°F for 1 ½ hours or until tester inserted in centre comes out clean. Cool on rack for 15 minutes before removing from pan.

- Cool thoroughly before icing with cream cheese frosting (see carrot pineapple cake).

Note: Cake may also be baked in 9 x 13-inch pan for an hour.

Variation: For chocolate zucchini cake, add 2 squares (2 ounces/60 g) melted unsweetened chocolate to batter.

Zucchini Cake

4 eggs
1 ½ cups vegetable oil
3 cups granulated sugar
3 cups finely grated raw
    zucchini
1 cup chopped nuts
1 cup raisins (optional)
3 cups all-purpose flour
1 ½ teaspoons baking powder
1 teaspoon baking soda
1 ½ teaspoons ground
    cinnamon
1 teaspoon salt

Here's another icing that is particularly nice on this cake.

- In a heavy-bottomed saucepan, combine butter, icing sugar, milk and egg yolk. Bring to a boil and cook for 2 minutes, stirring constantly.

- Remove from heat. Stir in vanilla, coconut and nuts.

- Cool slightly and spoon over warm cake.

Coconut Glaze

1/2 cup butter
1 cup icing sugar
1/2 cup evaporated milk
1 egg yolk
1 ½ teaspoons vanilla
1 cup shredded coconut
1/2 cup chopped nuts

Daffodil Cake

White Batter:
1 ¼ cups sifted cake flour (not all-purpose)
1 ½ cups granulated sugar
1 ¾ cups (12 to 14) egg whites, at room temperature
1/2 teaspoon salt
1 ½ teaspoons cream of tartar
1 ½ teaspoons vanilla

Yellow Batter:
5 egg yolks
2 tablespoons cake flour
2 tablespoons granulated sugar
2 tablespoons grated lemon peel

For me, spring brings an inevitable yearning for daffodil cake, a light, fluffy confection of white and yellow marbling. When making this cake a day ahead, leave it in the pan until it's time to serve it. To cut it, use a serrated knife in a light sawing motion.

• To make **white batter**, sift flour, then measure to make 1 ¼ cups. Combine with 1/2 cup of the sugar, then resift 3 times.

• With mixer at high speed, beat egg whites with salt and cream of tartar until soft peaks form.

• Add remaining 1 cup sugar, 1/4 cup at a time, beating well after each addition. Continue to beat until stiff peaks form.

• Using wire whisk, fold in vanilla.

• Sift flour mixture, 1/4 at a time, over egg whites and gently fold after each addition with the whisk. Do this in 15 strokes, using an under-and-over motion and rotating bowl a quarter turn after each addition. Fold 10 more strokes to blend completely. Turn 1/3 of the batter into a medium bowl.

• Prepare **yellow batter** in small bowl by combining egg yolks with 2 tablespoons flour and 2 tablespoons sugar. Beat at high speed until very thick.

• Add lemon peel.

• Fold yolk mixture into the reserved 1/3 white batter using an under-and-over motion with whisk in 15 strokes.

• Spoon batters alternately into ungreased 10-inch tube pan, ending with white batter on top.

• Cut through batter twice with knife. Using rubber spatula, gently smooth out batter until it touches sides of pan. Bake on lower rack at 375°F for 35 to 40 minutes or until cake springs back when lightly pressed.

• Invert pan over neck of a bottle to cool for 2 hours. Loosen cake with spatula before removing from pan. Sprinkle with icing sugar, if desired. Makes 10 servings.

This cake surfaced sometime during the late 1940s or early 50s. It's also been called screwball, crazy and depression cake, even quick and easy cake. It's deliciously moist and so chocolatey. The recipe is a keeper.

- Sift flour, granulated sugar, 3 tablespoons cocoa, baking powder, soda and salt into ungreased 8-inch cake pan.

- Make 3 depressions in dry ingredients and, without stirring, pour vanilla, vinegar and melted shortening into respective depressions. Cover with the warm water and stir thoroughly.

- Bake at 325°F for 45 minutes or until tester inserted in centre comes out clean. Cool in pan.

- To make **icing**, combine chocolate, icing sugar and milk or juice in top of double boiler and cook until smooth. (Plain butter icing is also delicious on this cake.)

The first time Laurie tasted this cake, he tried to tell the hostess how much he liked it. "It's so...so...so soggy," he stumbled. The word he was searching for was moist.

- Pour boiling water over dates. Add baking soda and set aside.

- In large bowl, thoroughly cream 1/4 cup butter and 1 cup brown sugar. Add beaten egg, blending well. Stir in date mixture.

- In separate bowl, combine flour, baking powder and salt.

- Add to creamed mixture, stirring just until blended.

- Add walnuts.

- Pour into greased 9-inch square pan and bake at 350°F for 20 minutes.

- To make **topping**, blend 1/4 cup brown sugar and 2 tablespoons butter. Mix in milk and coconut. Spread on cake and return to oven to brown lightly.

Wacky Woo Cake

Cake:
1 ½ cups sifted cake flour
1 cup granulated sugar
3 tablespoons cocoa
1 teaspoon baking powder
1 teaspoon baking soda
1/4 teaspoon salt
1 teaspoon vanilla
1 tablespoon vinegar
5 tablespoons shortening, melted
1 cup warm water

Icing:
2 squares semisweet chocolate or
    3 tablespoons cocoa
1 cup icing sugar
5 tablespoons milk or orange juice

Queen Elizabeth Cake

Cake:
1 cup boiling water
1 cup chopped dates
1 teaspoon baking soda
1/4 cup butter or margarine, softened
1 cup packed brown sugar
1 egg, beaten
1 ½ cups all-purpose flour
1 teaspoon baking powder
1/2 teaspoon salt
1/2 cup chopped walnuts

Topping:
1/4 cup brown sugar
2 tablespoons butter or margarine
2 tablespoons milk
1/2 cup flaked coconut

Oatmeal Cake

1 ½ cups boiling water
1 cup quick-cooking rolled oats
1/2 cup butter or margarine,
    softened
1 cup packed brown sugar
1 cup granulated sugar
2 eggs
1 ½ cups all-purpose flour
1 teaspoon baking powder
1 teaspoon baking soda
1 teaspoon ground cinnamon
1/2 teaspoon salt

Topping:
1/4 cup butter or margarine,
    softened
1/2 cup packed brown sugar
1/4 cup light cream or milk
1/2 teaspoon vanilla
1 cup flaked coconut
1 cup chopped walnuts

None of my sons complained about eating their oatmeal when it was prepared in the form of this delicious cake.

• In small mixer bowl, pour boiling water over rolled oats, stir to combine and let stand for 20 minutes.

• In large mixer bowl, cream butter until fluffy, gradually add sugars, beating until creamy.

• Add eggs and beat well.

• Add rolled oats mixture and beat well.

• Stir in combined flour, baking powder, soda, cinnamon and salt.

• Pour into a greased 9 x 13-inch pan and bake at 350°F for 35-40 minutes, or until a tester inserted in centre comes out clean.

• While cake is baking, prepare **topping**.

• Cream butter until fluffy.

• Add brown sugar and beat until creamy.

• Stir in cream, vanilla, coconut, and walnuts.

• Spread on hot cake as soon as it is removed from oven. Place under a preheated broiler for 4 to 5 minutes. Makes 12 servings.

Delight Cake

1 cup peeled and chopped
    apples
1 cup chopped dates
1 teaspoon baking soda
1 cup boiling water
1/2 cup shortening, softened
1 cup granulated sugar
1 egg
1 teaspoon vanilla
1 ½ cups all-purpose flour
1/2 teaspoon salt

This cake can be spread with the topping for Oatmeal Cake (above) or the Coconut Glaze on page 147. It's delightful either way.

• In a bowl, combine apples, dates, baking soda and water. Let cool.

• In large mixer bowl, cream together shortening and sugar. Add egg and beat well. Stir in vanilla.

• Combine flour and salt and add to creamed mixture alternately with fruit mixture. Pour into a greased 9-inch square pan and bake at 350°F for 45-50 minutes.

• Spread hot cake with choice of toppings suggested in recipe heading.

My mother followed in her mother's footsteps and made this pie, that isn't a pie, but a cake, every week. I didn't hold to the tradition, although it did make an occasional appearance in my kitchen. I include it here for Dorothy, my publisher, who ranks it high on her list of favourites.

- Sift flour before measuring and sift twice more to remove any tiny lumps. Then sift flour, baking powder, and salt into small bowl. Set aside.

- In large bowl, cream butter until fluffy.

- Gradually add sugar, beating until creamy. Add vanilla. Add beaten eggs and beat until well blended.

- Reduce mixer speed and add dry ingredients alternately with milk.

- Pour into two greased 8- or 9-inch layer cake pans and bake at 350°F for 25 to 30 minutes or until cakes test done. Allow to stand in pans for 5 minutes, then turn out on cake racks to cool.

- Use one layer to make Boston cream pie. Wrap and freeze the other for later use.

- Split cooled cake layer to make two layers. Spread custard cream filling over bottom layer. Cover with second layer.

- Dust with icing sugar or spread with chocolate glaze. Makes 8 servings.

- **Filling:** Gradually add milk to combined sugar, cornstarch, and salt in top of double boiler. Place over simmering water and cook, stirring constantly until mixture thickens, about 10 to 15 minutes.

- Add approximately 1/2 cup of hot mixture to beaten eggs. Stir until well mixed.

- Gently stir eggs into mixture in double boiler and cook, stirring constantly for about 3 minutes.

- Remove from heat. Stir in butter and vanilla.

- Cool. Makes approximately 1 ¼ cups.

- **Glaze:** Chop each chocolate square into quarters. Place, along with butter and water, in top of double boiler and set over hot, not boiling, water. Blend until smooth. Spread evenly over top of Boston Cream Pie.

Boston Cream Pie

2 cups sifted cake flour
2 teaspoons baking powder
1/2 teaspoon salt
1/3 cup butter, softened
1 cup granulated sugar
1/2 teaspoon vanilla
2 eggs, beaten
2/3 cup milk
custard cream filling (recipe
    follows)
icing sugar or chocolate glaze
    (recipe follows)

Filling:
1 cup milk, scalded
1/2 cup granulated sugar
3 tablespoons cornstarch
pinch of salt
2 eggs, slightly beaten
1 tablespoon butter or
    margarine
1 teaspoon vanilla

Chocolate Glaze:
2 ounces semisweet chocolate
1 tablespoon butter
1 tablespoon water

Sour Cream Coffee Cake

1 cup butter or margarine,
   softened
1 ½ cups granulated sugar
2 eggs
1 cup sour cream
1 teaspoon vanilla
2 cups all-purpose flour
1 teaspoon baking powder
1 teaspoon baking soda
1/2 teaspoon salt

Topping:
2/3 cup walnuts or pecans
2 teaspoons ground cinnamon
1/3 cup granulated sugar

This delicious coffee cake has been one of my favourites for at least 30 years. It still turns up in cookbooks today, sometimes with more sugar and sometimes with less. I've made it successfully with only one cup of sugar. This cake can also be made in a 10-inch springform pan but be sure to increase the cooking time by 15 minutes or more.

- Cream butter in large bowl. Add 1 ½ cups sugar gradually, beating until light and fluffy.

- Add eggs, one at a time, beating well after each addition.

- Fold in sour cream and vanilla.

- Combine flour, baking powder, soda, and salt in separate bowl. Fold into butter mixture.

- Pour half of the batter into greased and floured 10-inch tube pan.

- To make **topping**, combine nuts, cinnamon and 1/3 cup sugar. Reserve 1/4 of mixture and sprinkle the rest over batter in pan.

- Cover with remaining batter, then remaining topping.

- Bake at 350°F for 50 to 60 minutes or until tester inserted in centre comes out clean. Let cool on rack for 15 minutes before turning out to cool completely.

Quick Mix Coffee Cake

1 ⅓ cups dry biscuit mix
1/2 cup brown sugar
1/2 teaspoon cinnamon
1 egg
3 tablespoons melted butter or
   margarine
3/4 cup milk

Topping:
as in preceding recipe

Here's the fastest coffee cake in the east.

- Combine biscuit mix, sugar and cinnamon in small mixer bowl. Add egg, butter and milk. Beat 1 minute, scraping the bowl constantly.

- Spread batter in a greased 8-inch square pan. Sprinkle with topping used in Sour Cream Coffee Cake.

- Bake at 350°F for 40 to 45 minutes. Cut into 9 servings.

A friend in town from Toronto called me one day to see if she and her husband could drop by for a visit. "We're on our way," she said as I hung up the phone and hurried to the kitchen. The aroma of this coffee cake in the oven greeted their arrival. "How did you do it?" she asked. Everybody needs a reliable recipe like this one.

• Cream butter and shortening in large bowl. Gradually add sugar and beat until light and fluffy.

• Add eggs, one at a time, beating well after each addition.

• In separate bowl, combine flour, baking powder, soda and salt.

• Add to creamed mixture alternately with buttermilk, beginning and ending with dry ingredients.

• Spoon half the batter into greased and floured 9 x 13-inch baking dish. Arrange apple slices over batter and spread remaining batter evenly over top.

• To make **topping**, combine 1/4 cup flour, 1/4 cup sugar and cinnamon.

• Cut in 2 tablespoons butter until mixture resembles coarse meal.

• Stir in nuts. Sprinkle mixture evenly over batter.

• Bake at 350°F for 45 minutes. Cool completely before cutting into squares. Makes 15 servings.

Variation: For rhubarb coffee cake, replace apples with 2 cups rhubarb cut in 1/2-inch pieces.

Apple Walnut Coffee Cake

1/2 cup butter or margarine
1/2 cup shortening
2 cups granulated sugar
2 eggs
3 cups all-purpose flour
2 teaspoons baking powder
1 teaspoon baking soda
1/4 teaspoon salt (optional)
1 ¾ cups buttermilk (or milk soured with 2 tablespoons vinegar)
3 to 4 medium apples, peeled and sliced thinly

Topping:
1/4 cup all-purpose flour
1/4 cup granulated sugar
1 teaspoon ground cinnamon
2 tablespoons butter or margarine
1/4 cup finely chopped walnuts

Fresh Strawberry Coffee Cake

1 cup all-purpose flour
1/2 cup granulated sugar
2 teaspoons baking powder
1/2 teaspoon salt
1/2 cup milk
1 egg
2 tablespoons butter, melted
1 ½ cups sliced fresh
    strawberries

Topping:
1/2 cup all-purpose flour
1/2 cup granulated sugar
1/4 cup butter

Strawberry season lasts about six weeks in Nova Scotia and then we must either resort to more expensive imports or rely on our freezers. But during those six weeks, we live lavishly on fresh berries served every possible way.

• Combine 1 cup flour, 1/2 cup sugar, baking powder and salt in large bowl.

• Add milk, egg and melted butter, beating until blended.

• Pour or spread into greased 8-inch square baking pan. Top with strawberries.

• Make **topping** by combining 1/2 cup flour, 1/2 cup sugar and 1/4 cup butter. Mixture should resemble coarse crumbs. Sprinkle evenly over strawberries.

• Bake at 350°F for 45 minutes or until tester inserted in centre of cake comes out clean. Cut into 9 servings.

Blueberry Coffee Cake

2 cups all-purpose flour
1 ½ cups granulated sugar
2 teaspoons baking powder
1/2 teaspoon salt
2/3 cup butter or margarine,
    softened
1 cup milk
2 eggs
1 cup blueberries
1/4 cup granulated sugar
1/2 teaspoon cinnamon

We always watched for the young man near the head of St. Margaret's who would pick a quart or two of wild blueberries, sell them at roadside, then hurry back to pick more.

• In large mixer bowl, combine flour, sugar, baking powder, salt, butter, milk and eggs. Blend at low speed until dry ingredients are just moistened, Beat at medium speed for 3 minutes.

• Pour into a greased and floured 9 x 13-inch pan.

• Top with blueberries.

• Combine 1/4 cup sugar and cinnamon. Sprinkle over blueberries. Bake at 350°F for 40 to 50 minutes.

W hat do you mean you can't make pastry? Of course you can. All you have to do is get rid of the mental block, read the rules and go to it. If your first effort isn't the best, don't worry. Consider it a step towards perfection and remember, practice makes perfect.

A good pie crust should be tender enough to cut easily with a fork, yet not too crumbly. The colour should be golden brown. My simple rules for pastry making are as follows: measure accurately, handle lightly, use a good quality vegetable shortening or lard (never butter or margarine), use just enough water to bind the mixture, do not overmix, roll fairly thin and bake at the right temperature.

Cut the shortening into the flour with a pastry blender or two knives until the particles are about the size of small peas. If the particles are too small, the crust will be tender but it won't be flaky. If the particles are too large, the result will be a flaky crust that is not tender.

When adding the water, distribute it evenly, tossing the flour up lightly from the bottom with a fork. The dough should just barely hold when pressed together. Too little water makes the dough dry and hard to manage, while too much water makes the crust shrink while baking.

Roll the pastry on a flat surface, preferably on a pastry cloth with the rolling pin covered in a pastry stocking. With a cloth, you won't need to use an excessive amount of flour to keep the pastry from sticking. Roll from the centre out, applying light, even pressure. Do not use a back and forth motion and never stretch the pastry, since this will cause it to shrink during baking. You should also be careful not to stretch the pastry when fitting it into the pie plate.

Remember to work with chilled ingredients and utensils so that fat particles do not melt during mixing. Some cooks work with cold hands when handling the dough. Others even chill the pie before placing it in the oven. If you decide to chill the pie, don't let the plate get so cold that it cracks when it's placed in the hot oven.

PIES

No-Fail Pie Crust

4 cups all-purpose flour
1 ½ teaspoons salt
pinch of baking powder
1 ½ cups vegetable shortening
   (cold)
1 egg
1 tablespoon vinegar
1/3 cup ice water

For timid cooks, who just can't muster the courage to make pastry, here's a "no-fail" recipe.

• Mix flour, salt and baking powder together in large bowl.

• Add 3/4 cup shortening and cut into flour with pastry blender using short, cutting motion or with two knives cutting in opposite directions. Particles should be size of small peas.

• Cut in remaining 3/4 cup shortening until particles are size of dry beans.

• In small bowl, beat egg and vinegar into ice water.

• Sprinkle over flour mixture, drop by drop, tossing flour up from bottom with fork and working around bowl. As lumps get wet, push aside and continue working with dry mixture until all has been dampened.

• Press together into ball. Wrap dough and chill for an hour before rolling out.

• **To roll**, flatten and round 1/4 of dough and place on lightly floured surface. Roll out from centre with light, even pressure until circle measures 1/2 inch larger than pie plate (dough should be approximately 1/16-inch thick). Fold in half and lift gently into pie plate. Unfold and fit loosely in place, being careful not to stretch dough. Make sure no air is trapped between dough and plate. Trim excess, leaving up to 1/2-inch extra all around. Fold under and make decorative border.

• For **single shell**, prick pastry well with fork. Place in centre of oven at 450°F for 10 to 12 minutes.

• For **single shell pie with filling**, bake on lower oven shelf at 450°F for 10 to 15 minutes, then lower heat to 325°F and continue baking 20 to 30 minutes longer.

• For **double crust pies**, bake on lower shelf at 450°F for 10 minutes, then at 325°F for 25 to 30 minutes. Makes 4 single or 2 double crusts.

A crumb crust is the perfect solution for those who don't have time to make pastry. For the crumbs, finely roll graham wafers, chocolate wafers, gingersnaps, cereal flakes, zwieback or even oven-dried bread. Heighten the flavour of graham or bread crumbs by adding 1/2 teaspoon ground cinnamon.

- Combine crumbs and sugar in bowl. Stir in butter.

- Press firmly into bottom and up sides of greased 9-inch pie plate.

- Chill 20 minutes or bake at 350°F for 10 minutes and cool.

Crumb Pie Shell

1 ½ cups fine crumbs (see suggestions opposite)
1/4 cup granulated sugar
1/2 cup butter or margarine, melted

Why stop at crumb crusts? For ice cream pies, there's nothing like a coconut crust, either chocolate flavoured or simply toasted until crisp and browned.

- In top of double boiler over hot, not boiling, water, melt chocolate and butter, stirring until blended.

- Combine milk and sugar in small bowl. Add to chocolate mixture, stirring well.

- Add coconut and mix well.

- Spread on bottom and up sides of greased 9-inch pie plate.

- Chill until firm. Use for ice cream, chiffon or cream pie.

Chocolate-Coconut Crust

2 squares unsweetened chocolate
2 tablespoons butter
2 tablespoons hot milk or water
2/3 cup sifted icing sugar
1 ½ cups flaked or desiccated coconut, toasted or plain

- Spread butter evenly over bottom and up sides of 9-inch pie plate.

- Pat coconut into butter.

- Bake at 350°F for 8 to 10 minutes or until shell is crisp and browned. Cool.

Crisp Coconut Crust

2 tablespoons butter or margarine, softened
1 ½ cups shredded or flaked coconut

Meringue

8-Inch Pie:

2 large egg whites, at room
temperature
1/4 teaspoon cream of tartar
1/4 cup granulated or superfine
sugar

9-Inch Pie:

3 large egg whites, at room
temperature
1/4 teaspoon cream of tartar
6 tablespoons granulated or
superfine sugar

10-Inch Pie:

4 large egg whites, at room
temperature
1/2 teaspoon cream of tartar
1/2 cup granulated or superfine
sugar

There's no need to weep over "weeping" meringue. Just follow these simple directions. Granulated sugar works well but superfine is best, if it's available. For better volume, allow egg whites to stand at room temperature for 30 minutes.

•   Make sure bowl and beaters are clean and dry. Combine egg whites and cream of tartar in bowl and beat until foamy.

•   Gradually beat in sugar a tablespoon at a time.

•   Continue beating 1 ½ to 2 minutes or until mixture is glossy and stiff peaks form.

•   Carefully remove plastic wrap from pie while still warm and spread meringue over cream filling. Push some of meringue securely against crust to seal and to prevent it from shrinking. Pile meringue lightly and quickly, swirling and lifting to form attractive peaks (do not overwork).

•   Bake at 350°F for 15 minutes or until meringue is golden.

•   Cool on rack at room temperature away from drafts.

Note: Store cream pies in refrigerator when cooled.

Glazed Strawberry Pie

1 cup granulated sugar
6 teaspoons cornstarch
1 cup hot water
4 tablespoons strawberry-
flavoured gelatin
3 cups fresh whole
strawberries, rinsed and
hulled
baked 9-inch pie shell, cooled
whipping cream

The simple elegance of this pie makes it worth a trip to a "U-pick" strawberry field. On the way home, I like to stop by Marjorie Stirling's Evangeline Tea Room in Grand-Pré in hopes that she'll be serving her version of strawberry pie.

•   In saucepan, combine sugar and cornstarch. Add hot water and bring to boil. Cook until thickened.

•   Remove from heat. Add gelatin, stirring until dissolved. Cool.

•   Arrange strawberries, hulled side down, in pie shell to make attractive pattern.

•   Pour cooled gelatin mixture over berries.

•   Refrigerate until glaze has set.

•   Whip cream. Cover pie with cream and serve.

Our best memories of rhubarb pie are of those made by Viola of Glen Haven. With the car loaded, the five of us and Gyp, our black and gold Cocker Spaniel, would head for the cottage at Indian Point. "Can anyone hold a pie?" I would ask as we neared the roadside bakery. "I can, I can." There was always room for Viola's doughnuts too.

- Line 9-inch pie plate with pastry.

- In small bowl, mix flour and sugar thoroughly.

- Fold flour mixture into rhubarb until combined.

- Turn into pie plate. Dot with butter or margarine.

- Prepare lattice top and slide into place. Cut more strips of pastry and place around edge of pie. Flute.

- Bake at 425°F for 15 minutes. Reduce heat to 350°F and continue baking 50 to 60 minutes or until filling is set.

Rhubarb Pie

pastry for 2-crust, 9-inch pie
6 tablespoons all-purpose flour
1 ⅓ cups granulated sugar
4 cups fresh rhubarb, cut into
    1/2-inch pieces
2 tablespoons butter or
    margarine

Come blueberry season, Laurie could never drive by the little house in Glen Haven that served as Viola's bakery without stopping to pick up a blueberry pie.

- Line 9-inch pie plate with pastry.

- Combine sugar, cinnamon, salt and tapioca in small bowl. Sprinkle some over crust.

- Alternate layers of blueberries with sugar mixture, ending with berries.

- Sprinkle lemon juice over top. Dot with butter. Cover with top crust.

- Bake at 400°F for 30 minutes.

Fresh Blueberry Pie

pastry for 2-crust, 9-inch pie
1/2 cup granulated sugar
1/4 teaspoon ground cinnamon
1/8 teaspoon salt
1 tablespoon minute tapioca or
    2 tablespoons all-purpose
    flour
3 cups fresh blueberries
1 tablespoon lemon juice
1 teaspoon butter or margarine

Pumpkin Pies

3 unbaked 8-inch pie shells
4 cups cooked and mashed
    pumpkin
4 teaspoons ground cinnamon
1 teaspoon ground ginger
1 teaspoon ground allspice
1 teaspoon grated nutmeg
1/2 teaspoon salt
2 cups granulated sugar
4 eggs
2 cups milk
2 cups blend (light cream) or
    milk

Not only is this an excellent recipe, but it also fits my habit of stockpiling. My motto is "do one for now, two for the freezer." The filling is best mixed by hand in a very large bowl, since its volume tends to cause it to splatter in the mixer.

• Line three 8-inch pie plates with pastry.

• In large bowl, combine pumpkin, cinnamon, ginger, allspice, nutmeg and salt. Mix well.

• Stir in sugar.

• Add eggs, one at a time, beating well after each addition.

• Stir in milk and blend, mixing well.

• Divide mixture between pie shells.

• Bake at 375°F for 45 minutes or until knife inserted in centre comes out clean.

Banana Cream Pie

2 ⅔ cups milk
2 ½ tablespoons cornstarch
2 tablespoons all-purpose flour
1/2 teaspoon salt
2/3 cup granulated sugar
3 eggs, separated
1 tablespoon butter or
    margarine
1 teaspoon vanilla
2 or 3 well-ripened bananas
baked 9-inch pie shell
meringue for 9-inch pie (recipe
    page 158)

"When are you ever going to make another banana cream pie?" Laurie would ask soulfully over and over again. He could never get enough.

• In top of double boiler, over boiling water, heat 2 cups milk. Combine cornstarch, flour, salt and sugar in bowl. Mix with remaining 2/3 cup milk.

• Add to hot milk and cook, stirring constantly, until thickened. Continue cooking for 15 minutes, stirring occasionally.

• In small bowl, beat egg yolks slightly (reserve whites for meringue).

• Gradually stir in part of hot mixture, then add to remaining mixture in double boiler. Cook for 2 minutes.

• Remove from heat and blend in butter and vanilla.

• Peel bananas. Slice into bottom of baked pie shell.

• Pour hot cream mixture immediately over bananas. Top with meringue and refrigerate until ready to serve.

Not everyone in the family shares my love of certain foods. Even though I made Cape Breton pork pies a holiday tradition, it wasn't until grandson Craig came along that I found someone to share my enthusiasm. I wonder what Craig will think of this delightful pie?

- Line 9-inch pie plate with pastry.

- In saucepan, combine dates with just enough water to cover. Cook 5 minutes or until soft, stirring frequently.

- Stir in brown sugar. Remove from heat.

- In small bowl, beat egg yolks slightly (reserve whites for meringue).

- Add butter, vanilla, yolks, milk and salt to date mixture and mix well.

- Pour into pie shell and bake at 350°F for 30 minutes or until filling bubbles up well and knife inserted in centre comes out clean.

- Remove from oven and cover with plastic wrap to keep hot and prevent skin from forming.

- To make meringue, see recipe page 158 for 8-inch pie (using 2 egg whites).

Date Meringue Pie

pastry for single 9-inch pie
1 cup dates, cut up
water
1/2 cup packed brown sugar
2 eggs, separated
1 tablespoon butter or
  margarine
1 teaspoon vanilla
2 cups evaporated milk
1/2 teaspoon salt

Here's a delicious way to use my favourite berry.

- Drain raspberries, reserving syrup. Add water to syrup to make 1 cup.

- Dissolve gelatin in boiling water. Add marshmallows and stir until partially melted.

- Add syrup. Chill until partially set.

- With electric mixer, beat mixture until fluffy. Fold in raspberries and whipped cream.

- Line a 9-inch pie plate with vanilla wafers or use a crumb pie shell (see page 157). Fill with raspberry mixture. Chill until set. Serve with additional whipped cream, if desired. Makes 6 servings.

Raspberry Velvet Pie

1 (10 ounces/300 g) package frozen
  raspberries
1 (3 ounces/85 g) package raspberry
  gelatin
1 cup boiling water
4 ounces (125 g) marshmallows
1 cup whipping cream, whipped
vanilla wafers

Chocolate Meringue Pie

3 squares unsweetened
   chocolate
2 ½ cups milk
1 cup granulated sugar
3 tablespoons all-purpose flour
3 eggs, separated
1 tablespoon water
1 ½ tablespoons butter
1 teaspoon vanilla
1 teaspoon almond extract
2 baked 9-inch pie shells

This rich and delicious pie was satisfying other generations long before the word "chocoholic" became so popular.

• Place chocolate and milk in top of double boiler over boiling water and heat until chocolate has melted.

• In bowl, combine sugar, flour, egg yolks (reserve whites for meringue) and water.

• Blend in chocolate mixture.

• Return to top of double boiler and cook over boiling water, stirring constantly, until thickened.

• Add butter, vanilla and almond extract, stirring until butter has melted.

• Pour into baked pie shells and cover with plastic wrap to keep hot and prevent skin from forming.

• To make meringue, see recipe page 158 for 9-inch pie. (Double recipe for both pies.)

Apple–Cranberry–Mince Pie

pastry for 2-crust, 9-inch pie
4 cups thinly sliced apples,
   pared, cored
1 cup fresh cranberries, cut in
   half
1/4 cup mincemeat
1 ¼ cups granulated sugar
3 tablespoons all-purpose flour
2 tablespoons orange juice
1/2 teaspoon salt

Long before I met Madame Jehane Benoit, I was learning from her through her writings. Little did I dream that this "grand dame" of Canadian cuisine would one day write an introduction to the hard cover edition of Out of Old Nova Scotia Kitchens. *My job as food writer brought us together on several occasions. I was also the last person to interview her. She died without reading my final tribute.*

• Line 9-inch pie plate with pastry.

• In bowl, combine apples, cranberries and mincemeat.

• In separate bowl, combine sugar and flour.

• Sprinkle 1/4 cup sugar mixture over crust. Add fruit and spread evenly.

• Combine orange juice and salt in cup and sprinkle over fruit.

• Spoon remaining sugar mixture over fruit.

• Top with plain or lattice crust.

• Bake at 400°F for 10 minutes. Lower heat to 350°F and bake 30 to 40 minutes longer.

Still a popular dessert item, it's hard to believe this spectacular pie has been around since the 50s. Now that's lasting power!

- Combine 1/2 cup sugar and cornstarch in medium-sized bowl.

- In separate bowl, beat egg yolks slightly.

- Slowly add scalded milk, then stir into sugar mixture.

- Pour into top of double boiler set over hot, not boiling water. Cook, stirring, until custard coats spoon.

- Remove from heat and add vanilla.

- Pour 1 cup of custard into small bowl and add chocolate chips. Stir until chocolate has melted.

- Pour into bottom of baked and cooled pie shell. Chill.

- Soften gelatin in cold water. Add to remaining hot custard, stirring until dissolved. Chill until slightly thick.

- Meanwhile, beat egg whites in large bowl until soft peaks form. Gradually beat in 1/2 cup sugar and continue beating until stiff peaks form.

- Fold in chilled gelatin mixture.

- Pile over chocolate layer and chill until set.

- Whip cream, if using, and spread over pie. Garnish with shaved or grated chocolate.

Black Bottom Pie

1/2 cup granulated sugar
1 tablespoon cornstarch
4 eggs, separated
2 cups milk, scalded
1 teaspoon vanilla or rum
flavouring
1 cup semisweet chocolate
chips
baked 9-inch pie shell, cooled
1 envelope unflavoured gelatin
1/4 cup cold water
1/2 cup granulated sugar
1 cup whipping cream
(optional)
unsweetened chocolate for
garnish

This pie is as easy to make as it is delicious to eat but it's very rich. Cut smaller wedges and, if there's any left over, wrap it and return it to the freezer.

- Stir ice cream to soften. Add coffee granules and pecans.

- Spread into chilled crust. Decorate top with pecans, if desired.

- Place in freezer to harden.

Coffee Ice Cream Pie

1 quart (1 L) vanilla ice cream
2 teaspoons instant coffee
granules
1/4 cup chopped pecans
9-inch Chocolate Coconut
Crust, well chilled (recipe
page 157)

Ice Cream Sundae Pie

1 quart (1 L) vanilla ice cream, slightly softened
9-inch chocolate coconut crust, well chilled (recipe page 157)
1 ½ cups halved fresh strawberries, or 1 package (10 ounces/300 g) frozen strawberries, partially thawed
sugar
whipping cream (optional)

Nowadays, my family usually settles for ice cream as it comes from the container or topped with fresh or frozen fruit. In my early days in the kitchen, however, it was often a bigger production.

• Spoon half of ice cream into crust. Spread half of strawberries over top of ice cream and dust lightly with sugar. Repeat layers. Place in freezer to harden.

• Whip cream, if using. Remove pie from freezer 10 minutes before serving and decorate with whipped cream.

Note: A chocolate wafer crust may also be used. See recipe for Crumb Pie Shell (page 157) and add 1/2 cup chopped walnuts.

Peach Foam Pie

3 eggs, separated
1/4 cup granulated sugar
1/2 teaspoon salt
1/2 cup milk
1 ½ tablespoons unflavoured gelatin
6 tablespoons cold water
1/2 teaspoon vanilla
2 tablespoons lemon juice
1 cup mashed fresh, frozen or canned peaches
2 tablespoons grated lemon rind
6 tablespoons granulated sugar
9-inch Vanilla Wafer Pie Shell (recipe for Crumb Pie Shell, page 157)
whipping cream (optional)
pistachio nuts for garnish

I always depend on a chiffon pie to make an impression. It's delicate and rich and may be garnished elaborately, like this peach foam pie decorated with pistachio nuts.

• In top of double boiler, beat egg yolks until lemon coloured.

• Add 1/4 cup sugar, salt and milk. Set over boiling water and cook, stirring constantly, until custard coats spoon. Remove from heat.

• Dissolve gelatin in cold water. Stir into custard.

• Add vanilla and let cool.

• Pour lemon juice over peaches. Fold into cooled custard along with lemon rind.

• In bowl, beat egg whites until stiff. Gradually beat in 6 tablespoons sugar and continue beating until stiff and glossy.

• Fold into custard mixture. Pour into pie shell and chill until firm.

• Whip cream, is using. Garnish pie with cream and pistachio nuts.

"**W**hat'll I have for dessert?" harried mothers wondered as meal hour approached. If there wasn't a cake, pie, or pudding ready, at least there must be Jell-O to serve with cookies. No self-respecting mother ever allowed the cookie jar to be depleted.

And certainly, there was ice cream in the refrigerator and freezer. But, unless there was a homemade sauce for sundaes, or better still, banana splits, ice cream was used to top a fruit crisp or pie, or scooped into a cone for an after-school treat.

Today, we know the young mothers of the 50s and 60s were hard on themselves, shunning convenience for what they considered to be their duty. Sure, there would be a little "cheating" on occasion. Jell-O and the packaged puddings, albeit only those that needed cooking, are examples of the shortcuts Moms were forced to take once in awhile. Still, it didn't ease the guilt that came with not having baked something for the day's desserts. Nor did the child's preference for the jiggly stuff help.

"I don't know what I'm going to do with Gary—he won't eat anything but Jell-O for dessert," she would complain to hubby or friends.

While Laurie was content with tapioca or rice pudding, he was elated when custard was on the menu. Gary opted for anything flavoured with lemon. If it couldn't be lemon meringue pie, lemon meringue pudding or lemon fluff dessert would do nicely, thank you. Bob could be tempted with a strawberry whip or anything with raisins. And even to this day, we can pump a little enthusiasm from Frank with an Apple Crisp or Rhubarb Cobbler. (Both recipes are in *Out of Old Nova Scotia Kitchens.*)

Everybody came alive for the big production desserts, usually reserved for company or special parties. This is when a colourful bombe or glitter torte would make such an impression that no one believed how easy they were to prepare.

And in the days when cream flowed like water, it would be whipped and piled or spread on almost any dessert—from cheesecakes to tortes. Nobody thought about calories. Or if they did, nobody declined at least one helping of dessert.

DESSERTS

Tapioca Cream

3 tablespoons quick-cooking
   tapioca
2 cups milk
1 egg, separated
pinch of salt
2 tablespoons granulated sugar
1 teaspoon vanilla
2 tablespoons granulated sugar
1/2 cup whipping cream

Laurie and my Uncle Gordon both loved tapioca pudding, but Uncle Gordon preferred old-fashioned tapioca, which requires from three to 24 hours of soaking. Fortunately Laurie preferred the quick-cooking kind.

• In large saucepan, combine tapioca, milk, egg yolk, salt and 2 tablespoons sugar. Let stand 5 minutes. Then cook over medium heat, stirring constantly, until mixture comes to boil. Remove from heat and stir in vanilla.

• Pour mixture into bowl, cover and refrigerate for 2 hours or until chilled.

• Beat egg white until soft peaks form. Gradually beat in 2 tablespoons sugar and continue beating until stiff peaks form.

• With clean beaters, beat whipping cream in separate bowl until soft peaks form. Gently fold cream and egg white into chilled tapioca mixture with rubber spatula. Makes 6 servings.

Creamy Rice Pudding

3 cups milk
1 cup whipping cream (or
   milk)
1/2 cup converted rice
3 eggs, separated
1/2 cup packed brown sugar
1 teaspoon vanilla
1/2 teaspoon salt
1/2 cup golden raisins
freshly grated nutmeg

This old-fashioned rice pudding is delicious served lukewarm and unadorned. With a little custard or raspberry or chocolate sauce, it's sheer ambrosia.

• Combine milk and cream in top of double boiler and place over simmering water. Stir in rice. Cover and cook, stirring occasionally, for 1 to 1 ½ hours or until rice is tender and creamy. Remove from heat.

• In large bowl, beat egg yolks until frothy. Gradually beat in sugar, vanilla and salt.

• Add hot rice, a little at a time, stirring constantly. Stir in raisins.

• With clean beaters, beat egg whites in small bowl until soft peaks form. Fold into rice mixture.

• Turn into well-buttered, 2-quart (2 L) baking dish and sprinkle with nutmeg. Place dish in large, shallow pan and fill pan with enough hot water to cover 2 inches up sides of baking dish.

• Bake at 350°F for 45 minutes or until knife inserted in centre comes out clean. Remove baking dish to rack and cool to lukewarm before serving. Makes 6 servings.

Custard was another everyday dessert that young brides of the 1950s and 60s had to perfect in order to earn their culinary laurels. It was served either in the traditional little cups or as filling for a pie. When people talk about comfort foods, my mind turns to this rich, velvety-smooth dessert which I say tops the list.

- Heat milk to scalding (bubbles will form around edge of saucepan).

- In large bowl, beat together eggs and vanilla. Beat in sugar and salt just until mixed.

- Stir in scalded milk.

- Pour through small sieve directly into 8 unbuttered custard cups.

- Sprinkle lightly with nutmeg and place cups in large, shallow pan without letting cups touch. Partially pull out oven shelf and set pan on it. Fill pan with enough boiling water to cover 1 inch up sides of cups.

- Bake at 325°F for 30 minutes or until knife inserted in centre of a cup comes out clean. Lift cups out of pan and cool. Makes 8 servings.

Good things sometimes come in convenient packages. This simple dessert offers the flavour of lemon pie without the bother of making a crust. It was one of my son Gary's favourite desserts and I was happy to comply with his wishes, especially on busy days.

- In top of double boiler or heavy-bottomed saucepan, combine pudding mix, 1/3 cup sugar, egg yolks and 1/4 cup of the water. Blend well.

- Add remaining water and cook, stirring constantly, until thickened. Remove from heat.

- Beat egg whites until soft peaks form. Gradually add 4 tablespoons sugar, beating until stiff peaks form.

- With spatula, gradually fold into hot pudding.

- Spoon into individual dessert dishes and cool. Makes 6 servings.

Perfect Custard

3 cups milk
4 eggs
1 teaspoon vanilla
1/3 cup granulated sugar
pinch of salt
nutmeg (optional)

Lemon Meringue Pudding

1 package (3 ounces/85 g) lemon pudding and pie filling (not instant)
1/3 cup granulated sugar
2 eggs, separated
2 cups water
4 tablespoons granulated sugar

Pineapple Cream

2 packages unflavoured gelatin
1/2 cup cold water
1 cup boiling water
1 cup granulated sugar
1 can (19 ounces/540 mL)
   crushed pineapple, not
   drained
juice of a lemon
1 cup whipping cream

I remember once having given three dinner parties in as many nights and repeating the same, carefully prepared menu. I thought it a clever plan because each night there was a new guest list and my workload was considerably reduced. However, there was one important factor I hadn't considered. After the third party had ended and the guests departed, my husband said he hoped he wouldn't see that menu again for a long time. I've forgotten the other dishes but this was the dessert.

• In large bowl, soak gelatin in cold water for 5 to 10 minutes to soften. Then add boiling water, stirring well.

• Add sugar, undrained pineapple and lemon juice and stir well.

• Chill until mixture has consistency of honey.

• In separate bowl, whip cream.

• Fold into pineapple mixture, incorporating gently but thoroughly.

• Refrigerate. Serve in sherbet glasses. Makes 8 to 10 servings.

Note: To dress up dessert, set aside small amount of whipped cream and pineapple for garnishes.

Strawberry Whip

3/4 cup frozen strawberries,
   defrosted
1 egg white
1/2 cup granulated sugar
1 ½ teaspoons lime juice

When I first tried this recipe, I couldn't believe the volume that grew from so few ingredients. Just toss everything into the mixer, turn it on and make supper or clean up the kitchen for 20 minutes. The mixer will make the dessert. It's lovely served with a custard sauce but I have often served it without.

• Combine strawberries, egg white, sugar and lime juice in large mixer bowl. Whip at high speed for 20 minutes or until mixture is stiff.

• Serve with custard sauce, if desired (see index). Makes 10 servings.

This dessert always reminds me of folklorist Helen Creighton, who served it to me at lunch in her Dartmouth home. Helen probably didn't take the shortcut that I discovered after one of my babies refused to eat his prunes.

- Beat egg whites with salt until stiff.

- Beat in sugar.

- Fold in prunes and grated rind.

- Pour into dessert dishes and refrigerate until ready to serve. Makes 4 servings.

Prune Whip

2 egg whites
pinch salt
2 tablespoons granulated sugar
1 bottle (4 ½ ounces/128 mL) strained prunes for babies
grated orange or lemon rind to taste

There's probably some connection between my insatiable desire for chocolate and my use of the blender to make more than milk shakes.

- Beat egg whites in small mixer bowl until stiff but not dry.

- Break up chocolate chips in blender. Add boiling water or coffee and blend until smooth.

- Add egg yolks and rum or vanilla. Mix 1 minute or until thoroughly blended.

- Pour chocolate mixture slowly over egg whites, folding in gently until no white shows.

- Spoon into 4-cup serving dish or individual sherbet glasses.

- Refrigerate for an hour or until firm and well-chilled. Garnish with whipped cream, if desired. Makes 8 servings.

Quick Blender Chocolate Mousse

4 eggs, separated and at room temperature
1 package (6 ounces/175 g) semisweet chocolate chips
5 tablespoons boiling water or hot coffee
2 tablespoons golden rum or 2 teaspoons vanilla
whipped cream (optional)

Maple Ice-Box Dessert

1 cup pure maple syrup
3 eggs, separated
1 envelope unflavoured gelatin
1/4 cup cold water
1 cup whipping cream
1 teaspoon vanilla
10 to 12 macaroons, crumbled
1/4 cup slivered almonds,
    toasted

Shortly after my book Out of Old Nova Scotia Kitchens *was published in 1970, I heard from a friend that one of the recipes, maple mousse, was served at Rideau Hall during a dinner party for 12 ambassadors and their wives. I wonder if this dessert would go over just as well?*

- In small saucepan, heat maple syrup.

- Beat egg yolks well.

- Slowly pour maple syrup over yolks, stirring gently.

- Transfer mixture to top of double boiler and cook over simmering water for 20 minutes or until mixture thickens.

- In the meantime, soak gelatin in cold water to soften. Add to hot maple syrup mixture and stir to dissolve. Cool.

- Transfer to large bowl and beat until mixture is light and fluffy.

- Using clean beaters, beat egg whites in separate bowl until stiff peaks form.

- In another bowl, whip cream until soft peaks form. Fold in vanilla.

- Gently fold cream and egg whites into maple syrup mixture.

- Spread layer of broken macaroons in bottom of 2-quart (2 L) baking dish. Cover with layer of maple filling. Repeat layers and top with toasted almonds.

- Refrigerate overnight. Makes 8 servings.

The only trick to this dessert is remembering to refrigerate the evaporated milk overnight. If you forget, pour the milk into a metal pan and place in the freezer for about 45 minutes. At the same time, put the mixing bowl and beaters in the freezer. Once you have whipped the milk to soft peaks, add a tablespoon of lemon juice to make it stiffer.

- Combine wafer crumbs, brown sugar and melted butter in small bowl, mixing well. Set aside 1/2 cup for topping. Pat remainder into bottom of 9 x 13-inch pan.

- Dissolve gelatin in hot water. Add granulated sugar, lemon juice and rind, stirring until sugar is dissolved. Place in refrigerator until partially set.

- Whip the chilled evaporated milk until thick.

- Add gelatin and whip until well combined.

- Pour mixture evenly into crumb-lined pan. Sprinkle top with reserved crumb mixture.

- Chill thoroughly. Cut into squares and serve on dessert plates. Makes 20 servings.

It's been years since I've made this old favourite. When I dug it out of my oldest files, I had a strong urge to head for the kitchen and make it again, just to let my palate experience what my mind was remembering.

- Cream butter in large bowl. Gradually add sugar and continue beating until light and fluffy.

- Add egg yolks and beat well.

- Add lemon juice, rind and salt, blending well.

- Fold in coconut and flour, then stir in milk.

- In separate bowl, beat egg whites until stiff and fold into lemon mixture.

- Pour batter into greased 6-cup baking dish or casserole. Set in pan of hot water and bake at 375°F for 35 to 40 minutes.

- Chill, if desired, before serving. Serve unadorned or garnish with whipped cream and toasted coconut. Makes 8 servings.

Lemon Fluff Dessert

Crumb Crust:
34 graham wafers, finely crushed (about 2 cups)
1 cup brown sugar
1/2 cup butter or margarine, melted

Filling:
1 package (3 ounces/85 g) lemon-flavoured gelatin
1 cup hot water
1 scant cup granulated sugar
juice and rind of a lemon
1 can (13.5 ounces/385 mL) evaporated milk, refrigerated overnight

Coconut Sponge Surprise

2 tablespoons butter
1 cup granulated sugar
4 eggs, separated
1/3 cup lemon juice
1 teaspoon grated lemon rind
1/4 teaspoon salt
3/4 cup shredded or flaked coconut
2 tablespoons all-purpose flour
1 cup milk
whipped cream and toasted coconut for garnish (optional)

Forgotten Torte

Meringue:
6 egg whites, warmed to room
    temperature for 2 hours
1/2 teaspoon cream of tartar
1/4 teaspoon salt
1 ½ cups granulated sugar
1 teaspoon vanilla
1/8 teaspoon almond extract
few drops of red food
    colouring (optional)

Topping:
1 cup whipping cream
1 package (10 ounces/300 g)
    frozen raspberries or
    strawberries, thawed

This dessert bakes itself overnight and is a great ice breaker at a party. Although "forgotten" meringues are common these days, this recipe was a hot topic of conversation when it appeared in an ad around 1970. It is best made in the evening when the oven won't be in use.

• Place egg whites, warmed to room temperature, in large bowl with cream of tartar and salt. Beat at medium speed with electric mixer until foamy.

• Very gradually add sugar, beating well after each addition.

• Add vanilla, almond extract and food colouring. Continue beating until stiff, glossy peaks form.

• Butter bottom of 9-inch tube pan and spread mixture evenly in pan.

• Place pan in oven preheated to 450°F and *turn off heat immediately*. Let stand overnight. In the morning, loosen edge of torte with sharp, thin knife and turn onto serving platter (cake will settle slightly).

• Whip cream. Frost cake with cream and top with raspberries or strawberries, allowing a little of the juice to drizzle down sides. Cut into wedges to serve. Makes 8 to 10 servings.

Rhubarb Pudding

2 eggs, beaten
1 cup granulated sugar
1 teaspoon vanilla
1/4 cup all-purpose flour
4 cups cut-up rhubarb

Although classified as a vegetable, rhubarb is used as a fruit in pies, crisps, cobblers, puddings, cakes, breads and jams. The early crop is best for freezing. Wash the stalks, cut into 1¼-inch pieces, pack into plastic bags and store in the freezer for rhubarb desserts year-round.

• In large bowl, whisk together eggs, sugar, vanilla and flour.

• Stir in rhubarb.

• Pour into greased 6-cup baking dish and bake at 350°F for 40 to 50 minutes or until pudding is firm.

• Serve warm with whipped cream, if desired. Makes 4 servings.

Pat's Grandma's Apple Raisin Betty

My good friend Pat Crocker actually has a sister Betty. Perhaps their grandmother named this dessert in Betty's honour. Pat, who is now married and lives in Massachusetts, is a great cook herself. When she said this was the best dessert she'd ever eaten, I knew it belonged in this book.

4 large apples, peeled, cored and sliced
1/2 cup raisins or mincemeat
1/2 cup broken walnuts
1/2 cup butter or margarine, melted
2 cups cubed white bread
1/2 to 2/3 cup granulated sugar (depending on tartness of apples)
1/2 teaspoon cinnamon
dash of nutmeg
1/4 cup water
1 teaspoon lemon juice

- Place half the sliced apples in 2-quart (2 L) baking dish. Add half the raisins and half the nuts.

- In small bowl, toss butter and bread cubes lightly. Sprinkle half the crumbs over apples in baking dish.

- In another bowl, mix sugar, cinnamon and nutmeg. Sprinkle half over bread crumbs in baking dish. Repeat these same layers.

- Mix water and lemon juice and drizzle over other ingredients.

- Cover and bake at 350°F for 20 minutes. Uncover and bake 10 to 20 minutes longer.

- Serve warm with cream or ice cream.

Luscious Raspberry Cake

There's nothing quite like the mid-summer taste of freshly picked raspberries. But this cake is a luscious substitute and, with the help of today's freezers, can be made year round.

2 teaspoons unflavoured gelatin
1/2 cup water
1 package (15 ounces/425 g) frozen raspberries, thawed
raspberry juice plus water to make 1 cup
1 cup whipping cream
1 angel food cake

- Soften gelatin in 1/2 cup water.

- Drain berries well, reserving juice. In small saucepan, heat juice and water to make 1 cup.

- Add gelatin and stir to dissolve. Transfer to bowl and chill until partially set. Beat until fluffy.

- In separate bowl, whip cream. Fold into gelatin mixture.

- Add berries and chill until nearly set.

- Cut cake horizontally in three layers. Spread raspberry mixture between layers and on top and sides.

- Chill until set. Makes 8 to 10 servings.

Blueberry Buckle

Cake:
1/4 cup butter or margarine, softened
3/4 cup granulated sugar
1 egg
2 cups all-purpose flour
2 teaspoons baking powder
1/2 teaspoon salt
1/2 cup milk
2 cups fresh or frozen blueberries

Topping:
1/4 cup butter or margarine, softened
1/2 cup granulated sugar
1/3 cup all-purpose flour
1/2 teaspoon ground cinnamon

The little berry that makes the pie, stews the grunt and turns the tongue blue is never more delicious than when baked into a blueberry buckle.

• In large bowl, thoroughly cream 1/4 cup butter and 3/4 cup sugar. Add egg and beat well.

• Combine 2 cups flour, baking powder and salt in separate bowl. Add to creamed mixture alternately with milk, beginning and ending with dry ingredients.

• Fold in blueberries carefully so they will not break and turn batter blue (use frozen berries directly from the freezer). Spread batter into greased 8-inch square pan.

• To make **topping**, blend 1/4 cup butter, 1/2 cup sugar, 1/3 cup flour and cinnamon in small bowl with fork. Sprinkle evenly over batter in pan.

• Bake at 375°F for 35 to 40 minutes or until tester inserted in centre comes out clean. Serve warm with custard sauce (see index) or whipped cream, if desired. Makes 9 servings.

Pineapple Upside-Down Cake

3 tablespoons butter or margarine
12 maraschino cherries
12 walnut halves
2/3 cup packed brown sugar
2 ½ cups drained pineapple, crushed or tidbits (reserve juice)
1/3 cup shortening
1/2 cup granulated sugar
1 egg
1 teaspoon vanilla
1 ¼ cups sifted cake flour
1 ½ teaspoons baking powder
1/2 teaspoon salt
1/2 cup reserved pineapple juice

Although I adored my grandmother's pineapple upside-down cake made with pineapple slices, tidbits make slicing easier and the crushed pineapple is more economical.

• Melt butter in 9-inch round pan. Arrange cherries and nuts in decorative pattern in bottom of pan. Cover with brown sugar, then pineapple.

• To make cake, cream together shortening and sugar in large bowl. Add egg and vanilla and beat until fluffy.

• In separate bowl, sift together flour, baking powder and salt. Add to creamed mixture alternately with pineapple juice, beginning and ending with dry ingredients. Beat well after each addition. Spread over pineapple.

• Bake at 350°F for 45 to 50 minutes. Let stand 5 minutes, then invert pan on serving plate. Serve warm with whipped cream, if desired.

Note: If substituting all-purpose flour, use 2 tablespoons less flour for each cup to allow for the greater firmness of all-purpose flour.

Joan (Bailey) Martin shared this luscious dessert with me when we were both novices in the kitchen. We've survived— she in Vancouver and me in Halifax. So has the dessert although the required six egg yolks may tempt today's cholesterol watchers to turn the page.

Angel Lemon Custard Dessert

1 ½ tablespoons unflavoured
   gelatin
3/8 cup cold water
6 eggs, separated
3/4 cup granulated sugar
1 ½ teaspoons grated lemon
   rind
3/4 cup fresh lemon juice
3/4 cup granulated sugar
1 angel cake
1 cup whipping cream
maraschino cherries or
   chocolate curls for garnish

- Soak gelatin in cold water to soften.

- Beat egg yolks. Place in top of double boiler with 3/4 cup sugar. Set over boiling water and cook, stirring constantly, until thickened.

- Add gelatin and stir to dissolve.

- Remove from heat and transfer to large bowl. Cool until partially set, then stir in lemon rind and juice.

- In separate bowl, beat egg whites until foamy. Gradually add 3/4 cup sugar, beating until stiff peaks form.

- Fold into custard mixture.

- Tear angel cake into pieces, removing all crusts.

- Place a layer of angel cake pieces in a well-greased 10-inch tube cake pan. Pour on a layer of custard. Repeat layers until all is used, ending with custard.

- Refrigerate overnight.

- Turn out onto serving plate. Cover with a thin layer of whipped cream. Decorate with halved, drained, maraschino cherries or chocolate curls.

Bombe Glacée

3 pints (1.5 L) lime sherbet, softened
1 pint (500 mL) chocolate ice cream, softened
2 pints (1 L) raspberry sherbet, softened
1 cup whipping cream
2 tablespoons granulated sugar
grapes for garnish (optional)

Bombe Glacée is a pretty dessert that feeds and impresses a crowd. I like it because it's simple and can be made several days ahead. I have occasionally increased the recipe, using a bowl-shaped, 16-cup copper mold, to serve a group of 24 with leftovers for next day.

• Soften lime sherbet so that it can be spread with spoon. Press into 8-cup mold or bowl to make even layer that lines entire mold. Place in freezer until firm.

• Soften chocolate ice cream slightly and press evenly against lime sherbet to make second layer. Return to freezer until firm.

• Soften raspberry sherbet slightly and fill centre cavity of mold. Freeze until firm.

• Several hours before serving, place mold in cold water for few seconds. Invert onto serving plate, running a knife around edge if necessary. Return to freezer until firm again.

• Whip cream and sweeten with sugar. Decorate bombe with rosettes by putting whipped cream through pastry tube. Garnish with frosted grapes, if desired.

• Keep in freezer until serving time, then slice in wedges like a cake. Makes about 16 servings.

Note: This dessert can be made to fit in with various colour schemes. Lemon sherbet may replace raspberry and strawberry or vanilla ice cream may be used instead of chocolate.

This is another special occasion dessert which can be made 2 to 3 weeks ahead. Since I could not fit four meringues in my oven, I made two at a time. I have also sometimes substituted lemon sherbet for orange.

- On four 10-inch squares of brown paper, draw four 9-inch circles. Grease circles and place papers on cookie sheets or 12-inch pizza pans.

- Beat egg whites, cream of tartar and salt in large bowl until fluffy.

- Beat in sugar 2 to 3 tablespoons at a time.

- Add vanilla and continue beating until very stiff.

- Spread equal amounts of meringue in each circle. Dredge with almonds.

- Bake at 275°F for 50 to 60 minutes or until pale gold in colour. Turn off heat and leave overnight. Carefully peel paper off bottoms of meringues.

- Before assembling, whip cream and take ice cream and sherbet out of freezer to soften slightly.

- Place one layer of meringue on circle of foil-covered cardboard. Cover with chocolate ice cream. Spread about 3/4 cup whipped cream over ice cream. Cover with another meringue layer. Repeat procedure with sherbet and strawberry ice cream, chilling in freezer for few minutes during assembly if ice cream becomes too runny.

- Frost sides and top with remaining whipped cream. Place in freezer. When solid, wrap in plastic and return to freezer.

- To serve, defrost torte for 15 minutes or until whipped cream softens. Cut into wedges with warm cake knife. Makes 16 servings.

Neapolitan Torte

Meringue:
6 egg whites
1 ½ teaspoons cream of tartar
1/4 teaspoon salt
1 ½ cups granulated sugar
2 teaspoons vanilla
slivered almonds, toasted
   (optional)

Filling and Topping:
2 to 3 cups whipping cream
1 pint (500 mL) chocolate ice cream
1 pint (500 mL) strawberry ice cream
1 pint (500 mL) orange sherbet

Glitter Torte

Glitter:
1 package (3 ounces/85 g)
    orange-flavoured gelatin
1 package (3 ounces/85 g) lime-
    flavoured gelatin
2 cups hot water, divided
1 cup cold water, divided

Crumb Crust:
1 ½ cups fine graham wafer
    crumbs
1/3 cup granulated sugar
1/2 cup melted butter or
    margarine

Filling:
1 package (3 ounces/85 g)
    lemon-flavoured gelatin
1/4 cup granulated sugar
1 cup hot water
1 cup crushed pineapple,
    lightly drained
1/2 cup cold water
3 tablespoons lemon juice
pinch of salt
1 ½ cups whipping cream
1/4 cup chopped walnuts

The recipe for this very pretty dessert was clipped many years ago from a magazine, where it was featured as part of a Christmas buffet. The "glitter" needs to be prepared ahead to allow the gelatin to set.

• In separate bowls, dissolve orange and lime gelatin in 1 cup hot water each. Add 1/2 cup cold water to each and stir. Pour into separate 8-inch square pans and chill until firm. Cut into 1/2-inch cubes.

• Make **crumb crust** by combining wafer crumbs, 1/3 cup sugar and melted butter in small bowl. Press into bottom and 2 ½ inches up sides of buttered 9-inch springform pan. Chill.

• To prepare **filling**, dissolve lemon gelatin and 1/4 cup sugar in 1 cup hot water.

• Add pineapple, 1/2 cup cold water, lemon juice and salt. Chill until partially set, then whip until fluffy.

• Reserve a dozen or more glitter cubes to trim top. Fold remainder into pineapple mixture.

• Whip cream. Fold into pineapple mixture.

• Pour filling into crumb-lined pan. Sprinkle top with walnuts and reserved glitter. Chill until set.

• Cut in wedges to serve. Makes 12 servings.

Note: Make dessert more spectacular by surrounding cake with additional glitter. Use 4 packages of gelatin and jell in 4 separate pans.

Here's another dazzling dessert that some may consider too rich for the nutrition-conscious 90s. It can at least be lovingly remembered as a comfort food fit for royalty.

- Cover cookie sheet with piece of heavy paper. Draw an 8-inch circle in centre of paper.

- Beat egg whites, salt and vinegar in large bowl until soft peaks form.

- Combine 1/2 cup sugar and 1/4 teaspoon cinnamon.

- Gradually add to egg whites, beating until very stiff, glossy peaks form and all sugar is dissolved.

- Spread meringue inside circle, making centre 1/2-inch thick and mounding edges to 1 ¾ inches. Use back of teaspoon to form rippled edge on outside.

- Bake at 275°F for 1 hour. Turn off heat and let dry in oven with door closed for at least 2 hours. Peel paper off meringue.

- Melt chocolate in double boiler over hot, not boiling water. Cool slightly, then spread 2 tablespoons of chocolate over bottom of cooled meringue shell.

- To remaining chocolate, add egg yolks and water and blend. Chill until mixture is thick.

- Combine cream, 1/4 cup sugar and 1/4 teaspoon cinnamon in bowl and whip until stiff. Spread half the whipped cream over chocolate in shell.

- Fold remaining whipped cream into chilled chocolate mixture. Spread on top of torte.

- Chill several hours or overnight. Decorate with whipped cream and chopped pecans, if desired. Makes 8 to 10 servings.

Chocolate Torte Royale

Meringue:
2 egg whites
1/4 teaspoon salt
1/2 teaspoon vinegar
1/2 cup granulated sugar
1/4 teaspoon ground cinnamon

Filling and Topping:
1 cup semisweet chocolate
   chips
2 egg yolks, beaten
1/4 cup water
1 cup whipping cream
1/4 cup granulated sugar
1/4 teaspoon ground cinnamon
whipped cream and chopped
   pecans for garnish (optional)

Frozen Cheesecake

3 packages (3 ounces/85 g each)
    cream cheese
1 cup granulated sugar
3 eggs, separated
1 cup whipping cream
1 teaspoon vanilla
pinch of salt
24 graham wafers, finely
    crushed

The cheesecake era was in full swing when a friend in Gettysburg, Pennsylvania gave me this recipe for a frozen version. It's an excellent dessert on a hot, summer day. I sometimes use a 10-inch springform pan for a more traditional cheesecake look.

- Cream cheese and sugar.
- In large bowl, beat egg yolks. Add cheese mixture and beat until smooth.
- Whip cream until soft peaks form. Fold in vanilla and salt, then fold into cheese mixture.
- Beat egg whites until stiff but not dry. Fold into cheese mixture.
- Spread 3/4 of the cracker crumbs in bottom of 9 x 13-inch pan. Pour cheese mixture over crumbs. Sprinkle with remaining crumbs.
- Place in freezer until needed. Cut into squares and serve frozen. Makes 12 generous servings.

Frozen Cherry Jubilee Pie

Crust:
1/2 cup saltine cracker crumbs
2/3 cup granulated sugar
1/3 cup chopped pecans
    (optional)
2 egg whites
1/2 teaspoon vanilla

Filling:
1 pint (500 mL) vanilla ice
    cream, softened

Topping:
1 can (14 ounces/398 mL) pitted
    Bing cherries
1/2 cup of reserved cherry syrup
1 tablespoon cornstarch
1 tablespoon granulated sugar
1/8 teaspoon salt
1/4 cup light corn syrup
1 teaspoon brandy
3/4 teaspoon butter

To end this "sweet" chapter on a delicious note, here's a frozen dessert which my family wholeheartedly endorsed.

- Combine cracker crumbs, 1/3 cup of the sugar and pecans.
- In separate bowl, beat egg whites. Gradually add remaining 1/3 cup sugar and vanilla and continue beating until stiff peaks form.
- Fold cracker mixture into egg whites. Spoon into greased and floured 9-inch pie plate and spread to form shell.
- Bake at 350°F for 25 minutes. Cool thoroughly (crust will fall as it cools).
- Fill centre of crust with softened ice cream and place in freezer for an hour.
- Drain cherries, reserving 1/2 cup syrup. In saucepan, combine cherry syrup with cornstarch, 1 tablespoon sugar, salt and corn syrup. Cook, stirring until sauce is thick and smooth. Simmer for 2 minutes, stirring constantly.
- Remove from heat and add cherries, brandy and butter.
- Cool thoroughly. Spread over frozen ice cream. Wrap securely in foil and freeze. Makes 6 to 8 servings.

I remember the first time I ever made Hollandaise sauce to serve over eggs for a luncheon dish when I was entertaining women friends. I had prepared it ahead in a double boiler, and by the time I was ready to serve it, it had curdled. With everyone already seated at the table, this was a disaster. I quickly tried a little reheating and hard whipping, but it was beyond help.

Maybe they won't notice, I soothed myself as I ladled the separated "curds" over the Eggs Benedict. But it didn't pass muster. How could it?

"Oh, Marie, your Hollandaise has curdled," one of my helpful guests informed me. Why couldn't she have just let it go, so I could have at least saved face if not the sauce and the meal? Wasn't it enough that they could go away and talk about Marie's dreadful sauce, and her inability in the kitchen?

"Oh, no!" I cried—with as much sarcasm as faked surprise. It's such a painful memory that, I still make the foolproof version included here.

Gravy was another problem for this young cook. At first I was so intimidated with the task that I used to avoid making it whenever I could. But Laurie loves his gravy, and I learned to appreciate it as a cover-up when meat got a little overdone. Once I got the knack I often wondered how it could ever have been a problem.

At that time, I considered barbecue sauce to be something you buy in bottles, the same way you get tartar sauce, seafood cocktail sauce, mint sauce, and yes, salad dressing.

But I soon learned the difference between "bought" and homemade. My first taste of success came when I made a hot sauce to serve with appetizer shrimps at a cocktail party. One friend was so taken with the sauce that he almost insisted that I write out the recipe then and there. Being the hostess, and trying to keep the food flowing, I put him off with the promise of writing it out for him the next day. I hope I did. If not, it's included here, almost 40 years later.

We all had our favourite dessert sauces, as well. Custard sauce was a natural to pour over fruit or puddings, and anything else. And there had to be chocolate or hot fudge sauce to serve over ice cream, which could never go naked to the table.

SAUCES AND DRESSINGS

Best Ever Barbecue Sauce

1 cup ketchup
grated zest of a lemon
juice of 2 lemons
1 teaspoon prepared mustard
10 drops Tabasco sauce
1 tablespoon Worcestershire
    sauce
2 tablespoons brown sugar
2 tablespoons cider vinegar
1/4 teaspoon salt

Whatever barbecue sauce I used in my early days in the kitchen has long since disappeared. Maybe that's our good fortune. This "best ever" sauce came from former cooking school instructor Karen Neal, when she was doing promotional work for the Nova Scotia Chicken Marketing Board.

• In non-aluminum pan, combine ketchup, lemon zest and juice, mustard, Tabasco and Worcestershire sauces, brown sugar, vinegar and salt. Heat gently. Do not allow to simmer.

• Remove and reserve until ready to use. Sauce will keep, covered and stored in refrigerator.

Pan Gravy for Roasts

drippings from roast
water
2 tablespoons all-purpose flour
salt and pepper to taste

The secret to good gravy is not to use too much fat. It's also important to scrape the brown bits from the bottom of the pan as they are the flavour buds. A quarter teaspoon of sugar added to the pan will also help darken the gravy.

• Remove roast from roasting pan and keep warm.

• Pour drippings from pan into large glass measuring cup. Let stand a minute or so until fat rises to top. Spoon 2 tablespoons fat into a saucepan. Skim off remaining fat and discard.

• Pour 1/4 cup water into roasting pan. Stir to loosen any brown bits. Add to meat juice in measuring cup. Add water to make 2 cups liquid.

• Place saucepan over medium heat and stir in 2 tablespoons flour, salt and pepper. Gradually stir in liquid. Cook, stirring, until thickened.

Mint Sauce for Roast Lamb

1 cup red currant jelly
1/4 cup tarragon vinegar
1/2 teaspoon fresh sweet basil
3 tablespoons chopped fresh
    mint

Our little herb garden disappeared one year when we asked our son Frank to help with the spring clean-up. Our young rhubarb plants also fell under his heavy hand. He never did any weeding after that. Maybe that was his strategy all along. Anyhow, it's worth buying fresh herbs for this delightful sauce, served with fresh Nova Scotia lamb.

• Melt jelly in top of double boiler over hot water. Add vinegar, basil and mint, stirring to blend.

• Serve hot or cold with roast lamb. Makes approximately 1 cup.

Classic hollandaise sauce is a bit tricky to make. It can separate in the blink of an eye if the butter is too hot or added too quickly or if the egg yolks are not whipped well enough. That's why I opt for this foolproof recipe to serve over Eggs Benedict or fish.

- Melt butter in top of double boiler over hot water. Stir in flour and cook for 1 to 2 minutes or until bubbly.

- Add egg yolk, salt and water. Stir until mixture thickens.

- Remove from heat and add mayonnaise and vinegar.

- Return to heat over hot water. Makes 1 cup.

Foolproof Mock Hollandaise Sauce

4 tablespoons butter
2 tablespoons all-purpose flour
1 egg yolk, beaten
1/4 teaspoon salt
1/2 cup water
5 tablespoons mayonnaise
1 ½ teaspoons vinegar or lemon juice

Probably no sauce is used more often by busy homemakers than what the English call white sauce and the French call béchamel. It begins with a roux—butter and flour blended together and cooked for a minute or two, just until it begins to bubble. Then milk is added and the sauce is whisked until it thickens.

- In saucepan or top of double boiler, melt butter. Add flour and cook, stirring, for 1 to 2 minutes.

- Blend in salt. Gradually stir in milk. Cook, stirring constantly, until sauce boils and thickens.

- Cook longer over low heat to improve texture and flavour. Makes approximately 1 cup.

White Sauce

Thin:
1 tablespoon butter
1 tablespoon all-purpose flour
1/4 teaspoon salt
1 cup cold milk

Medium:
2 tablespoons butter
2 tablespoons all-purpose flour
1/4 teaspoon salt
1 cup cold milk

Thick:
3 tablespoons butter
3 tablespoons all-purpose flour
1/4 teaspoon salt
1 cup cold milk

Raisin Sauce for Ham

1/2 cup brown sugar
1 ½ teaspoons dry mustard
1 tablespoon all-purpose flour
1/4 teaspoon salt
1/4 teaspoon pepper
1/4 teaspoon ground cloves
dash of nutmeg
dash of cinnamon
1/4 cup vinegar
1 ½ cups water
1/2 cup seedless raisins

Although there appear to be numerous ingredients, this sauce is excellent and requires little effort. In our house, ham is naked without it.

- In saucepan, combine brown sugar, mustard, flour, salt, pepper, cloves, nutmeg and cinnamon.

- Stir in vinegar, water and raisins. Cook until mixture reaches syrup stage. Serve hot. Makes 2 cups.

Tartar Sauce

1 cup mayonnaise
1 tablespoon minced dill
   pickles
1 tablespoon minced capers
1 tablespoon minced olives
1 tablespoon chopped fresh
   parsley

For a long time, I thought tartar sauce was bought in a bottle to eat with scallops. Then I discovered how easy it is to make.

- In small bowl, combine mayonnaise, pickles, capers, olives and parsley.

- Store in refrigerator to serve with fish or shellfish or as an appetizer with raw vegetables. Makes approximately 1 cup.

Hot Cocktail Sauce for Shrimp

1 cup ketchup
1/2 cup finely chopped celery
1 tablespoon finely chopped
   onion
1/4 cup prepared horseradish
1/2 cup lemon juice
1/4 teaspoon Tabasco sauce

Many years ago I served this sauce at a cocktail party in our home on Greenwood Avenue. I clearly remember the rave reviews it received and the requests I had for the recipe. It's still going strong today.

- In small bowl, combine ketchup, celery, onion, horseradish, lemon juice and Tabasco.

- Chill sauce before serving with cooked, chilled shrimp. Makes approximately 2 cups.

Since I didn't get Nanna Johnston's recipe for salad dressing from her before she died, it was lost to me for many years. My memories of it were sharp enough to provoke a search equal to that for the Holy Grail. Finally one of her friends sent it to me. It is still my taste of home.

- In top of double boiler, combine mustard, sugar, salt and flour and mix well.

- Add egg and blend thoroughly.

- Stir in vinegar and enough milk to make desired consistency. Cook over boiling water until bubbly, then add butter.

- Stir well, bottle and cool. Keep covered in refrigerator. Use within a week. Makes approximately 1 ½ cups.

Nanna Johnston's Salad Dressing

1 tablespoon or more dry
    mustard
1/2 cup granulated sugar
1/2 teaspoon salt
2 scant tablespoons all-purpose
    flour
1 egg
1/2 cup vinegar
1 cup or more milk
1 tablespoon butter

We were married before the blender became a popular wedding gift and it was a few years before one came along and changed my life. Since then I've run two into obscurity and am working on my third.

- In blender, combine oil, vinegar, ketchup, sugar, paprika, pepper, mustard, salt, onion and parsley. Blend thoroughly.

- Makes approximately 1 ½ cups.

Blender French Dressing

3/4 cup vegetable oil
1/2 cup tarragon vinegar
1/4 cup ketchup
2 teaspoons granulated sugar
1 teaspoon paprika
1/4 teaspoon pepper
1 teaspoon dry mustard
1 teaspoon salt
thin slice of onion, chopped
2 sprigs parsley, chopped and
    stems removed

Mason Jar Dressing

1 can (10 ounces/284 mL)
    condensed tomato soup
1 ½ cups vegetable oil
3/4 cup vinegar
1 teaspoon onion juice*
1/2 cup granulated sugar
1 tablespoon dry mustard
1/2 teaspoon salt
1/2 teaspoon pepper
1/2 teaspoon paprika
1 or 2 cloves garlic, crushed

With a can of condensed tomato soup in the house, I always had the base for a salad dressing or marinade. This is still a handy recipe and one which can be seasoned to suit individual tastes.

- In small bowl, combine soup, oil, vinegar and onion juice.

- In separate bowl, combine sugar, mustard, salt, pepper, paprika and garlic.

- Moisten dry ingredients with a little of the wet, then pour both into 1 quart (1 L) mason jar.

- Shake thoroughly and store in refrigerator. Always shake before using. Makes 4 cups.

*To extract onion juice, cut in half and press on a juicer.

Note: To vary flavour, add Worcestershire sauce or liquid from dill pickles.

Easy Chocolate Sauce

1 ½ cups granulated sugar
1 cup cocoa powder
1 ¼ cups boiling water
1/2 teaspoon vanilla

Our family ate so much chocolate sauce that I switched from chocolate to cocoa powder, which made a great tasting but less expensive topping.

- In saucepan, combine sugar and cocoa.

- Gradually stir in boiling water. Boil gently, stirring, for 5 minutes.

- Remove from heat and stir in vanilla.

- Let cool. Store in covered jar in refrigerator. Makes 2 cups.

Hot Fudge Sauce

3/4 cup light corn syrup
1/2 cup cocoa powder
pinch of salt
1/3 cup butter or margarine

To me, comfort food sometimes means a hot fudge sundae—and I can stand a lot of comforting.

- In saucepan, combine corn syrup, cocoa and salt.

- Add butter. Heat slowly, stirring constantly, until butter melts and sauce is smooth.

- Pour over vanilla ice cream or plain cake. Makes 1 ¼ cups.

Custard sauce, also known as crème Anglaise, is England's most famous sauce. It can be served hot or cold on puddings, fruit, cakes or many other desserts. A little patience is needed in the stirring of this sauce, which should be cooked until it coats the back of a spoon.

Custard Sauce

1 ½ cups milk
3 egg yolks
3 tablespoons granulated sugar
pinch of salt
1/2 teaspoon vanilla

- In top of double boiler over direct heat, scald milk.

- Place top over simmering (not boiling) water.

- Beat egg yolks in small bowl. Gradually add sugar.

- Stir in small amount of hot milk, then gradually add yolk mixture to milk in double boiler.

- Add salt and cook, stirring, until thickened.

- Cool. Stir in vanilla.

- Makes approximately 1 ¾ cups.

Long before nouvelle cuisine had everyone putting fruit purée under slices of meat or delicate desserts, our family was enjoying frozen fruit over ice cream and other desserts. This raspberry sauce couldn't be quicker or more palatable.

Quick Raspberry Sauce

1 package (10 ounces/300 g)
**   frozen raspberries, thawed**
2 tablespoons granulated sugar
1 tablespoon fresh lemon juice

- In food processor or blender, purée raspberries (with their juice) and sugar.

- Press through sieve to remove seeds.

- Stir in lemon juice.

- Makes 3/4 cup.

Blueberry Sauce

2 cups fresh blueberries
1/3 cup granulated sugar
1 tablespoon fresh lemon juice
1/4 teaspoon salt
1/2 teaspoon vanilla

While the raspberry is probably the most popular berry for fruit sauces, in Nova Scotia we don't overlook the indigenous blueberry. Fresh lemon juice heightens the flavour of this sauce.

- In saucepan, crush blueberries.

- Add sugar, lemon juice and salt and mix well.

- Bring to boiling point, then boil for 1 minute.

- Remove from heat. Add vanilla.

- Let cool and then chill in refrigerator. Serve over pudding, cake or ice cream. Makes 1 ½ cups.

Orange Sauce Supreme

1/2 cup granulated sugar
1 tablespoon cornstarch
pinch of salt
1 cup orange juice
1/4 cup butter
1 teaspoon grated orange rind
3 tablespoons lemon juice
1/4 cup orange juice (or orange
    liqueur)
1 cup orange segments

This beautiful sauce was intended to accompany charlotte russe, but I discovered it was also delightful over plain cake or vanilla ice cream. I have always used orange juice for my family but an orange liqueur would add elegance for company.

- In small saucepan, combine sugar, cornstarch and salt.

- Gradually blend in 1 cup orange juice.

- Cook over low heat, stirring constantly, until mixture thickens and comes to a boil.

- Cover and cook over very low heat, stirring occasionally, for 5 minutes longer.

- Remove from heat. Add butter and stir until blended.

- Stir in orange rind, lemon juice, 1/4 cup orange juice and orange segments.

- Chill thoroughly. Makes approximately 3 cups.

The tradition of pickling has always been strong in the Maritimes. It sort of goes with the territory that as the fruits and vegetables come off the vines and bushes, at least some of it is "put by" in jars.

In fact, when CTV's "Live It Up" program decided to seek out the country's best pickles, they headed for Halifax and the prize-winning entries of the Atlantic Winter Fair. It seems that every call made during their research offered the same recommendation—if it's homemade pickles you want, you'd best go to Nova Scotia.

Young women learned from their mothers or grandmothers that the preservation of food for winter meals was as necessary to homemaking as washing the dishes or making the beds.

Even today, a whole new generation of working parents are driven to find time for preserving, claiming satisfaction and pride when the job is accomplished, or guilt when it isn't.

During the 20-year period that this book covers, pickling went on much the same as it had for generations. Homemakers (we used the term 'housewives' then) saved peanut butter, mayonnaise, and baby food jars all year in order to have plenty available at pickling time.

This practice is no longer recommended. Commercial jars are made to withstand one heat treatment but the glass is not tempered to allow repeated contracting.

Another process that has fallen into disfavour is the open kettle method of boiling food in a kettle and then transferring it to hot, sterilized jars and sealing with paraffin wax.

Even jams and jellies which contain large amounts of sugar (usually considered a preservative) are no longer thought to be absolutely safe without proper sealing in a boiling water bath. This is because the paraffin seal may loosen, or little pinholes can form in the wax, causing spoilage.

So how, you might ask, did our ancestors, who relied on canned and preserved foods much more than we do, survive? And how did we, ourselves survive by using the same methods?

PRESERVES

Bernardin's Boiling Water Bath

The recipes included in this chapter are some of the favourites made in my earlier kitchens. Should you wish to process these pickles in a boiling water bath, here is the modern method (1990) supplied by Bernardin, one of the leading makers of canning jars and lids.

- Place snap lids in boiling water and boil 5 minutes to soften sealing compound.

- Ladle pickles or relish into hot jars to within one-half inch of top of rim (head space).

- Remove air bubbles by sliding a rubber spatula between glass and food; readjust head space to one-half inch. Wipe jar rim to remove any stickiness.

- Centre snap lid on jar; apply screw band just until fingertip tight.

- Place jars in canner with boiling water to cover the jars by at least one inch, while still leaving room for the water to boil. Cover canner; return water to a boil; process 10 minutes.

- Remove jars. Cool 24 hours. Check jar seals. (Sealed lids curve downward.) Remove screw bands. Wipe jars, label, and store in a cool, dark, place.

Bread and Butter Pickles

16 cups thinly-sliced small
    pickling cucumbers
1/2 cup coarse salt
8 cups sliced small onions
4 cups white vinegar
5 cups granulated sugar
1 tablespoon celery seeds
2 tablespoons mustard seeds
1 ½ teaspoons turmeric
1/2 teaspoon pepper,
    preferably white

At pickling time, the smell of onions mingling with spices is a delightful aroma. But, the smell of onions on your hands at the bridge table or social event is embarrassing. Try rubbing your hands with salt before washing.

- In a large bowl or enamel kettle, layer cucumbers, salt, and onions. Cover with ice cubes. Let stand 3 hours. Drain.

- In a large kettle, combine vinegar, sugar, seeds, and spices. Bring quickly to the boil; boil 10 minutes.

- Add drained cucumbers and onions. Return to the boiling point.

- Remove from heat and ladle immediately into hot, sterilized jars. Seal. Makes 5 pints.

A "jam" closet built into a cool corner of the basement allowed for hundreds of jars of jams and pickles to be "put by" every year. Alas! The heated storage rooms in apartments don't provide the same keeping quality.

- Wash beans, trim ends, and cut into 1-inch lengths. Cook in boiling salted water until just tender. Drain.

- In a bowl, combine brown sugar, mustard, flour, salt, and turmeric to a smooth paste with 1/2 cup of the vinegar.

- In an enamel kettle, heat remaining vinegar and celery seeds to the boiling point.

- Slowly add a little of the hot vinegar to the mustard paste, blending well. Add paste to kettle and cook, stirring constantly until slightly thickened, about 5 minutes.

- Add drained beans to mustard sauce and bring to boiling point.

- Remove from heat and ladle into hot sterilized jars. Seal. Makes about 4 pints.

Mustard Beans

2 pounds yellow beans
2 cups packed brown sugar
1/2 cup dry mustard
1/2 cup all-purpose flour
2 teaspoons salt
1 teaspoon turmeric
3 cups vinegar
1 tablespoon celery seeds

Don't spoil the flavour of a perfectly good relish by using spices left over from last year. An investment of all that time and effort deserves the best and freshest ingredients available.

- Put all vegetables through the coarse blade of a meat grinder or food processor.

- Put in a large enamel kettle, sprinkle with salt; cover, and let stand overnight.

- Rinse with cold water. Drain, pressing out as much water as possible.

- Return drained vegetables to large kettle, add sugar, vinegar and spices. Bring to boiling point. Uncover and boil for 5 minutes. Reduce heat and cook slowly for 15 minutes.

- Remove from heat, ladle into hot sterilized jars. Makes 4 pints.

Piccalilli

5 green tomatoes, quartered
5 sweet green peppers, cored
  and seeded
2 sweet red peppers, cored and
  seeded
5 onions, peeled and quartered
1 small head cabbage, cut in
  wedges
1/4 cup coarse salt
2 cups packed brown sugar
2 cups cider vinegar
1 tablespoon mustard seeds
1 ½ teaspoons celery seeds
1 teaspoon whole allspice

Cucumber Relish

12 large cucumbers
2 cups chopped onions
1/4 cup coarse salt
4 cups cider vinegar
3 cups granulated sugar
1 teaspoon turmeric
1 teaspoon celery seeds
2 tablespoons all-purpose flour

Laurie's favourite "pickle" was, and still is, this cucumber relish, made and shared by his Aunt Mame.

• Peel and seed cucumbers. Put through grinder, or chop fine.

• Combine with onions in a large bowl or enamel kettle. Sprinkle with salt; let stand overnight. Drain.

• In a large kettle, combine vinegar, sugar, turmeric and celery seeds. Bring quickly to boil.

• Add drained cucumber mixture. Return to boil. Cook 20 minutes.

• Combine flour with a little cold water; stir into mixture to thicken slightly. Cook 2 minutes longer.

• Remove from heat, ladle into hot, sterilized jars, and seal. Makes about 8 pints.

Hot Dog Relish

5 cups ground cucumber
3 cups ground onions
2 hot red peppers, chopped
2 sweet green peppers,
   chopped
3 cups finely chopped celery
3/4 cup coarse salt
8 cups water
4 cups vinegar
3 cups granulated sugar
2 tablespoons celery seeds
2 teaspoons mustard seeds

Between 50 and 60 pints of this relish had to be made every year to back the demand for hot dogs—barbecued, grilled, or simmered.

• In a large bowl or enamel kettle, combine cucumber, onions, red and green peppers, and celery. Sprinkle with the salt. Add water. Let stand overnight. Drain.

• In a large kettle, combine vinegar, sugar, celery and mustard seeds. Bring quickly to boil.

• Add drained vegetables; return to boil. Cook 10 minutes.

• Remove from heat and ladle immediately into hot, sterilized jars. Seal. Makes 5 pints.

One of our favourite summer desserts was chilled wedges of watermelon. I used to caution the family not to eat too deep, so I could trim away the bite (or fork) marks, and prepare the rind for pickles. Gary and I competed for first place in the watermelon-rind-pickle-eating-contest. They're so sweet and spicy, not to mention the economy of utilizing something that would have been thrown away.

Spiced Watermelon Pickle

rind of half a large watermelon (about 8 cups)
8 cups water (for brine)
1/2 cup salt
4 cups sugar
1 lemon, thinly sliced
1 tablespoon whole cloves
1 tablespoon whole allspice
6 one-inch sticks of cinnamon
2 cups vinegar
2 cups water (for syrup)

• Pare green skin from watermelon; cut rind into 1-inch cubes.

• Soak overnight in brine of 8 cups of water and salt in large bowl.

• Drain, place in kettle, cover with fresh water. Heat to boiling, then simmer 10 minutes, or just until cubes are tender but still firm; drain.

• While rind drains, combine sugar, lemon, cloves, allspice, cinnamon, vinegar, and 2 cups water in same kettle; heat to boiling; stir in drained rind. Simmer, stirring often from bottom of pan, 1 hour, or until rind is clear and syrup is thick.

• Ladle rind and spice evenly into hot sterilized jars; fill to brim with remaining hot syrup. Seal, label, and store in a cool dry place.

Note: You might prefer to add the spices in a cheesecloth bag, but I like the look of them in the jars. They do tend, however, to darken the fruit and the syrup over long storage.

Rhubarb Marmalade

1 pound rhubarb
1 lemon
2 ½ cups granulated sugar

Clifton Dauphinee, of Indian Point, had enough rhubarb to supply anyone who wanted it. He'd even pull it and trim the leaves for you. Then, when the bag was full (with maybe 5 or 10 pounds) and you insisted on paying, he'd say, "Well, okay, give me a dollar."

- Wash rhubarb and cut into thin slices without peeling.

- Wash lemon and shave off the thin yellow rind.

- Add rind to rhubarb with sugar, mix and let stand overnight.

- Add juice of lemon and cook quickly until thick.

- Remove from heat and ladle into hot sterilized jars. Seal. Makes 3 half-pint jars.

Heavenly Peach Jam

20 medium-sized peaches
2 oranges, juice and rind
6 cups granulated sugar
small bottle of maraschino
  cherries

Use the plate test to determine if jam is set: put a spoonful of hot mixture on a plate that has been stored in the freezer. Return plate to freezer for 2 minutes. If the mixture moves slowly when the plate is tilted, the jam is done. If not, return to heat and cook 2 more minutes. Test again.

- Dip peaches into boiling water; remove skins and pits; mash or chop fine.

- Combine with orange juice in a large saucepan or kettle. Bring to boil, cover, and cook until soft.

- Add sugar and orange rind, which as been put through the medium blade of meat grinder. Boil until it reaches the jellying point. (It should set quickly if a portion is dropped on a cool plate.)

- Stir in chopped cherries.

- Remove from heat and ladle into hot sterilized jars. Seal. Makes approximately 8 half-pint jars.

To the boys, jam usually meant strawberry jam, made according to the recipe in Out of Old Nova Scotia Kitchens. *But Bobby was willing to bear the discomfort of picking wild raspberries from the canes surrounding the cottage. The trick was getting them into the jam pot before he had them eaten.*

• Pick over the berries, mash and cook gently for 10 minutes, stirring often.

• Add sugar, cook 15 minutes more, or until it reaches the jellying point.

• Remove from heat. Ladle into hot sterilized jars. Seal. Makes approximately 7 half-pint jars.

I always used to peel and core the apples before making apple butter, but now I sometimes skip this time-consuming step. However, if you're worried about pesticide residue on the skins, you might prefer to peel the apples first.

• Thoroughly wash apples (a little vinegar added to the water will cut pesticide residue). Leaving skins on, cut into quarters. Core, if desired, and slice.

• In a large enamel or stainless steel kettle, bring apples and liquid to a boil. Cook uncovered over medium heat, stirring frequently, until apples are very soft. This might take about 20 minutes.

• Remove from heat and press pulp through a sieve to trap skins and cores (if left in). Measure pulp and return to clean kettle. Depending on sweetness of apples, add 1/3 to 1/2 cup sugar (lightly packed, if using brown) for each cup of pulp. Stir in spices, lemon rind and juice, if using, and cook uncovered over very low heat, until thick. At first, frequent stirring with a wooden spoon should prevent mixture from sticking, but as it thickens, it will require constant stirring. Cooking may take 1 ½ to 2 hours, depending on juiceness of apples.

• To test for doneness, spoon a little of the mixture onto a cold plate. If it's firm, with no liquid oozing out around the edge, the butter is done.

• Ladle into hot sterilized jars and seal. Makes 4 to 5 half-pint jars.

Raspberry Jam

8 cups raspberries
6 cups granulated sugar

Apple Butter

4 pounds apples (16 cups sliced apples)
2 cups apple juice, cider, cider vinegar or water
Sugar, brown or granulated
1 to 2 teaspoons ground cinnamon, according to taste
1/2 teaspoon ground allspice
1/2 teaspoon salt
Grated rind and juice of 1 lemon (optional)

Brandied Fruit (Rumtoff)

fresh fruit, as it comes into
    season, i.e., strawberries,
    raspberries, sliced peaches,
    halved plums, blueberries,
    etc.
granulated sugar
brandy

I had my first taste of this delicious sauce while visiting my Uncle Merv in Toronto. Aunt Myrtie served it over ice cream. But no coaxing could get her to reveal the "secret" which she had sworn to protect.

Spurred by stubborn determination, I began a search to equal that of the Holy Grail.

Months later I found the recipe attached to an expensive "rumtoff" pot in an American kitchen shop. Trying not to be noticed, I made notes of the procedure. Well, how could I get that pot across the border!

You will need a large wide-mouthed jar or crock with a cover, that can be stored in the refrigerator, if you don't have a cold room.

•   Start with the first fruit of summer. Wash and hull 2 cups strawberries, halving any large ones. Put in a bowl with 1/2 cup of sugar. Let stand at room temperature for an hour.

•   Stir to dissolve sugar. Transfer to the sterilized jar. Pour in enough brandy to cover fruit by 1 inch.

•   Crumble a wad of plastic wrap and fit over the berries, then weight it with a small sterilized plate to keep berries submerged and prevent discolouration. Place crock in a cool, dark place, or refrigerator.

•   Repeat procedure as other fruits come in season, adding 1/2 cup of sugar for each 2 cups of fruit, top with brandy to maintain liquid level. Give fruit a gentle stir with each addition.

•   If you make your last addition of fruit and sugar around Hallowe'en, you can enjoy the first fruits of your labour by Christmas. During the final resting period, be sure the jar is tightly covered, and do not stir.

Note: Other fruits that can be added to the rumtoff include pitted cherries, currants, gooseberries, and cubed cantaloupe.

Not suitable are: apples (too hard), bananas and pears (too mushy), blackberries (too seedy), and grapes (skins become tough).

To prolong the rumtoff, add 1 cup fruit and 1/2 cup sugar for every cup removed. Be sure to keep liquid up with brandy, as needed.

CANDY

P art of the Christmas tradition in our house, at least when the boys were in grade school, was to make lots of candy. It didn't seem like Christmas without several varieties of fudge, brittles, taffy, fondants, glazed nuts and popcorn, made and packed into decorated boxes for aunts, teachers, and other special people.

It became a challenge to make these gift boxes as attractive as possible and, as time went by, I began trying my hand at turtles, Turkish delights, pralines, and even chocolates. But fudge always remained the favourite, perhaps because licking the pot tasted so good.

I remember one day I was making fudge when a young neighbour dropped in for a visit. He was a very serious seven-year-old and far too worried about current issues of international importance. As I continued to beat the fudge, I tried to steer the conversation towards lighter subjects. Suddenly he asked, "What do you think of the U-2 situation?"

I looked at that sweet, innocent face and wished he didn't have to be troubled about such things. "Would you like to lick the pot?" I asked.

"Would I!" The serious little man suddenly became a child again.

This little boy grew up to be a very talented and successful artist. I wonder if he remembered that day. I remember every time I'm looking for someone to lick the pot as I continue to make fudge to share with others at Christmas.

Candy making is not the awesome task some people think it is but, as with most worthwhile endeavours, there are rules to be followed. One of the most important is to make it on a clear day. High humidity plays havoc with sugar crystals. If you can't wait for the sun to shine, try boiling the syrup a little longer than is called for in the recipe.

Use a heavy, flat-bottomed saucepan with high sides to prevent spillovers. Butter the sides of the pot so that grains of sugar cannot cling and start crystallizing. If crystals do form, brush them down with a pastry brush that has been dipped in hot water.

Watch the boiling process carefully, testing

frequently by dropping a bit of the syrup into a cup of ice water to determine if it's ready. Or do as I do and rely on a candy thermometer.

If candy needs to be beaten, set the saucepan in a sink half filled with cold water and cool the candy to 110°F. Then beat it vigorously without resting—change hands or call in a helper but don't stop beating—until the mixture begins to stiffen and lose its gloss. If you're making fudge, this is the time to add nuts or coconut. Move quickly, stirring only until the nuts are distributed.

If the candy is being put into a pan, use a rubber or wooden spatula to spread it into the corners. Don't scrape the pot or you'll lose some of the creaminess. Then store the candy in airtight containers and, if you have room, in the freezer.

Cooking to the right temperature is critical to candy making. But the right temperature is not easy to determine. Depending on which candy thermometer you have, or which cookbook you use, the various stages of the cooking syrup can differ.

It would be so easy if I could tell you that the soft ball stage is reached when the candy thermometer (always read at eye level) rests at 238°F. But because ingredients play a role in determining just when the syrup reaches a certain stage, temperatures can only serve as a guide, not a hard-fast rule.

For instance, because fudge contains milk and butter, it will reach the required soft-ball stage at a lower temperature than a plain sugar and water syrup.

I suggest you use the thermometer and the chart given below, but also use the cold water test as a backup.

For the cold water test, put some cold water in a cup. Remove saucepan from the heat so it doesn't continue to cook. Drop about 1/2 teaspoon of the hot mixture into the water. Let stand 1 minute. Then pick the mixture up between your thumb and index finger to determine the stage to which it has cooked.

Thread stage: (223-234°F) forms a fine, thin thread from the side of a spoon.

Soft ball: (234–240°F) makes a soft ball, but doesn't hold its shape.

Firm ball: (244–248°F) holds its firm shape.

Hard ball: (250–266°F) feels hard; but while still sticky, it can be molded.

Soft crack: (270–290°F) can be pulled into separate hard, but not brittle strands.

Hard crack: (300–310°F) brittle threads snap when bent.

I wish I had a dime for every pan of fudge I've made over the past 40 years, for candy tables and other money-raising events, for Christmas gift boxes and for passing around the office. If the weather was fine and Laurie was around to spell me with the beating, I would turn out one batch after another. Finally, in November of 1991, it caught up with me. Seven continuous hours of fudge making brought on a stress fracture in my left foot. Still, there must always be fudge for Christmas.

Fudge

4 cups packed brown sugar
1 cup evaporated milk
1/4 cup butter or margarine (in 1 piece)
1 teaspoon vanilla
3/4 cup chopped nuts or desiccated coconut

• In large, heavy-bottomed saucepan, combine sugar, milk and butter. Stir over moderate heat until butter has melted and sugar has dissolved.

• Bring to boil. Clip candy thermometer in place, making sure it is deep into the mixture but does not touch the bottom of pan. Cook, stirring, until mixture reaches the soft ball stage. (See chart page 198.)

• Remove from heat and, leaving thermometer in place, cool to 110°F. Don't move saucepan while cooling or sugar crystals may start to form.

• Stir in vanilla. Beat vigorously until fudge begins to lose its gloss and seems to stiffen.

• Add chopped nuts or coconut.

• Work quickly to push mixture from saucepan into buttered 8- or 9-inch square pan with rubber spatula or wooden spurtle. Don't scrape sides.

• Score fudge while still warm and cut when cold. Makes 25 or 36 pieces, depending on size of pan.

Variation: To make chocolate fudge, mix 3 tablespoons cocoa powder with the sugar.

White Christmas Fudge

3 cups granulated sugar
1/4 teaspoon cream of tartar
1/4 teaspoon salt
1 cup evaporated milk or blend
   (light cream)
1 tablespoon butter
1 ½ teaspoons vanilla
1/2 cup chopped walnuts
1/4 cup finely chopped dates
1/4 cup finely chopped glazed
   cherries

In my house, fudge means variations of the previous recipe. But, in earlier years, I provided a wider variety in my Christmas gift boxes. This was my favourite.

• In large, heavy-bottomed saucepan, combine sugar, cream of tartar, salt and evaporated milk. Stir, over low heat, until sugar has dissolved.

• Increase heat to moderate, cover and heat to boiling, stirring occasionally.

• Uncover and clip candy thermometer in place. Cook, without stirring, until mixture reaches soft ball stage. (See chart page 198.)

• Remove from heat, add butter and let cool to 110°F. Stir in vanilla. Beat until mixture begins to lose its gloss.

• Quickly stir in nuts, dates and cherries and pour into buttered 8-inch square pan. Cool and cut into 25 squares.

Turtles

1 package (14 ounces/397 g)
   vanilla caramels
1 ½ tablespoons butter
2 teaspoons butter
72 pecan halves (approximately
   1 cup)
salt
1/2 cup chocolate chips

Buying Turtles means a missed opportunity for family fun. When grouping the pecans into threes, be sure to have them almost touching in the centre. Spread the two "legs" apart, as if the turtle is crawling.

• Unwrap caramels and place in top of double boiler with 1 ½ tablespoons butter. Set over boiling water, cover and let melt, stirring occasionally.

• Put 2 teaspoons butter in shallow baking pan and melt in oven at 300°F.

• Add pecans, stirring lightly to coat. Sprinkle with salt. Toast in oven for approximately 12 minutes, stirring often. Cool.

• Arrange pecans in groups of 3 on buttered cookie sheet (1 for turtle's head and 2 for legs). Drop spoonful of caramel mixture on top of each group of nuts.

• Set chocolate chips in saucepan over hot water until partially melted. Remove from heat and stir until completely melted and smooth. For each turtle, spread a little chocolate over caramel. Cool. Makes 24 turtles.

Cooked divinity was traditionally shaped with two teaspoons—one to pick up the right amount of candy and the other to push it into the pan. I have since adopted a neat and efficient method in which I put the divinity into a plastic bag, snip off one corner and squeeze the candy through into attractive, uniform shapes.

• In large, heavy-bottomed saucepan, combine sugar, corn syrup, salt and water. Stir over moderate heat until sugar has dissolved.

• Cook, without stirring, until mixture reaches hard ball stage on candy thermometer. (See chart page 198.) Wipe off any sugar crystals that form on side of saucepan.

• In the meantime, beat egg whites until stiff.

• Pour hot syrup slowly over egg whites and beat with mixer at medium speed until mixture fluffs up.

• Add vanilla and continue beating until mixture begins to lose its gloss (small amount dropped from spoon should hold soft peaks). If candy gets too stiff for mixer, finish beating with wooden spoon.

• Fold in nuts.

• Working quickly, drop candy by teaspoonfuls onto waxed paper or turn into lightly buttered 8-inch square pan. If divinity becomes too stiff, stir in a few drops of hot water.

• Makes approximately 24 pieces or 1 pound (500 g).

Divinity

2 ¼ cups granulated sugar
1/3 cup white corn syrup
1/4 teaspoon salt
1/3 cup water
2 egg whites
1 teaspoon vanilla
2/3 cup chopped walnuts

Coconut Ice

3 cups granulated sugar
1/2 teaspoon cream of tartar
1 cup milk
2 packages (7 ounces/200 g
    each) desiccated coconut
red food colouring

For a variation of this sweet, sweet treat, make a pink batch and a white batch and layer one colour over the other in the same pan. In this case, use a 9-inch square pan. Allow the first batch to sit at room temperature while the second is cooking.

• Butter an 8-inch square pan. Fold and place piece of aluminum foil down middle to divide pan into two sections.

• In large, heavy-bottomed saucepan, combine sugar, cream of tartar and milk. Stir over low heat until sugar has dissolved.

• Cook, without stirring, until mixture reaches thread stage on candy thermometer. (See chart page 198.)

• Remove from heat and stir in coconut.

• Spoon half the mixture into one section of pan.

• Blend food colouring into remaining candy to tint pale pink. Pour into other half of pan.

• Chill 2 to 3 hours or until firm. Cut into 25 squares.

Raisin Peanut Clusters

8 ounces (250 g) semisweet
    chocolate
2 ½ cups seedless raisins
1 cup salted peanuts

For those who feel intimidated by candy making and all its proper stages of cooking, this recipe is a good place to begin. The only caution is to prevent even a drop of water from getting into the chocolate or the whole batch could be spoiled.

• Melt chocolate in top of double boiler over hot, not boiling, water. Remove from heat and cool slightly.

• Stir in raisins and peanuts.

• Drop by teaspoonfuls onto cookie sheets lined with waxed paper.

• Chill overnight in refrigerator. Makes about 40 pieces.

Taffy pulling is another way to share the fun of candy making. Each of my sons had his own technique but laughter and a little "whip lashing" were always a part of it. Once the pulling was over, they were quite willing to let me wrap the taffy and do the cleaning up.

- Butter sides of heavy, 2-quart (2 L) saucepan. Add sugar, molasses and water. Stir to combine. Continue stirring over low heat until sugar has dissolved.

- Bring to boil, clip candy thermometer in place and add vinegar. Continue cooking until mixture has reached soft crack stage. (See chart page 198.)

- Remove from heat, add butter and sift in baking soda. Stir to mix.

- Without scraping pan, turn out onto buttered platter or large shallow pan. For even cooling, use spatula to turn edges to centre.

- Pull taffy while still as warm as possible, using only fingertips. If candy sticks, dip fingers in cornstarch. When candy is light, taffy colour and becomes hard to pull, cut in quarters and pull each piece into a long strand, approximately 1/2-inch thick.

- With buttered scissors, quickly snip into bite-sized pieces. Wrap each piece in wax paper, twisting ends.

- Makes approximately 1 ¾ pounds.

Molasses Taffy

2 cups granulated sugar
1 cup molasses
1/4 cup water
2 teaspoons vinegar
2 tablespoons butter or
   margarine
1/2 teaspoon baking soda

Sponge Taffy

2 ½ cups brown sugar
1/2 cup light corn syrup
1/2 cup water
1 tablespoon baking soda

There's nothing quite like sponge taffy to satisfy a craving for something sweet. All that's needed is brown sugar, a little corn syrup and baking soda to aerate the mixture. Then enjoy that tingling sensation as it slowly melts in your mouth.

• In large, heavy-bottomed saucepan, combine sugar, syrup and water. Stir over low heat until sugar has dissolved.

• Increase heat to moderate and cook, stirring occasionally, until candy thermometer reaches hard crack stage. (See chart page 198.) This takes about an hour of gentle boiling.

• Remove from heat. Add baking soda and beat well to distribute soda evenly.

• Pour, while mixture is foaming, into 9-inch square pan. Let stand at room temperature, undisturbed, until cold.

• Loosen sides, invert pan and turn out. Cut into large squares. Makes approximately 25 2-inch pieces.

Easy Toffee Squares

35 unsalted soda crackers
1 cup unsalted butter
1 cup packed brown sugar
1 package (6 ounces/175 g)
    chocolate chips

This recipe belongs to the 70s. But it is so delicious and easy to make that I just had to include it.

• Line bottom of lightly greased 10 x 15-inch jelly roll pan with soda crackers.

• In medium-sized saucepan, combine butter and brown sugar. Cook over medium heat, stirring constantly, until mixture comes to boil. Cook 3 more minutes, stirring constantly.

• Pour mixture evenly over crackers. Bake at 375°F for approximately 15 minutes, watching carefully during last few minutes to prevent burning.

• Remove from oven and sprinkle with chocolate chips. Let stand 5 minutes.

• Spread melted chocolate over crackers. While still warm, cut between crackers.

• Chill in refrigerator until set. Makes 35 squares.

As a confection, dates may be stuffed with peanut butter, fondant, softened cream cheese, finely chopped candied ginger or pineapple, snipped marshmallows or even chopped nuts. I usually follow my mother's lead, with orange flavoured icing.

- Cream butter and 2 tablespoons icing sugar.

- Add orange juice and enough of remaining icing sugar to make mixture which can be kneaded.

- Knead and shape into pencil-like rolls. Cut and fit into slitted dates.

- If desired, garnish by topping each date with piece of red or green cherry, nut or sprinkling of cake decorations.

- Makes approximately 25 pieces, depending on number of dates in package.

Stuffed Dates

1 tablespoon butter
2 cups icing sugar
2 tablespoons orange juice
1 package (8 ounces/250 g) pitted dates
cherries and nuts for garnish (optional)

To find new variations of Rice Krispies squares has been an on-going quest in North America for at least three decades, encouraged by the company that makes the cereal. For my boys, it was a toss-up between the original marshmallow recipe (page 137) and this one.

- Combine cereal and peanuts. Set aside.

- In large, heavy-bottomed saucepan, combine sugar and corn syrup. Stir over moderate heat until mixture comes to full rolling boil.

- Remove from heat and stir in peanut butter and vanilla. Immediately pour over cereal mixture, stirring gently to coat.

- Pat evenly into buttered 8- or 9-inch square pan. Cool and cut into 2-inch squares or bars. Makes 16 or 25 squares, depending on size of pan.

Peanut Butter Cereal Candy

3 cups crisp rice cereal
1 cup salted peanuts
1/2 cup granulated sugar
1/2 cup light corn syrup
1/2 cup peanut butter
1/2 teaspoon vanilla

Peanut Brittle

2 cups granulated sugar
1 cup light corn syrup
1/4 cup water
1 ½ cups salted peanuts
3 tablespoons butter or
 margarine
1/2 teaspoon vanilla
2 teaspoons baking soda

Crisp brittles are not only fun to eat but also fun to make. It's important to remove any sugar crystals, which may form on the side of the saucepan during cooking, with a pastry brush dipped in cold water. Rinse the brush thoroughly after each use. Cooking temperatures are precise for this recipe.

• In large heavy-bottomed saucepan, combine sugar, corn syrup and water. Stir over medium heat until sugar dissolves.

• Continue cooking, stirring frequently, until mixture reaches 285°F. Immediately remove from heat.

• Stir in peanuts and butter. Return to heat and cook, stirring constantly, until mixture reaches 295°F.

• Remove from heat at once. Quickly stir in vanilla and baking soda. Mixture will foam up.

• Pour into 2 large buttered baking sheets, spreading as thinly as possible with spatula.

• Let sit 5 minutes or until cool enough to handle, then turn over and stretch as thinly as possible.

• When cold, break into pieces. Makes 2 pounds .

Popcorn, dressed in one way or another, is a treat for all ages. This recipe gives us both the candy and the corn. Temperatures are precise in this recipe.

- In large, heavy-bottomed saucepan, combine granulated and brown sugar, corn syrup, water and salt. Set over medium heat and cook, stirring, until sugar has dissolved.

- Continue cooking, without stirring, until mixture reaches 260°F on candy thermometer or until hard ball forms when small amount is dipped in cold water.

- Add butter and cook until mixtures reaches 270°F or until hard threads form when tested in cold water.

- Stir in popcorn, peanuts, vanilla and almond extract. Pour into buttered jelly roll pan, spreading as thinly as possible with 2 forks.

- Break into pieces when cold. Makes approximately 2 pounds.

Popcorn Peanut Brittle

1 cup granulated sugar
1 cup packed brown sugar
3/4 cup corn syrup
3/4 cup water
1/2 teaspoon salt
6 tablespoons butter
2 cups popped corn
1 cup roasted salted peanuts
1 teaspoon vanilla
1/2 teaspoon almond extract

I first made these little Christmas trees as favours for my son Gary's December birthday. For a while, we made them every Christmas. Then, in 1991, they made a fresh appearance when our then 6-year-old granddaughter Ashley was looking for something fun to do.

- Make smooth icing of sugar, egg white and water.

- Gradually add few drops food colouring, mixing well, to make delicate shade of green.

- Using approximately 2 tablespoons icing, spread on each cone to cover completely.

- While icing is still soft, press approximately 1/2 cup popcorn on each cone.

- Place red cinnamon candies here and there between pieces of popcorn. Makes 6 trees.

Popcorn Christmas Trees

2 ½ cups sifted icing sugar
1 egg white
1 teaspoon water
green food colouring
6 pointed ice cream cones
3 cups popped corn
red cinnamon candies

Oven-Made Caramel Corn

5 quarts freshly popped corn
1 cup butter or margarine
2 cups packed brown sugar
1/2 cup light corn syrup
1 teaspoon salt
1/2 teaspoon baking soda

Was it the caramel corn or the prizes in every box that kept my boys spending nickels? They liked it even better when I made it for them for free.

• Spread popcorn in large roasting pan and place in oven at 250°F to keep warm.

• In 2-quart heavy-bottomed saucepan, combine butter, brown sugar, corn syrup and salt. Cook over medium heat, stirring, until sugar has dissolved.

• Continue cooking, without stirring, until mixture reaches firm ball stage on candy thermometer. (See chart page 198.)

• Remove from heat and stir in baking soda. Mixture will foam up.

• Remove popcorn from oven. Pour hot caramel mixture over popcorn in fine stream and stir to mix well.

• Return to oven for 45 to 50 minutes, stirring every 15 minutes.

• Cool. Makes approximately 5 quarts.

INDEX